CASE STUDIES IN
CULTURAL ANTHROPOLOGY

GENERAL EDITORS
George and Louise Spindler
STANFORD UNIVERSITY

COLONIAL CAKCHIQUELS:

Highland Maya Adaptations to Spanish Rule, 1600–1700

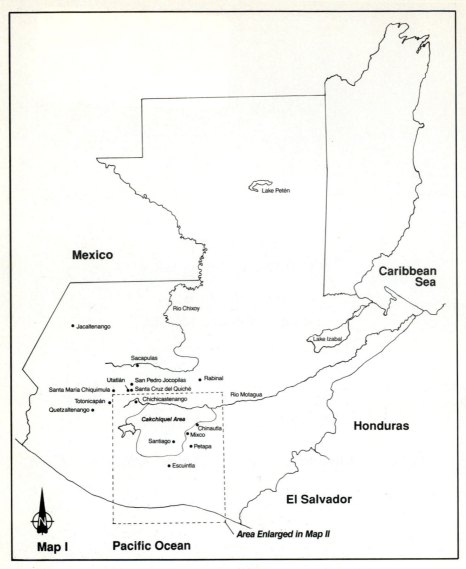

Mexico

Caribbean
Sea

Lake Petén

Rio Chixoy

Lake Izabal

• Jacaltenango

Sacapulas

Utatlán   San Pedro Jocopilas   • Rabinal
Santa María Chiquimula •   • Santa Cruz del Quiché   Rio Motagua
Totonicapán •   • Chichicastenango
Quetzaltenango •

Cakchiquel Area

• Chinautla
• Mixco
Santiago •   • Petapa

• Escuintla

Honduras

El Salvador

Area Enlarged in Map II

N

Map I   **Pacific Ocean**

Guatemala and adjacent countries, showing the location of the Cakchiquel region.

COLONIAL CAKCHIQUELS:

Highland Maya Adaptations to Spanish Rule, 1600–1700

BY

ROBERT M. HILL, II

Harcourt Brace Jovanovich, Publishers
Fort Worth   Philadelphia   San Diego   New York   Orlando   Austin   San Antonio
Toronto   Montreal   London   Sydney   Tokyo

Publisher Ted Buchholz
Acquisitions Editor Christopher P. Klein
Senior Project Editor Dawn Youngblood
Production Manager Thomas Urquhart
Art & Design Supervisor John Ritland

Library of Congress Cataloging-in-Publication Data

Hill, Robert M., 1952–
    Colonial Cakchiquels: highland Maya adaptations to Spanish rule, 1600–1700 / by
Robert M. Hill II.
      p.   cm. — (Case studies in cultural anthropology)
    Includes bibliographical references and index.
    ISBN 0-03-073444-4 (paperback)
    1. Cakchiquel Indians—Social life and customs. 2. Cakchiquel Indians—Social
conditions. 3. Cakchiquel Indians—Government relations. 4. Guatemala—Social
conditions. I. Title.
II. Series.
F1465.2.C3H55 1991
972.81'03—dc20   91-15326
                                            CIP

      ISBN 0-03-073444-4

Address Editorial Correspondence to:
301 Commerce Street, Suite 3700, Fort Worth, TX 76102

Address Orders to:
6277 Sea Harbor Drive, Orlando, FL 32887
1-800-782-4479, or 1-800-433-0001 (in Florida)

Printed in the United States of America

2 3 4 5   016   9 8 7 6 5 4 3 2 1

To the Colonial Cakchiquel ancestors and their present-day descendants, who have taught me that tenacity in the face of adversity is the greatest human virtue.

Foreword

ABOUT THE SERIES

These case studies in cultural anthropology are designed to bring to students, in beginning and intermediate courses in the social sciences, insights into the richness and complexity of human life as it is lived in different ways and in different places. They are written by men and women who have lived in the societies they write about and who are professionally trained as observers and interpreters of human behavior. The authors are also teachers, and in writing their books they have kept the students who will read them foremost in their minds. It is our belief that when an understanding of ways of life very different from one's own is gained, abstractions and generalizations about social structure, cultural values, subsistence techniques, and the other universal categories of human social behavior become meaningful.

ABOUT THE AUTHOR

Robert M. Hill, II, was born in Elizabeth, New Jersey, in 1952. A graduate of the Pingry School, he went on to earn A.B., A.M., and PhD (1980) degrees in anthropology at the University of Pennsylvania. In addition to his ethnohistorical studies, Dr. Hill has conducted ethnographic research and archeological investigations (with the University Museum and the Franco-Guatemalan Scientific Mission), all focusing on the Highland Maya people. Dr. Hill is a member of the American Society for Ethnohistory and the American Anthropological Association. He recently received a Fulbright Foundation Senior Fellowship to continue his Cakchiquel research. Dr. Hill is the author or coauthor of several books, including *The Traditional Pottery of Guatemala* (with Ruben E. Reina), *Continuities in Highland Maya Social Organization: Ethnohistory in Sacapulas, Guatemala* (with John Monaghan), and *The Pirir Papers,* as well as numerous articles for international journals.

ABOUT THIS CASE STUDY

Cultural responses to colonial rule—beliefs, practices, organization, and more—of the Cakchiquel, a highland Maya people, during the seventeenth century are the topic of this case study. That century is not, perhaps, for us as dramatic a period as the preceding one, during which the conquistadors overwhelmed the indigenous Mesoamerican states. It was, nevertheless, an important period for both the Cakchiquel and, retrospectively, for anyone interested in the phenomenon of colonialism and the Age of Empire.

After the initial shocks of population decimation caused by epidemics of newly introduced diseases from the Old World, military conquest, and the subsequent loss of political autonomy, the Cakchiquels and their Spanish overlords gradually established a more or less stable relationship which endured three centuries and which set the tone for the postindependence republic of Guatemala as well. The Cakchiquels did not benefit much from this relationship, but their adaptations to the colonial system were creative and generally quite successful. This is a study of those adaptations, based on historical records—documents left by observers of the period, including a criollo descendant of a conquistador named Díaz del Castillo, an English friar who wrote about Spanish exploitation of the Indians for his compatriots, a Franciscan friar-linguist who lived among the Cakchiquels and studied their language for half a century, Spanish officials concerned with land disputes, and even some statements from the Cakchiquels of the period themselves.

A remarkably full picture of Cakchiquel life during the seventeenth century emerges. Dr. Hill is to be congratulated for producing a synthesis of historical materials and relevant contemporary scholarship that is a detailed and coherent representation of a way of life that is underrepresented in the literatures on colonialism and on empire building in Spanish America.

This case study exemplifies the utility of ethnohistory as an approach to understanding human behavior and cultural dynamics in times remote from the present. Dr. Hill brings to his reconstruction of seventeenth-century Cakchiquel life the sensitivity to meaning and interpretive constructs of the ethnographer as well as both a historian's awareness of cultural processes as a diachronic phenomenon and a broad knowledge of Mesoamerican culture and history.

This case study should prove valuable to students of indigenous Mesoamerican cultures, students of Latin American history, and to all those interested in imperialism, colonialism, and human adaptations to adversity, domination, and exploitation. Since, as Dr. Hill points out, the Cakchiquel are still very much with us, this book is also a tribute to their determination and vitality as a people.

George and Louise Spindler
Series Editors
Ethnographics Series Eds.
Calistoga, California

Preface

This case study presents a reconstruction of the culture of the Cakchiquel Maya people of highland Guatemala during the seventeenth century. Therefore, it is by definition a historical ethnography and is based in large part on documents and descriptions produced by people (mostly Spaniards) who did not have a participant's understanding of the customs, beliefs, institutions, and rituals they described. This presents some problems of interpretation and topical coverage, but having reference to three centuries of written records also makes it possible to discuss long-term trends and processes of change that analyses based on synchronic description cannot easily detect.

However, the objective here is more than just the description of an exotic people at some remote time. The Cakchiquel were also a people who, by the seventeenth century, had been swept up in an early phase of European empire building and who were fully incorporated within the Spanish regime. This involved much more than the loss of political sovereignty. These Maya people were also subject to a wide range of demands from their Spanish overlords: that they adopt a new faith, that they change their settlement patterns and political organization, that they pay tribute in goods, services, and money, and many more. The Cakchiquel were, in addition, exposed to some unintentional but nevertheless severe pressures, most notably the precipitous and continuing population losses due to the introduction of Old World diseases to which they had no natural immunities or other defense. Factors such as population loss (and its eventual resurgence) combined with Spanish demands created conditions to which these highland Maya people had to adapt physically, emotionally, and socially in order to survive as a culturally distinct population. The fact that the Cakchiquel are still very much with us today (to the number of about half a million) is ample testament to their ancestors' tenacity and success.

Yet, the Cakchiquel and their situation were not unique. The same range of Spanish-introduced institutions and pressures for change were present to some degree throughout Mesoamerica, and indeed, all of Spanish America. In a wider sense, the Cakchiquel experience is also representative of that of peoples in many parts of the world—in Africa, Oceania, Asia, and the rest of the Americas during the last half-millennium or so—who found themselves inescapably in the path of European expansion and empire building. In that sense, the Cakchiquel of the seventeenth century help to illustrate the cultural dynamics of an entire era and provide an important perspective on human behavior and resilience in general.

It is a pleasure to acknowledge the assistance and support of the many individuals and institutions that made this volume possible. Pride of place must go to my mentor, Dr. Ruben E. Reina, who both introduced me to Maya culture and developed my ethnohistorical interests and skills. I am indebted to the late Dr. William R. Swezey, who suggested to me the importance of studying the Cakchiquel. Licenciada Marcia Galindo provided invaluable aid in making photocopies, and sometimes transcriptions, of the many documents from Guatemalan archives used in this study and many more besides. Both Reina and Dr. Daniel J. Gelo took the time to read my original manuscript and offered many insightful suggestions. Finally, George and Louise Spindler are to be thanked for offering me every encouragement in the preparation of this volume and for sharing with me some of the insights they have gained through their long association with the Case Study series.

Institutionally, both the Archivo General de Centro America and the Instituto Nacional de Antropología e Historia de Guatemala and their respective staffs have consistently offered me every assistance in my investigations, helping to ensure that my stays in Guatemala have always been both productive and enjoyable. In the same vein, thanks are due to the Centro de Investigaciones Regionales de Meso-America and its staff. I am also grateful to the National Endowment for the Humanities for a summer stipend awarded under its Columbian Quincentenary initiative (Grant FT 34109-90), which afforded me time to write most of this volume.

Finally, I am grateful to my family, especially to Charlotte, Rebecca, and Alexander, for their love and support through trying times.

Contents

FIGURES

MAPS

1 / A Commemoration

FIESTA DEL VOLCÁN (FESTIVAL OF THE VOLCANO)

It is late afternoon on the fifth day of November in the year 1680. As they have on this occasion for the last century and a half, scores of Cakchiquel-Maya Indians are working feverishly under the eyes of Spanish officials to complete their project. This year, as in every other, Cakchiquel from towns around the Colonial capital, Santiago de los Caballeros de Guatemala (present-day Antigua), have been ordered to gather materials and bring them to the main plaza. There they build and realistically decorate a huge timber-frame replica of a volcano. The Cakchiquel workers have already spent much time and effort just collecting materials for the project. In addition to the many large timbers needed for construction, they are also required to bring many different kinds of flowering plants and even small trees, which are all used to decorate the volcano. The Indians must also capture wild birds and animals. They place brilliant red and blue varieties of guacamayas and green parrots in the trees along with noisy, capering monkeys. Small, cave-like openings or grottoes built in the sides of the volcano contain a variety of deer, javalinas (wild pigs), tapirs, coatis, and any other creatures the workers have been able to catch. At the volcano's summit the Cakchiquel workers have constructed a small house and, as night falls, Cakchiquel musicians take their places in it, where they will play all night on flutes, conch shell horns, and drums. Spaniards find the strange music entertaining and a large crowd begins to form on the plaza. Wealthier Spaniards arrive in carriages with their ladies, other gentlemen ride gaudily caparisoned horses. Tradesmen and lower-class people arrive on foot. There is room for all in the spacious plaza, and the Cakchiquel have built platforms and grandstands all around it. The evening air is quite mild, for the rains have ended and, even though the city lies within the tropics, it also lies in the high, cool Panchoy valley some 1500 meters above sea level, surrounded by heavily forested volcanoes and mountains.

Early the next morning Cakchiquel work crews are once again busy. They replace flowers which have wilted or been crushed and boughs which have fallen or been broken. Work continues nonstop until midafternoon. By three o'clock the grandstands are full of Spanish observers of every walk of life, as is every balcony providing a view of the plaza. Members of the royal administration look out from the balcony of the massive, two-storied Palace of the Governor, which spans the entire south side of the plaza. City council members are over a hundred yards away across the plaza, on the balcony of the only slightly less impressive ayuntamiento, or city hall. The newly finished cathedral dominates the east side of the plaza.

1

The Cathedral and part of the Plaza Mayor of Santiago de los Caballeros de Guate-mala ca. 1680 (unknown artist). Photo courtesy of the Latin American Library, Tulane University and Dr. Sidney D. Markman.

Statues of the Virgin and eighteen saints gaze out on the proceedings from their niches in the cathedral's elaborately stuccoed facade. On the west is the Portal de Mercaderes, the commercial heart of the city.

The spectacle for which the crowd has gathered begins with a trumpet call as two companies of Spanish cavalry parade in. The troopers then change formation to open order and line the edge of half the plaza. Two companies of infantry follow, who also shift from marching order to line the rest of the plaza. The stage is now fully set and shortly many groups of Cakchiquel, in total numbering perhaps a thousand, begin entering the plaza from the Mercaderes side. However, instead of their everyday clothing, all are dressed and adorned in the style of their preconquest ancestors. All the men wear *maztlates* (loincloths) and have both face and body paint. Gaudy parrot and guacamaya feathers worn as arm or ankle bands or as part of a frame worn on the back complete their outfits. They come as warriors but their weapons have been rendered relatively harmless by the prudent Spanish officials. The warriors all carry shields; some have bows with blunted arrows, others trail spears with no points.

It takes time for so many people to enter the plaza, and following the warriors are musicians who provide the accompaniment for an array of different dances performed by separate troupes of men. The Spanish crowd is enthralled by the performances; the costumes and music are exotic and the colors dazzle their eyes. A final dance with a greater number of participants precedes the next event, the arrival of the Spanish-appointed Cakchiquel governor of the nearby town of Jocotenango. He has the honor of playing the role of "Sinacam," the last Cakchiquel "king," whose unsuccessful "revolt" against Spanish domination in 1526 is to be commemorated this day. The Cakchiquel consider it a high honor indeed to portray Sinacam, the governor of the town of Itzapa once having offered his Jocotenango counterpart the substantial sum of 500 pesos in a vain attempt to persuade him to cede the role. The "king" is carried on a gilded throne adorned with the long, green, and extremely costly tail feathers of the quetzal bird, borne on the shoulders of members of his retinue. Others carry sunshades and fans both for his comfort and as symbols of his rank. All are dressed in fine and richly decorated cloth and wear necklaces of precious metals or jade and feathered headgear. The "king" carries a feather fan in one hand (the Cakchiquel term for a "lord," *ahau,* means literally "he of the fan") and a scepter in the other. He also wears a small but very costly crown, which like the scepter, is a symbol of royalty borrowed from Spanish practice. This group makes its way slowly and with great ceremony directly to the volcano and climbs to the summit with the "king" still in his litter. There, he and his throne are stationed in the small house in which the musicians had played the night before. This action is intended to represent Sinacam's flight from Spanish forces to a mountain on which he made his last stand. All the other warriors array themselves on the slopes of the volcano, sounding their whistles while the musicians play their loudest.

At this point, two companies of men dressed as Spaniards enter the plaza, armed with swords, harquebuses, and pikes and accompanied by a color guard. However, these are not Spaniards but the descendants of Tlaxcalan Indians who had originally come from central Mexico with the conquistadors as auxiliary troops. Now they come from their homes in Ciudad Vieja (the Old City, first site of the Spanish capital, largely destroyed by mudslides in 1541). As the descendants of allies the Spaniards afford them certain privileges such as freedom from tribute and labor obligations owed by other Indians. These "Spaniards" are commanded by their town's governor, accompanied by its council members, all richly dressed in traditional Tlaxcalan style, and a retinue of Tlaxcalan "commoners," also armed like warriors.

As soon as the "Spaniards" and their allies enter, they begin a mock battle, advancing on the volcano and firing their harquebuses into the air. The Cakchiquel defenders shoot their blunt arrows into the air with shouts and whistles and put on an entertaining defense. They move in coordination from one point to another to throw back the assaults, then spread out again. "Officers," recognizable by the devices on their shields, the quetzal feathers they wear, and the gold insignias on their sandals, direct the defenders' movements. The battle lasts quite some time, to the great diversion of the Spanish observers, many of whose ancestors had fought in the campaign.

In a final assault, the "Spaniards" charge up the volcano, driving the Cakchiquel defenders up and over the summit, taking the house there, and making Sinacam their prisoner. He is bound in chains by the governor and councilmen of Ciudad Vieja, who lead him down from the volcano to be presented to the royal governor of Guatemala. With this, the Cakchiquel and Tlaxcalans parade out of the plaza with the same order and pomp as which they entered. The Spaniards then stage a bullfight to end an afternoon of spectacles.

COMMENTARY

This sketch of the Fiesta del Volcán is an appropriate beginning for a description of seventeenth-century Cakchiquel life because all the themes and realities of the Colonial system in which they found themselves are nakedly and unambiguously displayed. In ethnically homogeneous societies, such public observances are typically integrative, drawing together the different component groups or strata for a shared experience based on a common set of meanings. Such is emphatically *not* the case with the Fiesta del Volcán. The groups comprising the larger Colonial society do not intermingle, have vastly different roles, and attach totally different meanings to the symbols and performances.

For the Spaniards, the fiesta is a celebration of violence, the basis of all Colonial systems. Significantly, however, it is not the initial conquest of the area in 1524 that is commemorated. Rather, it is the final battle of a successful campaign two years later against Cakchiquel and Quiché rebels that the Spaniards observe and that legitimizes the Colonial regime with themselves at the top. From the Spaniards' legalistic viewpoint the conquest and accompanying destruction and enslavement of the Highland Maya were barely justifiable acts, especially in the seventeenth century, by which time the royal administration had long since corrected some of the worst excesses of the conquistadors.

The Spaniards themselves were not a homogeneous group. There were marked differences in social station, wealth, and education. There were also three major "interest groups": the *criollos* (descendants of the conquistadors and other New World–born Spaniards), the clergy (especially the religious orders), and members of the royal administration. Tension was also growing between the criollos and the *peninsulares* (European-born Spaniards) because most of the important administrative and ecclesiastical posts were filled by peninsulares sent out for the purpose. For their part, peninsulares thought that the criollos had lost the drive and spirit of their conquistador ancestors and that they looked instead to the king for their continued support through grants of Indian laborers or their products. Whatever their internal differences, all Spaniards found their places and interests legitimized in the Fiesta del Volcán.

The status and livelihood of the criollos in particular depended on appropriating Indian labor and its products. How could such continued exploitation be justified in the face of laws and peninsular officials whose stated aim was to afford the Indians a degree of protection as Spanish subjects? One way was by creating myths concerning the conquest and maintaining self-serving stereotypes about the Indians. The Fiesta del Volcán was a vital and vivid part of their ideology. If the conquest itself was hard to justify, suppression of a revolt against royal authority was not. Indeed, it was the greatest show of loyalty to the Crown that Spanish subjects could make. The criollos chose to believe that, since the indigenous highland Maya (including the Cakchiquel) had technically submitted to the Spanish Crown (in the person of conquistador Pedro de Alvarado), their revolt against endless conquistador demands for gold and for laborers to work as miners was *really* a threat to royal authority. Vanquishing such renegade Maya leaders and their followers was, therefore, a patriotic act and one which also entitled the Spanish participants to the labor and products of the defeated "rebels." Their descendants perpetuated these claims and continued to justify them by maintaining that the Maya were still barbaric, unconverted to Christianity, and untrustworthy. They could, however, be kept loyal, or at least obedient, through the unceasing vigilance of criollo colonists with their superior élan and fighting ability, even in the face of overwhelming numbers. For the criollos, the Fiesta del Volcán kept the ideology alive. As in real life, the criollos directed and observed the Indians, but performed no physical labor. Nor did they participate. They did not even deign to act out their ancestors' role in the performance and thus be forced into close proximity with Indians, instead leaving it to the Tlaxcalans to fill. Spaniards ideally did not work, nor did they typically associate on anything like equal terms (such as combatants) with Indians. They probably felt that even the suggestion that a Spaniard and an Indian could be combatants was too potentially dangerous to the Colonial order to be allowed. The Cakchiquel, by appearing in traditional dress, by performing their own music and dance, and by arranging themselves on the volcano for battle, simply reinforced criollo stereotypes of them as unredeemed savages. The inevitable Spanish victory served to remind criollos *and* peninsular officials of the invaluable service performed by the first colonists and of the need for continual vigilance. It also reassured them that, as in the past, Spanish arms would always triumph. Viewed in this light, the initial parade of Spanish troops that later lined the plaza was both an exhibition of military might to awe the natives and a necessary precaution should the mock battle get out of hand.

Probably both Spaniards and Cakchiquels perceived the volcano (the dominant feature of the landscape) as a symbol for the land, made all the more universal by its decoration with all the different native plants, birds, and other animals. Certainly gaining the summit and driving the defenders off the volcano while capturing their leader was, for the Spaniards, a clear metaphor for taking possession of the country as a whole.

Viewed from this perspective, the Fiesta del Volcán was clearly a Spanish-inspired celebration which symbolically achieved a variety of ends. Spanish rule and the prominence of the criollos in Colonial society were both legitimized. Criollos and peninsulares alike were reassured as to the supremacy of Spanish arms. Self-serving stereotypes of the Indians were perpetuated. Finally, through their humiliating defeat every year, the Cakchiquels were supposedly reminded of their place in Colonial society.

However, it is just as clear that the Cakchiquel did not feel humiliated by the experience. Although it is true that they were ordered to participate by the Spanish authorities, they would have done so with the apparent enthusiasm and dignity that they brought to their performance only if it served some of their own ends as well. Just the fact that the Cakchiquel governor of one town tried to buy the honor of playing Sinacam (who is ultimately brought in chains before the royal representatives) indicates that their participation was not the degrading experience that the Spaniards intended it to be. We cannot know the full range of meanings the Fiesta del Volcán held for the Cakchiquel, because the surviving descriptions were written by and for Spaniards and many important details were omitted. Yet it is still possible to identify a range of symbolic associations (some of which are Pan-Mesoamerican in nature) that provide some clues as to the significance of the fiesta for the Cakchiquel.

As noted previously, both Spaniards and Cakchiquels probably perceived the volcano as a symbol of the land. But for the Cakchiquel this symbol was much richer and contained more profound, even cosmic, associations. In Maya cosmology the volcano or mountain is the home of the Earth Lord, the supernatural being who provides, among other things, the rains essential for agriculture. The volcano/mountain is also the place where the *tonas*, the animal-spirit companions of each individual, are kept. The security of these tonas was of great concern to each individual, for if one's own tona escaped or was set free onto the surface of the world, both would share the same fate. In particular, if the tona were killed by a hunter or by some other animal, its human counterpart would also die. Thus, to the Cakchiquel, the construction of caves or grottoes containing wild animals in the timber-frame volcano was much more than merely ingenious decoration. It was a portrayal of a fundamental component of their traditional worldview. The fact that they were able to present it publicly to the Spaniards, who were too ignorant of the symbolism to object, must have made the exercise all the more satisfying.

The volcano/mountain was also the home of the Cakchiquels' ancestors' spirits. These beings kept watch over their living descendants, who believed quite strongly that their ancestors would one day return to reclaim the land. The volcano/mountain with a small house on top additionally represented a traditional Maya temple-pyramid, or rather vice versa: Maya temple-pyramids were symbols of volcanoes with all the associations outlined above. With the imposition of Christianity as the only legitimate religion, open ritual at the now abandoned temple-pyramids was forbidden. Yet here, in the very center of the Spanish regime, the Cakchiquel had, at the Spaniards' instigation, erected a temporary temple-pyramid. Again, the symbolism would have been obvious to the Cakchiquel but lost on the Spaniards.

The course of the performance was also highly symbolic. The "Spaniards" and their Tlaxcalan allies do overrun the volcano, but, in native Mesoamerican terms, their victory is both literally and figuratively superficial. Only the surface of the land was taken; the domains of the Earth Lord, the ancestors, and the tonas were unscathed. The house atop the volcano represented the temple on the pyramid to the Cakchiquel. In Mesoamerican warfare of the immediate preconquest period, the taking and burning of an enemy's temple was what conventionally constituted defeat. The typical sign for conquest in many of the surviving Mexican pictorial documents is, in fact, a burning temple atop its pyramid. The Spaniards who organized the drama evidently had no familiarity with these Mesoamerican symbols of defeat. In their eyes the taking of the house and its "royal" occupant were enough. But, to the Cakchiquel, "Spanish" actions in the ritual did not go far enough. The house/temple was not desecrated. Therefore, once again, the Spanish conquest was incomplete.

Yet it is in the figure of Sinacam, the last Cakchiquel "king," that we see the most profound divergence between Spanish and Maya symbols. To the Spaniards, Sinacam was a villain who had reneged on his submission to the Crown and helped lead an open revolt that had only barely been suppressed by the meager Spanish forces at hand. His capture and presentation in chains were the greatest humiliation they could imagine, because to professional European officers of the time it was (at least in theory) better to die gloriously in battle than to be taken prisoner and have one's honor questioned. Mesoamerican peoples, including the Cakchiquel, had almost the very opposite idea. For them, an honorable death required that one be captured in order to be sacrificed subsequently by the enemy at their temple, the heart torn from the body being used to feed the gods, which in turn perpetuated the cosmic order. Thus, at one level for the Cakchiquel, their "king" was captured but not sacrificed. Again, the Spanish conquest was incomplete. Yet there is still a more esoteric, mythical interpretation for the role of Sinacam, one which changes the entire meaning of the Fiesta del Volcán from a straightforward celebration of Spanish domination to an event on the cyclical round of cosmic time.

Sinacam can be interpreted as a figure in the Mesoamerican tradition of the man-god ruler. In late preconquest Mesoamerica, the ruler ruled because he partook of the divine, had some special relationship with his group's tutelary deity, or even served as the medium through which the will of the deity could be made manifest. Perhaps the best-known example of such a man-god is Quetzalcoatl (in Maya, Q'uq' Kumatz), or Feathered Serpent. The association is made obvious by the decoration of Sinacam's litter (and probably the impersonator himself) with the long, green tail feathers of the quetzal bird, an almost universal symbol of Quetzalcoatl throughout the region. In Mesoamerican myth Quetzalcoatl was the symbol of civilization: inventor of writing, calendrical record keeping, and divination; patron of the arts, promoter of peace, and the model of the benign priestly role. As a benevolent ruler of the legendary city of Tollan during a golden age of peace, Quetzalcoatl was also opposed to human sacrifice. For this he was ultimately deposed by an opposing faction, ushering in a dark age of militarism and human blood offerings. However, Quetzalcoatl himself was not killed. He fled to the "East" with some of his followers, promising someday to return, reclaim his domain, and bring about a new golden age. Although some scholars question the existence of a historic Quetzalcoatl, and some even suggest that the myths concerning him were postconquest fabrications, the structure of the myth is entirely indigenous. The man-god does not die; he leaves, usually as the result of some conflict. For a people with an understanding of time as cyclical, the act of leaving presupposes an eventual return.

Such myths were not just stories told to children. All Mesoamerican peoples have (or traditionally had) a cyclical view of time quite different from the linear European view. For ourselves, the past is past and its events will never "happen" again. Our future is often uncertain but we do not expect that it will ever be the same as it was in the past. But, for Mesoamerican peoples, like the Cakchiquel, time was indeed cyclical. Days, weeks, months, years, and centuries, as they reckoned them, were all recurring cycles. More significantly, events which had occurred in the past would occur again in the future. Events were just points on a gigantic cycle of cosmic time. It is widely accepted, for example, that the power of these concepts caused the Aztec emperor Moctezuma to vacillate in dealing with the conquistador Hernán Cortés, with tragic results for himself and his people, thinking that the Spaniard just might be the returning Quetzalcoatl, to whom Moctezuma would surrender his domain.

In the Fiesta del Volcán the historical Sinacam is merged with the man-god. The latter's myth is the script that the Cakchiquel participants play out. Like Quetzalcoatl, Sinacam rules in a golden age (of which by 1680 no one had any direct experience) before the coming of the Spaniards and their Tlaxcalan allies. They do overthrow and even capture Sinacam, but, just as in the Quetzalcoatl myth, the "king" is not killed. Sinacam is presented in chains to the Spanish governor but then is released and allowed to exit the plaza with his followers with the same splendor and dignity with which they entered. This is exactly parallel to the departure of Quetzalcoatl and his followers. Quetzalcoatl promised to return. As Sinacam, he returns cyclically, symbolically each year. In this way, the Cakchiquel placed the event of the Spanish conquest and their own current misery in an understandable mythico-historic framework. Events were not chaotic or unpredictable, nor were they or their ancestors to blame for what befell them. Rather, the Spaniards came and deposed them (represented by Sinacam) as an independent people. Implicit in that event is the belief that the deposed man-god and his followers will some day return to reclaim the land. Then the revered ancestors and their descendants will live once again in the future as they had in the past.

Thus, in the Fiesta del Volcán we see the Colonial order in microcosm. The two main groups, Cakchiquels and Spaniards, have fundamentally different realities and vastly divergent interpretations of their situations and experience. This does not mean that the Spanish conquest, associated events, and imported institutions had no effect on Cakchiquel life. Nor does it mean that the Cakchiquel meekly accepted and responded to Spanish demands. But, like their role in the Fiesta del Volcán, their responses, their *adaptations* to the demands of the Colonial situation were largely worked out by the Cakchiquel themselves, usually without the Spaniards' knowledge or understanding. The adaptive process involved innovative combinations of both traditional and imported practices, beliefs, technologies, and institutions. The resulting synthesis was a Colonial Cakchiquel culture, as different from that of their preconquest ancestors as it is from their present-day descendants, that provided the means for the Cakchiquel to endure *as* Cakchiquel through three centuries of Colonial rule, and indeed, down to today.

BIBLIOGRAPHIC NOTE

The most complete account of the Fiesta del Volcán is contained in the writings of the criollo historian Fuentes y Guzmán (1969–1972, I:346–350), who was himself responsible for organizing the event in 1682 (Archivo General de Centro America, document A 1.2.9 Leg.2840 Exp.25350). Juarros (first English edition 1823) relied heavily on Fuentes in his account, adding only that the fiesta had been discontinued due to the expenses incurred by the Indian participants (part of the general process of Cakchiquel impoverishment in the later Colonial period). Tovilla (1960:153) penned a much briefer account of the fiesta as performed in the 1630s. The man-god concept of Mesoamerican rulers was advanced by López Austin (1973) and has been elaborated upon by Gruzinski (1989) and Gillespie (1989). Hunt (1977) presents a good, English-language introduction to the vast topic of Mesoamerican symbolism.

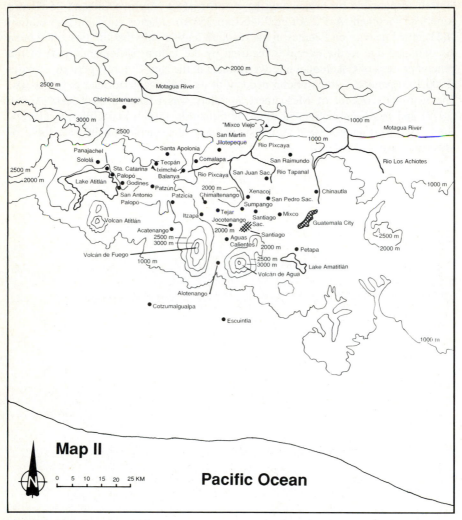

Map II

0 5 10 15 20 25 KM

Pacific Ocean

2500 m

2000 m

Chichicastenango

3000 m

2500

2000 m

Motagua River

"Mixco Viejo"

San Martín
Jilotepeque

Río Pixcaya

1000 m

Motagua River

1000 m

Río Los Achiotes

Santa Apolonia

Panajachel
Solalá

Tecpán

Comalapa

San Raimundo

Sta. Catarina
Palopó

Iximché

Río Pixcaya

San Juan Sac.

Río Tapanal

Lake Atitlán

Balanya

Godines

Patzún

2000 m

Xenacoj

San Pedro Sac.

Chinautla

1000 m

San Antonio
Palopo

Patzicia

Chimaltenango

Sumpango

Volcan Atitlán

Itzapa

Tejar

Jocotenango

Santiago
Sac.

2000 m

Mixco

Guatemala City

2500 m

2000 m

Acatenango

Santiago

2500 m
3000 m

Aguas
Calientes

2000 m

Petapa

Volcán de Fuego

1000 m

2500 m
3000 m

Lake Amatitlán

Volcán de Agua

Alotenango

Cotzumalgualpa

Escuintla

1000 m

N

The Cakchiquel region with important towns and other places mentioned in the text.

2 / Background

HIGHLAND GUATEMALA

At the time of the Spanish conquest in 1524, the people we call the Cakchiquel occupied a considerable portion of the highland area of what is today Guatemala. Their combined territory stretched from the edge of the Valley of Guatemala on the east to the shores of Lake Atitlán on the west, and from the Motagua River on the north to the edge of the Pacific slope. Though almost entirely in the highlands, this area is far from uniform. Several major geological and altitudinal variations exist, with corresponding environmental differences. These, in turn, have for millennia been a stimulus for trade both through the highlands and with the rest of preconquest Mesoamerica.

Tierra caliente; the Motagua River valley just west of "Mixco Viejo" (photo by the author).

11

The whole of Guatemala lies south of the Tropic of Cancer, so seasonal differences (especially in terms of temperature) are generally much less pronounced than in the temperate regions of North America or Europe. These general conditions are complicated by the mountains which form the highlands, since temperature varies with altitude. Also, the relatively narrow land mass of Central America permits the movement of humid ocean air entirely across it. These factors produce two important effects. The first is the existence of two seasons, the rainy season from about May through October, during which about 70 percent of the region's precipitation occurs; and the dry season from November through April. The reliability and predictability of this rainy season–dry season cycle have made cultivation of one sort or another a dependable source of subsistence and required people to schedule their activities accordingly. The second effect is the presence of distinct altitudinal/environmental zones, referred to using Spanish terms since Colonial times.

Tierra caliente is land less than about 800 meters above sea level, with a median temperature of 27°C. This zone is normally thought of in terms of the lush, humid lowlands of the broad Pacific coastal plain and the Petén jungle of the north. But, it also refers to the region's hot, dry interior river valleys such as the Chixoy, the Grijalva, and, especially for the Cakchiquel, the Motagua. *Tierra templada* is normally defined as ranging in altitude between about 800 and 1500 meters. As the name indicates, temperatures here are moderate, with a median of 23°C. It is this

Tierra templada; looking northeast across the upper Pixcaya River valley, on the road to San Martín Jilotepéque (photo by the author).

Tierra fría; looking northeast across the Chimaltenango basin near Tecpán (photo by the author).

zone that gives Guatemala its reputation as "the land of eternal spring." *Tierra fría* lies above 1500 meters. Above the 2500-meter level, median temperatures may range as low as 10° to 17°C. Using these parameters, much of the Cakchiquel territory lies within the tierra fría zone, with bands of tierra templada and tierra caliente as one descends toward the coast or the Motagua valley.

However, the geological variation in the region is still more complex. The highlands themselves can be subdivided. The so-called volcanic highlands are part of the string of occasionally active volcanoes that rim the Pacific. They constitute roughly the southern third of the Cakchiquel country between Lake Atitlán (dominated by the Tolimón volcano) and the Valley of Guatemala (dominated in turn by the Volcán de Agua). The ejecta of the volcanoes have accumulated in the high basins between them. Over time, these deposits have weathered into excellent soils for cultivation. However, erosion has also occurred in these massive deposits so that most valleys are cut by deep, steep-sided ravines *(barrancas)*, which constitute serious impediments to ground travel, whether on foot, mule, or by motor vehicle. Parallel and to the north of the string of volcanoes lies a region sometimes known as the tropical highlands. This area is primarily formed of geologically older igneous and metamorphic rocks, and the resulting soils are neither as deep nor as good as those of the volcanic zone. However, the generally lower altitude and warmer temperatures encourage the growth of a wide range of plants and animals. The tierra caliente of the Motagua valley lies within this metamorphic zone. The Motagua is the main drainage from the Guatemala highlands to the Caribbean and follows a major geologic fault line. Slippage along this fault has been the cause of severe earthquakes, such as the one which devastated a large portion of the highlands in 1976. While hot because of the low altitude, the valley tends to be very dry and supports only a semidesert range of plants (such as cactus) except along the actual water courses of the river and its tributaries. There, larger trees such as the giant ceiba can find enough soil and water to flourish. The valley is dry due to a "rain shadow" effect, in which the mountains on both the north and south catch the rain coming up either from the Pacific or the Caribbean and Gulf of Mexico. While water flow is heavy, even furious, during the rainy season, it is low during the rest of the year. The great variation in flow and the narrow valley floor preclude the development of irrigation agriculture on any great scale, but the basin is an area from which important resources were and are drawn.

The main food plants—corn, beans, and squash—can be grown successfully at all altitudes where soil and moisture are adequate, providing a basic vegetarian subsistence. Other plants, some of which are economically very important, are more limited in range. The avocado, tomato, ubiquitous chile, and most other fruits require a great deal of water and produce best in tierra templada and tierra caliente. Similarly, cacao (chocolate beans) and cotton are also essentially tierra caliente crops. On the other hand, the *agave* (century plant), from which both cordage and textiles are made, grows best in the drier parts of the highlands above 1500 meters.

Other important natural resources are also irregularly distributed. Obsidian (volcanic glass) was fashioned into blades as the universal cutting tools of pre-conquest Mesoamerica. Its use, at the very least for arrow-points, continued well into the Colonial period. Indeed, one reason for the Chajomá-Cakchiquel expansion in the late preconquest period was to control a major obsidian source near San Martín Jilotepéque. Another volcanic material, basalt, was the preferred material for *metates* (grinding stones) and *manos* (handstones), which were needed in every household for the preparation of corn dough for *tortillas,* the basic food staple. Reeds occurred only in well-watered places but were woven into *petates* (rush mats) used by everyone as floor or wall coverings, doors, mattresses, and work surfaces for activities such as pottery making. Clay, as the raw material for pottery, tends to occur as strata or veins in geologically older formations outside the highland volcanic zone, and such deposits are often exposed through erosion. All these plants and substances may be considered commodities of primary importance because they underlie the life-style of the Cakchiquel, as they did for nearly all Mesoamerican people.

However, there were a number of other commodities that, while not crucial for physical survival, were necessary for the functioning of the preconquest Cakchi-quels' stratified society. Jade ornaments were markers of aristocratic status and included beads strung as necklaces and bracelets, pendants, ear plugs (inserted through artificially enlarged holes in the ear lobes), and nose plugs or pendants (either inserted through the nasal septum or suspended from it). They were valued for their scarcity and for the labor involved in their manufacture, but jade also had symbolic associations. Its green color symbolized the lush plant life that flourished during the rainy season. By extension, it symbolized life itself, a single jade bead often being placed in the mouth of a corpse before burial in hopes of an eventual return to the living. Finally, as we have seen in part, feathers were also valuable commodities, both for signaling differences in social rank and for their symbolic associations. Especially valued were the long, green tail feathers of the quetzal bird, whose habitat lay well outside the Cakchiquel country to the north in the lower tropical highlands of the Verapaz. Many other brightly colored tropical birds were also valued for their plumage, and these tended to be dwellers of the tierra caliente or, at most, tierra templada.

Even from this brief discussion it is clear that people living in or controlling one geological, altitudinal, or environmental zone needed products from the others in order to maintain their way of life. In fact, there is scant evidence that any Maya polity ever directly controlled production in all major zones in the way that was common in Andean civilization. Instead, the Cakchiquel, like Mesoamerican people in general, relied on merchants and markets for the distribution of goods from their diverse points of origin. Until the Spanish conquest, this was purely a matter of human porters, carrying goods on the ubiquitous *cacaste* (pack frame) supported with a *mecapal* (tumpline), either as individual, small-scale vendors or as part of an important merchant's train. Through these mechanisms, people created a network through which goods and commodities made their way from zone to zone, polity to polity, and even well beyond the region. For example, quetzal feathers from the Verapaz and cacao from the Pacific slope of Guatemala both were traded through intermediaries all the way to the Valley of Mexico, where Aztec nobles sipped hot chocolate laced with chile and royalty adorned themselves with the long, green feathers.

THE CAKCHIQUEL AND MAYA CIVILIZATION

Despite the need to obtain products from different zones, the Guatemala highlands on the eve of the Spanish conquest were not unified politically. The different ethnolinguistic groups (Cakchiquel, Quiché, Tzutujil, Mam, Pokóm, and Pipil, among others) were all at odds with one another and were themselves divided into smaller polities, engaged in an incessant, Machiavellian web of negotiations, alliance, betrayal, and war, which the conquistadors used to their own advantage in subduing the individual groups. In particular, the people whom we have come to call the Cakchiquel were never a single political entity. There appear instead to have been at least four independent confederations *(amaq')*, whose conflicts with each other were, perhaps, slightly less frequent than those with other peoples. The Zotzil amaq' and that of the Cakchiquel proper had their combined capital, Iximché (also known as Tecpán Guatemala), on the western edge of the broad and fertile Chimaltenango basin. From there they controlled communication routes between the upper Motagua valley and the Pacific coast, while dominating the eastern and northern shores of Lake Atitlán. On the east were the people referred to by their Cakchiquel neighbors as the Akahal. Their own name for themselves was Chajomá, and their occupation focused on the Motagua valley and its tributaries. Just before the

Partially restored temple-pyramids at Iximché in tierra fría country (photo by the author).

Foundations of palace structures at Iximché (photo by the author).

Restored temple-pyramids at "Mixco Viejo" in tierra caliente country (photo by the author).

conquest they appear to have begun a process of separation. Those Chajomá west of the Pixcaya River controlled an area that would later become San Martín Jilotepéque. They seem still to have shared with some of the eastern Chajomá an important center near the junction of the Pixcaya and Motagua rivers (restored, the site is popularly known as "Mixco Viejo," a result of its misidentification by Colonial chronicler Fuentes y Guzmán). The eastern Chajomá claimed the territory defined by the Pixcaya, Motagua, and Los Achiotes rivers on the west, north, and east respectively and by a series of streams and hills running just north of the Valley of Guatemala. Finally, the Tukuché were originally part of the Iximché polity but had revolted in 1493 and had been pushed out as a result. Apparently, they initially gravitated back north toward the Quiché, but at least some of them moved east into the Chajomá territory, where they were numbered in the 1560s as a distinct group *(parcialidad)* within the town of San Pedro Sacatepéquez. All of these Cakchiquel polities were relatively recent creations, the people themselves (or at least their aristocratic leadership) being late arrivals in highland Guatemala. Yet they were still Maya people within the larger Mesoamerican area and thus heirs to a highly developed cultural tradition that, in 1524, spanned some two millennia.

Maya civilization attained its highest development in the Petén lowlands during the millennium between about 300 B.C. and 900 A.D. This period saw the development of a complex, urban society with a high degree of social stratification and a

Another group of restored structures at "Mixco Viejo" (photo by the author).

political organization on something like a state level with a number of larger, at times competing, lowland "kingdoms." Long-distance trade both in bulk commodities and luxury goods ranged far beyond the lowlands. The Maya developed a system of mathematics based on the common Mesoamerican vigesimal (by twenties) system and innovated the concept of a zero notation. These mathematics were undoubtedly applied to a wide array of administrative tasks but were also used in astronomical calculations that were central to their ideas concerning time, history, and divination. They developed a unique representational style, expressed in a variety of media (including stone, wood, pottery, and bone) that had great continuity across the region and through time. These characteristics together define what has come to be known as "Classic" Maya civilization.

But, by 900 A.D., lowland Maya civilization was in a state of collapse. The explanations for the apparently rapid disintegration of this seemingly successful society vary and a discussion of them goes beyond the scope of this volume. However, many Maya groups, perhaps mostly on the fringes of the Petén lowlands, survived more or less intact. Among these, probably from the eastern Gulf coast near the mouth of the Usumacinta, were groups of Maya heavily influenced by Central Mexican culture. At some point, numbers of these aggressive, adventurous people began migrating up the Usumacinta and, after about 1200 A.D., pushed up the narrow valley of the Chixoy River into the Guatemala highlands. Among them were the ancestors of the Cakchiquel and Quiché rulers who met the Spaniards. It is not clear just what form this migration took. One view is that it was essentially a military operation, in which basically only men went up into the highlands, there to intermarry with indigenous women whose language they also adopted (Carmack 1981:43–61). Other evidence suggests something more like a true migration of entire peoples (Reina and Hill 1978:205–206). This interpretation is supported by the seemingly complete changes in such components of the archeological record as ceramics, styles of art and architecture, construction techniques, and site placement (Smith 1955, 1965). In any event, these newcomers found something of a power vacuum in the midwestern highlands and shouldered aside or incorporated some of the indigenous people they found there, while coming into long-term conflicts with the Pokomám on the east and the Mam on the west. The Cakchiquel groups seem to have served as dependent allies and military auxiliaries of the central Quiché of the Santa Cruz basin until the later 1400s. At that time the Cakchiquel began carving out their own independent territories, moving south and east of their former Quiché associates, into the areas where the Spaniards first met them.

THE SPANISH CONQUEST

Very little documentation concerning the conquest appears to have been produced at the time by individuals involved in it. Most accounts were written long after the events they describe, by authors with ulterior motives such as glorifying the conquerors or vilifying their deeds. The few surviving accounts written by the Maya themselves are not effusive in terms of details and are spotty in their coverage of events.

To the extent that we can reconstruct occurrences, it seems that the Iximché polity was visited by emissaries from the Aztec emperor Moctezuma as early as 1510, advising them of rumors concerning newly arrived strangers in the Caribbean and, perhaps, the Atlantic coast of the Yucatán. There was no further news about the Europeans until 1520. That year witnessed two pivotal events in highland Maya history. One was the arrival of the first in a long, agonizing series of pandemics, probably involving both smallpox and plague. As we know from European history, the effects of these new diseases on a population with no immunities must have been devastating. One scholar has estimated that at least one-third of the highland Guatemala population died as a direct result of these diseases, while many of the survivors were so weakened as to be susceptible to a host of secondary infections such as pneumonia and influenza (MacLeod 1973:41). The second event, and perhaps in part a product of the first, was the sending of ambassadors from Iximché to Hernán Cortés, the Spanish conqueror of the Aztecs, requesting an alliance and his aid against their former friends and now bitter enemies, the Quiché.

Cortés and his small force were occupied with the subjugation of Mexico for some three more years, but late in 1523 his lieutenant, Don Pedro de Alvarado, set out toward the south to locate the lands that the Aztecs referred to as Xoconochco and Quauhtemallan. He took with him only a small force of Spaniards: some 120 horsemen, 300 infantry (armed with arquebuses, crossbows, or sword and buckler), and four small artillery pieces. The bulk of his force consisted of a contingent of as many as several thousand native Mexican troops. In advance of this force, Cortés sent emissaries to the Quiché of Utatlán, requesting their submission to the Spanish crown and offering his friendship in return. This offer was evidently refused, and the Quiché set about arranging an alliance among the many highland groups. However, old enmities were too strong and the two other most powerful groups, the Iximché Cakchiquels and the Tzutujil from the south side of Lake Atitlán, refused to cooperate. This left the Quiché alone to face Alvarado.

Their first encounter occurred in February of 1524 as Alvarado entered the Quetzaltenango Valley. There a Quiché army was routed and its commander killed (reputedly in single combat against a mounted Alvarado). How could such a small force of Spaniards have prevailed against the combined might of the Quiché? The same question has been asked regarding Cortés' success against the much larger and more powerful Aztec state. While both events had some unique circumstances, they also shared some common elements. Mesoamerican warfare was conducted by combatants using bows and arrows, spear-throwers and darts, obsidian-tipped lances, and obsidian-bladed wooden clubs or swords. These were all weapons that were only effective when used at close range or against massed troop formations. Such large blocks of men were ideal targets for the inaccurate firearms and artillery of the early sixteenth century. There is a tendency in the literature on the Spanish conquests to suggest some lack of courage or childlike fear on the part of the Indians resulting from their first exposure to gunfire, as if this were an unusual reaction or something to be expected only from "primitive" or "savage" peoples. In fact, it is impossible to overestimate the terror caused by massed firearms and artillery fire when directed at people (including European troops of the period) with no previous experience of them. The noise is tremendous, the smoke produced by the ignition of large volumes of black powder overpowering, and the effect of the projectiles on human flesh terrific. It might be argued that the Aztecs and Maya should simply have overwhelmed the Spaniards by weight of numbers, taking advantage of the long loading procedure required by firearms of the period to close with the enemy. The problem here is twofold. First, Spanish commanders knew full well the limits of their weapons and how to cover reloading infantry and guns with cavalry, the effect of which was as devastating psychologically as that of firearms. Second, both Cortés and Alvarado had many times the number of Spanish troops in Indian auxiliary troops. These constituted the shaft behind the iron Spanish spearpoint. They could be relied upon to protect the flanks or close with the enemy to give the Spaniards time to load or rally. Another important reason for Alvarado's successes was the nature of Mesoamerican warfare. As we currently understand it, Mesoamerican warfare had a strong ritual element in which the capture of enemy prisoners for later sacrifice was often more important than killing the enemy on the field or achieving some tactical advantage. This attitude would have put the Quiché at a fatal (literally!) disadvantage vis-à-vis their Spanish adversaries, who had a much more pragmatic approach to waging war. Probably the single most important factor in Alvarado's victories was the fact (referred to above) that the highland Maya had been decimated by Old World diseases two years before his arrival. These microbes have been dubbed "the shock troops of the conquest" (MacLeod 1973:40). After their onslaught it was only "the sickly survivors of a disaster" whom Alvarado and his men encountered on their campaign (MacLeod 1973:41).

After several more defeats, the Quiché offered to negotiate an end to hostilities. This was evidently just a *ruse de guerre,* however, in order to get the Spaniards into the densely built center of Utatlán, which the Quiché reportedly planned to burn in order to eliminate their powerful enemy. Somehow, the Spaniards became suspicious or were warned of Quiché intentions and were able to exit the town with a number of high-ranking prisoners. A drumhead court was convened in which one of the prisoners confessed to the plot and was pardoned. The others, apparently defiant to the end, were executed on Alvarado's order.

To continue his campaign against the Quiché, Alvarado sent messengers to Iximché requesting troops. Some 2000 warriors were sent immediately to participate in the long-anticipated end to Quiché power. At the conclusion of this phase of his expedition, Alvarado made a triumphal entry into Iximché, where he was greeted by the dual rulers, Cahi Imox (Four Lizard, a calendrical name), the ahpozotzil, or head of the Zotzil amaq', and Belehe Qat (Nine Loads of Maize), the ahpoxahil, or Xahil leader. When questioned about their other enemies, the Iximché rulers identified the Tzutujil people. Shortly thereafter, in April of 1524, Alvarado and his force, presumably well reinforced with eager Cakchiquel warriors, met and defeated the Tzutujil forces. Ever restless for greater conquests and more gold than he had found in Guatemala, Alvarado pressed on in early May for Cuscatlán (present-day El Salvador), eliminating the Pipil-speaking polity (and enemies of the Cakchiquel) at Escuintla.

Late in July he returned to Iximché. Things must have looked very good indeed to its people. Their traditional enemies had all been crushed and they had the most powerful military force in the region as their ally. The possibilities for expanding Iximché control over still more of the country must have seemed limitless. Suddenly, however, the self-satisfaction and dreams of domination over their enemies were shattered. Frustrated by his failure to take as much gold booty during his conquests as he had hoped, and perhaps feeling that he was running out of both time and new, richer lands to conquer, Alvarado began almost psychotically to extort tribute from his Cakchiquel allies and to demand crews of workers by the hundreds to pan gold for him in the area's few placer deposits. The Iximché leaders tried to negotiate but were brusquely dismissed. This was not how they, as Spanish allies, expected to be treated. Only then did they begin to realize the implications of the new order. Not having any other options against Spanish military power, the Iximché people placed their faith in one of their religious leaders, who warned all residents of the town to leave by night late in August of 1524. However, his magic had no effect; the Spaniards were not destroyed. In fact, just the opposite was about to occur. Alvarado, evidently expecting an attack after the town's abandonment, decided to take the initiative, cruelly hunting the people down as they attempted to flee into the surrounding hills and condemning the captives as slaves.

The Cakchiquel fought back as best they could, digging pitfalls planted with stakes to help defend passes and other natural strongpoints against Spanish cavalry. But, by 1528, the Xahil division of the Iximché polity had again submitted to Alvarado's tribute demands and were being resettled in a new town that would later become known as Sololá. Sporadic uprisings continued, but with the death of Ahpoxahil Belehe Qat in 1532 and the appointment of a puppet to his office by

Alvarado, even Cahi Imox (the Sinacam of the Fiesta del Volcán), the ahpozotzil, gave up and went to live in the new Spanish capital (unlike the legend enacted in the fiesta, Cahi Imox was later hanged by Alvarado's order in 1540 out of fear that he and his Quiché counterpart, Tepepul, *might* lead another uprising).

The conquest of the Chajomá is even less well documented than that of the Iximché polity but was, perhaps, even more drawn out, due to their greater decentralization. Our only source for this episode is the account of Fuentes y Guzmán, written over a century and a half after the event. According to this account, the Chajomá began raiding other groups (probably other Cakchiquel and Quiché) that had submitted to Spanish rule as early as 1524 or 1525. After his defeat of the Tzutujil, Alvarado reportedly sent a detachment of Spanish infantry supported by Iximché and Mexican warriors against the Chajomá (in Fuentes' account they are referred to by their Colonial and modern name, the Sacatepéquez). After a quick series of victories, the Chajomá were defeated and surrendered many of their number as slaves to the Spaniards. By 1526 the Chajomá were evidently in revolt against Spanish domination, urged on by one of their priests. He had declared that one of their gods (Camanelon) was angered that the Chajomá had apparently lost faith in him and had surrendered to the Spaniards and their gods (including the saints). This was probably the uprising commemorated in the Fiesta del Volcán, although "Sinacam" was not involved in it directly. After another series of battles, the Spaniards were again in command and the captured priest was executed.

In the wake of all these "rebellions" and the continuing failure to amass large quantities of gold, the Spaniards in general, and Alvarado in particular, felt justified in enslaving many hundreds (if not thousands) of highland Maya people, including many former leaders and members of the indigenous aristocracy. Whatever their former rank, these people were used to build the first Spanish capital (ruined in 1541 and henceforth known as Ciudad Vieja, the Old City), to pan for gold, to serve as bearers and servants, and to cultivate the lands around the capital for a variety of Spanish masters. Alvarado had been brought up before a royal tribunal *(audiencia)* in Mexico in 1529 on charges for his excesses, but in the absence of Maya witnesses, he easily deflected the accusations against him. Indeed, Alvarado's power and that of his fellow conquistadors over their emperor's new Maya subjects were unrestrained until after his death, which occurred while he was preparing for yet another campaign in search of gold in 1541.

Shortly thereafter, a proper royal administration began. Before this time, Alvarado (in his capacity as *adelantado* and by virtue of the authority given him by Cortés) and his followers, organized as a municipal government *(ayuntamiento),* had held virtually all power. The promulgation of the New Laws in 1542 (which abolished slavery and other excesses) and the appointment of Alonso López de Cerrato in 1548 as president of the governing audiencia of Guatemala were acts which, to a significant degree, challenged and even partially dismantled the early conquest state.

The initial conquest of Guatemala was more of an organized raiding expedition than an attempt to bring the new land under effective control. By 1550 this phase of the Colonial period was effectively over. The easily worked placer deposits of precious metals were exhausted and slavery had been abolished. Partly replacing it was the practice of *encomienda,* whereby the Crown granted the tribute otherwise due it to a Spaniard in return for his service in the conquest of the region. Only prominent or well-connected Spaniards benefited from this, however, and many of them (including Alvarado) even wanted to leave, either to return to Spain or to move on to more promising adventures. Those who stayed searched for other natural resources which they could quickly and profitably turn into valuable commodities. Cacao provided one short-lived economic boom but was labor-intensive and difficult to grow. Spanish mismanagement of the delicate crop, maltreatment of the Indians, and the latter's continuing population loss combined so that the boom was over by 1600. From the Europeans' viewpoint, the region then declined into a century-long economic depression. During this later period a fairly stable relationship was established between the Cakchiquel and the Spaniards, their institutions, and their practices. It was not an equal relationship, nor one in which the Cakchiquel benefited much. However, as exemplified by the Fiesta del Volcán, the Cakchiquel, while required to conform to Spanish demands, responded innovatively to their situation, especially in those aspects of their lives (the majority) in which the Spaniards had no specific interest. The following chapters, then, describe the Cakchiquel adaptation to Colonial rule as it developed in the relatively depressed and stable conditions of the seventeenth century.

A WORD ON SOURCES

The following description of Colonial Cakchiquel culture is, by definition, a historical ethnography, a reconstruction based on documentary sources. Rather than relying on information provided by live informants, the ethnohistorian uses evidence gleaned from written records. It may thus be appropriate here to describe and briefly evaluate some of the main sources and categories of documents relied upon in this study.

All the documents used here are primary historical sources in the sense that they were written during the time period described, by individuals with some direct experience of the events, customs, beliefs, or institutions they report. Beyond this, a useful distinction can be made between descriptive and episodic documents. As the name indicates, descriptive documents are composed by their authors for the specific purpose of portraying some custom, belief, or institution to the reader. Histories (in the original sense of a description of contemporary conditions), memoirs, and dictionaries are the main descriptive documents used in this study. In contrast, episodic documents are created to serve some immediate, utilitarian purpose rather than to describe some custom. Administrative records, litigation proceedings, wills, and agreements between individuals or groups are included here.

As is typical in ethnohistory, the descriptive documents used here were all written by individuals who were not themselves Cakchiquel and who thus did not have an insider's understanding of the things they reported. Yet, the authors of all the descriptions used here had fairly intimate knowledge of at least some aspects of Colonial Maya culture resulting from long association with the people or intentional investigations of their language.

Francisco Antonio de Fuentes y Guzmán was born, raised, and spent his entire life in the Kingdom of Guatemala. He was thus a criollo and proudly traced his descent from an original conquistador and chronicler, Bernal Díaz del Castillo. Fuentes wrote his monumental Recordación Florida near the end of the seventeenth century. In it he combined the history of the kingdom up to that time with natural history and contemporary social conditions. Like other criollos, Fuentes saw the Indians as a race to serve their conquerors, and he fully expresses all the stereotypes of Indians as lazy, drunken, only partly Christianized, and thus untrustworthy, which his class used to justify their exploitation. But Fuentes had grown up around Cakchiquel Indians living near the Colonial capital and, as an adult, had even served as a royal administrator over an overwhelmingly Indian district of the kingdom. He thus had an unusually broad (if not especially deep) knowledge of Indian culture for a criollo. He also had intense local pride, which compelled him to describe many aspects of Indian culture at some length. They may have been to him ignorant, superstitious, and little better than barbarians, but they were, in a sense, *his* Indians and thus worthy of at least some attention in his work.

In contrast, the English friar Thomas Gage was in many respects sympathetic to the Indians. He lived in several Pokomám towns (especially Mixco, which lay on the eastern border of the Cakchiquel region) in the 1630s. In his polemical memoir intended to inflame English readers against Spain and Catholicism, he spared no effort to describe Spanish exploitation of the Indians and to depict any unsavory (to European eyes) Indian characteristic as a result of defective Spanish administration. Because his work was written to inform an audience with absolutely no experience of Guatemala or its people, Gage's descriptions are often quite fulsome, though not always on subjects which an ethnographer would deem all that important.

Finally, in terms of descriptive sources, Thomás Coto was a Franciscan friar-linguist who lived among the Cakchiquel and studied their language for over half a century, before his death in the last decade of the seventeenth century. His massive *Thesaurus Verborum* is a combination dictionary and grammar compiled from his own investigations plus those of earlier members of his order, going back to the mid 1500s. His dictionary is organized on a Spanish-to-Cakchiquel basis and constitutes an exhaustive inventory of seventeenth-century Cakchiquel culture. Coto is especially useful in that he explains the meanings and usage of the Cakchiquel terms rather than just presenting them as rough equivalents of Spanish words. The result is glimpses of nearly ethnographic quality into many aspects of Colonial Cakchiquel life.

Despite some occasional insights, all of these descriptive sources were written by individuals whose knowledge and understanding of Indian culture were incomplete, and many important topics (such as family organization, for example) go completely unaddressed. Fortunately, we have a variety of episodic sources that make up these deficits to some extent, and some of these were written by and for Cakchiquel people themselves. The day-to-day Spanish civil and ecclesiastical administration produced an enormous quantity of documents, with the Indians figuring prominently in many of them. Most important in this study are the records of litigations concerning land, which are especially prominent in Chapter 4. Such litigation records also frequently contain as evidence Cakchiquel documents such as wills, histories, bills of sale, and contractual agreements. These sorts of documents conveniently complement the European sources, covering topics not otherwise addressed anywhere else. These documents are described in detail in Chapter 9. Information from Cakchiquel documents was used extensively in Chapters 3, 4, 8, and 9.

The documentary record is, by definition, incomplete and imperfect. Even if they had set out to do so, seventeenth-century Europeans could not have produced a full description of Cakchiquel culture. Even a present-day ethnographer achieves only an approximation and focuses on topics defined by the concerns of anthropology as a discipline. Errors and inaccuracies are also inevitable. However, by using a wide range of documents, multiple sources for specific topics, and documents produced by both Spaniards and Cakchiquel, the ethnohistorian can overcome most of these inadequacies and create a picture (remarkably detailed in some respects) of Colonial Cakchiquel.

BIBLIOGRAPHIC NOTE

MacBryde (1947) is still the best introduction to highland Maya cultural geography and was relied upon heavily for this chapter. For an overview of Maya archeology see Coe (1984). Some of the results of archeological investigations appear in Guillemin (1967, 1977). Cakchiquel protohistory and the Spanish conquest are discussed by Polo (1977) and Borg (1986). Carmack (1973) discusses in detail the variety of historical sources pertaining to the highland Maya, and Hill and Monaghan (1987) discuss the potentials and pitfalls of litigation records in particular.

3 / The Social Universe

The social universe of the seventeenth-century Cakchiquel was complex. They were heirs to a preconquest system of organization and stratification, but the Spanish conquest had drastically changed the situation. Cakchiquel population fell precipitously in the sixteenth century as a result of both military resistance to Spanish rule and introduced diseases. Some traditional institutions disintegrated under the strain, while the Cakchiquel successfully modified others to meet or even exploit the new conditions. By the seventeenth century the basic form of Colonial Cakchiquel society was set.

POPULATION

As in any preindustrial, overwhelmingly agricultural society, population trends, such as growth and decline, and the person/land ratio conditioned the entire range of social, economic, and even religious relationships and institutions. The general history of highland Maya population involved a catastrophic decline in the sixteenth century, reaching the lowest level in the late sixteenth and early seventeenth centuries. Populations remained at depressed levels through much of the seventeenth century but began to grow by its end, initiating a trend that would continue down to the present.

Unfortunately, we cannot know with any precision the size of the preconquest Cakchiquel population, or that of any other indigenous group. The archeological remains at some of the larger excavated preconquest centers suggest resident populations numbering in the thousands. However, as today, the bulk of the population was probably dispersed throughout the countryside, with families living near the lands they cultivated. Seldom does any trace remain of their perishable dwellings, built in most cases of wattle and daub with thatched roofs. Therefore, archeology provides only an incomplete and ambiguous picture of the region's preconquest population.

The Spaniards made no attempt to compile anything like a census of their emperor's new subjects until the late 1540s, more than twenty years after the first, devastating pandemic. Despite the lack of detailed information, the Spaniards were quite aware that the indigenous populations, and especially the Cakchiquel, had greatly declined and were continuing to do so at an alarming rate, as they had increasing difficulty in finding sufficient laborers for their fields, mines, and construction projects.

No true, detailed censuses exist for the Colonial Cakchiquel, only an occasional detailed enumeration of the people living in a particular community. Usually the Spaniards only compiled figures useful to their civil and ecclesiastical administration of the area, the number of *tributarios enteros* and *indios de confesión,* respectively. The tributario entero (full tributary) was a unit of taxation ideally composed of a married couple and their children. Unmarried adults, such as widows and widowers, counted as *medios,* or half-tributaries, while people over age 55 were exempt. Indios de confesión were individuals of either sex and any age who regularly took confession. Both kinds of figures are difficult to interpret. The tributario counts took no account of children, people over 55, and *reservados* (those exempted from tribute on account of their participation in the civil government or ritual obligations of their community). Confesión figures do not distinguish age or sex at all. How, then, can one establish the average number of people— including children, old people, and reservados—represented by one tributario? What percentage of a population is represented by a given number of indios de confesión?

The problem is made still more difficult by chronic underreporting. By the beginning of the seventeenth century at the latest, significant parts of the populations that had been brought together by the Spaniards to form towns *(congregaciones)* began drifting out to the lands they worked, often far from the town itself. Spanish civil and church officials constantly complained about the difficulty, if not impossibility, of counting such people or rounding them up for regular attendance at church.

The figures cited are taken from the Franciscan chronicler Vázquez and Colonial-period historian Fuentes y Guzmán. The indios de confesión figures provided by Vázquez have been increased by a factor of one and a half, on the assumption that the counts are moderately accurate representations of the adult and adolescent portions of the population and that they underreport children and families living far from town. The tributario figures have been converted by multiplying by two and a half, because only adults under age 55 were counted, leaving children, adolescents, old people, and reservados completely unrepresented. Even so, the estimates given here are probably low, especially since populations were increasing by the 1690s, when these figures were collected.

We can gain some perspective on the degree of growth thanks to a fairly detailed head count of four Cakchiquel towns in the early 1560s. At that time, San Juan Sacatepéquez and San Pedro Sacatepéquez had populations of just under and just over 1300 people, respectively, while Comalapa numbered about 3200 and Chimaltenango almost 2300 residents. By 1690 these towns had grown considerably and had each developed daughter settlements as one way of managing the increase. Thus, San Juan and its dependency, San Raimundo, had a combined population of just under 3200, San Pedro and Xenacoj about 2700, Comalapa and Balanyá about 4400, and Chimaltenango some 4000. These represent increases of almost 150 percent, 100 percent, over 33 percent, and about 50 percent in just over a century and a half. Although similar data are lacking for the other Cakchiquel towns, one can assume a similar trajectory for them as well.

TABLE 1   CAKCHIQUEL TOWNS AND POPULATION ESTIMATES

| | About 1690[1] | | About 1770[2] |
Town	Confession/ Tributary Count	Estimated Population	Estimated Population
Sololá	1,650[1]	2,500	5,455
San Jorge	600	900	688
Santa Cruz	300	450	393
San Marcos	260	390	——
San José	290	430	1,332
Santa Lucía	400	600	——
Panajachel	800	1,200	1,167
Paquixalá	300	450	482
Semetabaj	297	450	320
Santa Catarina	180	270	293
Palopó	190	285	654
Tecpán Guatemala	1,900	2,800	5,708
Santa Apolonia	330	500	500
Patzicía	2,000	3,000	3,701
Patzún	1,600	2,400	3,600
Acatenango	500	750	521
Yepocapa	436	650	1,139[3]
Comalapa	2,600	3,900	7,000
Balanyá	350	500	500
San Andrés Itzapa	1,400	2,100	1,856
Parramos	900	1,300	2,362
Ziquinalá	340	500	31
Asunción	400	600	——
San Andrés	230	350	——
Magdalena	35	50	——
Alotenango	1,800	2,700	629
San Pedro	193	300	122
San Diego	10	15	82
San Sebastián	15	20	(189?)
Almolonga			
Barrio San Miguel	180	270	——
Santiago	331	500	812
San Juan Dueñas	368	550	——
Santa Catarina	283	400	584
San Antonio	400	600	554
San Lorenzo	262	400	300
San Andrés	74	110	116
San Juan de Obispo			
San Juan	700	1,000	498
San Cristóbal Abajo	350	500	263
San Cristóbal Alto	70	100	189
San Bartolo. Carmona	110	160	——
Santa Isabel	210	300	318
San Lúcas	60	90	50
San Bartolo. Becerra	36	50	104
Santa María de Jesús	1,600	2,400	2,122

TABLE 1   (CONTINUED)

| Town | About 1690[1] | | About 1770[2] |
	Confession/ Tributary Count	Estimated Population	Estimated Population
Cotzumalguapa	120	180	453
San Francisco	140	210	—
San Andrés	60	90	—
San Juan	140	210	—
Santa Lucía	160	240	—
San Cristóbal	80	120	—
Santo Domingo	60	90	31
San Martín Jilo.	497[4]	1,250	5,000
San Jacinto	87	200	—
San Juan Sacatepéquez	1,089	2,700	2,802
San Raimundo	191	470	597
San Pedro Sacatepéquez	632	1,580	2,000[5]
Xenacoj	448	1,120	1,400
Chimaltenango	1,602	4,000	3,492
San Sebastián	128	300	416
San Miguel	47	100	224
Sumpango	815	2,000	4,969
San Lorenzo	160	400	177
Santiago Sacatepéquez	501	1,000	1,303
San Lucas	475	1,200	1,048
San Bartolomé	78	200	—
Cauqué	120	300	191
Jocotenango			
Guatimaltecas	694	1,700	3,735[6]
San Felipe	114	285	—
San Luís	56	140	452
Pastores	52	130	525
San Pedro de Las Huertas	307	750	663
San Gaspar Vivar	71	175	136
San Andrés Deán	45	110	100
Santa Catarina	108	270	195
Santa Ana	40	100	359
Barrio Santa Cruz	37	100	—
Santo Tomás M.A.	91	225	667
Magdalena M.A.	172	430	562
Santa Lucía	42	100	—
San Mateo	34	85	—
San Miguel	15	35	—
		60,385	76,131

[1]These data are from Vázquez (1944).
[2]These data are from Cortés y Larraz (1958).
[3]Includes San Bernabé with 887 people.
[4]These and the following data are from Fuentes y Guzmán (1969–72).
[5]Includes estimate of at least 500 people living in dispersed settlements outside the town.
[6]Combined population of Guatimalteca and Utatleca *parcialidades*. Cakchiquel-speaking Guatimaltecas probably constituted two-thirds of the total, or some 2400 people.

Thus, by 1690, there were about 60,000 Cakchiquel living in some eighty settlements, ranging in size from large towns with several thousand inhabitants to tiny hamlets with only a few dozen. As in the case of the four towns discussed above, many of the smaller settlements were probably daughter communities that developed in naturally favored areas as the population of the mother towns grew. However, this process does not apply to the immediate hinterland of Santiago, the Spanish capital. The many small settlements there were the remains of farming enterprises established by Spaniards early in the Colonial period, using Cakchiquel and other Indian slaves captured during the conquest and the subsequent revolts of the 1520s. After slavery was abolished in 1548, many of the ex-slaves continued to live on the lands of their former masters, either paying rent or, occasionally, gaining eventual title and status as an officially recognized town (Lutz 1982:81–105).

Despite the apparent resurgence, by 1690 the Cakchiquel population was only a portion of its preconquest level. Though the region had undoubtedly supported several times the 1690 estimate before the conquest, the increasing population of the late seventeenth and eighteenth centuries was harder to support. This difficulty is attributable to two main factors: changes in land ownership and new kinds of agricultural activities.

During the late sixteenth century, when the Cakchiquel population was at its nadir, Spaniards acquired royal titles to large tracts of land which, at the time, were unoccupied and seemingly unused. This was especially common in the area of the Sacatepéquez towns, where Spaniards sought tierra fría for growing wheat, tierra caliente of the Motagua basin for sugarcane, and streams to power their grist and sugar mills. Initially this removal of land from Cakchiquel ownership had little adverse impact on the Indian communities' ability to support themselves. Later, however, as populations grew, the Spanish-owned lands could not generally be reclaimed.

The other source of difficulty in supporting the resurgent Cakchiquel populations of the late seventeenth and eighteenth centuries was changes in agriculture, especially the introduction of livestock as part of the Indian economy. Cattle in particular were uncontrolled by pens or fences and roamed where they pleased, destroying crops and, in some cases, even reverting to a semiferal state. Large areas were given over to this nonintensive agricultural activity in the late sixteenth and early seventeenth centuries when, again, Indian populations were at their low point and there was a relative abundance of unused land. However, cattle raising became such an integral part of both the Indian and Spanish economies that it could not be displaced easily or reduced as an activity later when populations grew.

Although difficult to document in quantitative terms, the rising pressures of a progressively worsening person/land ratio in highland Maya communities are reflected in three increasingly common phenomena. First, there was population dispersal. Daughter settlements had already appeared by the early seventeenth century, but as it wore on, more and more people began living in dispersed settlements strung out across the countryside and along water courses, near their ever more remote landholdings. Second, disputes over land multiplied, both within and among communities. Finally, it is possible to detect an increasing peasantization and pauperization of the Cakchiquel, largely unrelated to tribute obligations and other Spanish demands, which resulted in the disappearance of an entire class of wealthy Indians.

STRATIFICATION

Given our ethnographically derived characterization of the highland Maya as peasants, or, more recently, as postpeasants, one of the most striking and unexpected features of seventeenth-century Cakchiquel society is the extent to which it was stratified. Social stratification involving an aristocracy had been an attribute of preconquest society. By aristocracy we mean a social stratum, the members of which are presumed to be somehow "better" than other people in the society, because of their birth into particular elite families or lines of descent (see Goldman 1970: xvi–xxi). The preconquest nobility per se were much reduced as a result of the conquest and the "rebellions" they led against Spanish domination. If not killed outright or cast into slavery, survivors of the Cakchiquel aristocracy were not likely to have their status recognized formally, and thus perpetuated, by the Colonial regime, this despite the fact that Spanish law explicitly recognized the rights and status of indigenous elites.

Social stratification among the Colonial Cakchiquel was based as much on wealth as on birth, or, more specifically, the use of wealth in ways that benefited and were approved by the community, especially in the sphere of ritual observances. Wealth, in turn, was a function of land ownership, family size and organization, and economic diversification, taking advantage wherever possible of the opportunities created by the new Colonial situation. Although probably always numerically small, this stratum of wealthy, aristocratic Indians was nonetheless a socially and economically significant group, but one which was made possible by the peculiar and, ultimately, fleeting conditions of the time.

KINSHIP AND FAMILY

Kinship and the family are basic, universal human institutions. Whereas other forms of organization may lapse or fail because of some population catastrophe (caused by famine, disease, war, etc.), "institutions of lineage" endure as elemental building blocks of society (LeRoy Ladurie 1974:29–36). At the same time, kinship systems (the way in which a people categorize their relatives) are flexible. People can change their system in response to wider social and environmental developments. Especially in preindustrial societies (even in ones with a degree of social stratification, such as the preconquest and Colonial Cakchiquel) kin-based groups may be important social and economic units. Despite its significance, the Spaniards had little interest in documenting Cakchiquel kinship per se. The friars who compiled several dictionaries of the Cakchiquel language in the sixteenth and seventeenth centuries recorded a number of the kinship terms but in an unsystematic way. Their entries are, therefore, incomplete and some characteristics of the kinship system are unclear.

The available terms appear in Figures 1 and 2. It seems clear that either the kinship system was changing in response to the new realities of the Colonial period, or that the friars erred in their compilation and translation of terms, or both. Most frustrating is the equivocal evidence of bifurcation in the parental generation. *Bifurcation* refers to the use of different kinship terms for structurally similar people on different "sides" of the family. Thus, ego's (the reference point of the diagram) father and paternal uncles are classed together (with variations depending on relative age, as discussed later), whereas a separate term, *viq'an,* is used to refer to the maternal uncle. Such bifurcation usually denotes some form of unilineal descent reckoning: tracing descent through females on the mother's side (matrilineal descent) or through males on the father's side (patrilineal descent). However, the Cakchiquel data are confusing since there is no corresponding bifurcation on the father's side of the family, the paternal aunt being classed together terminologically with ego's mother and maternal aunts. This may simply be an instance in which the friar-linguists failed to note a distinct term for an "aunt" on the father's side of the family, but such an explanation is called into question by the fact that they *did* detect such a terminological difference on the mother's side. Patrilineal descent reckoning in particular is suggested by the fact that a male ego classes his children with those of his male siblings, yet refers to those of his female siblings simply as "offspring" *(al),* without even distinguishing them according to sex. However, as far as can be seen from the available data, cousins were all classed together with siblings, with due regard for relative age distinctions, with only the modifier *naht* (distant or far) to distinguish them from true siblings.

Besides bifurcation, the other striking characteristic of the Colonial Cakchiquel kinship terminology is the extent to which the criterion of relative age or birth order was used. An ego of either sex used the same terms to distinguish same-sex older and younger siblings *(nimal, chaq')* and used distinct terms for older and younger siblings of the opposite sex *(anabixel, ch'uti ana,* older and younger sisters, male ego speaking; *xibal, ch'uti xibal,* older and younger brothers, female ego speaking). As noted above, these sibling terms were extended to all cousins (with the possible and important exception of the maternal cross cousins or mother's brother's children) with the addition of the qualifier *naht.* Thus, a male ego referred to his older and younger male cousins as *nahti nimal* and *chaq',* respectively, a female ego using the same terms to refer to her older and younger female cousins, respectively. A male ego's older and younger female cousins were apparently classed together under the term *nahti ana;* a female ego's male cousins were similarly classed under the term *nahti xibal.*

There is no evidence that relative age distinctions extended to the grandparental generation, and it appears that the same terms were used on both sides of the family and that they were extended to include their siblings (great aunts and great uncles) as well. Similarly, we see no recorded distinctions based on birth order among ego's children. Unfortunately, no terms are recorded for the children of any of ego's cousins, so the hints about unilineal descent are difficult to expand upon.

As far as they go, these data are consistent with those of other, better-documented Colonial and comtemporary Maya groups. A convincing case has been made that the Tzeltal Maya of the Copanaguastla area of Chiapas in the sixteenth century had a strongly patrilineal descent system with an Omaha terminology (Ruz 1985:162–180). A similar terminology has endured until modern times among the Tzotzil Maya of San Pablo Chalchihuitan, also in Chiapas (Guiteras-Holmes 1954). Structurally, an Omaha system is distinguished by the fact that ego classes his or her maternal cross cousins (mother's brother's children) terminologically with the mother, maternal aunt, and maternal uncle. Thus, in strong contrast to the way we do things, terms are applied to individuals of different generations. It cannot be determined from the present data if the preconquest Cakchiquel also had an Omaha terminology or a less strongly patrilineal system of the Dakota type (Murdock 1949:236–238). Under a Dakota system, ego's parallel cousins (mother's sister's children and father's brother's children) are classed with siblings, and the cross cousins (mother's brother's children and father's sister's children) are classed separately. It does seem clear, however, that the Colonial Cakchiquel modified their preconquest terminology or the application of terms to fit their emerging, postconquest society and economy.

Interpersonal relationships among kin and family organization constitute a degree of intimate knowledge apparently not attained by any Spanish observer. Yet the Pirir wills (discussed in the next section) allow us to address these topics partially and to understand how both kin terminology and domestic organization in the seventeenth century were responses to general demographic and socioeconomic conditions.

THE PIRIR FAMILY

In the middle of the rainy season of 1642, a ninety-year-old Cakchiquel man lay on what he believed to be his deathbed in the town of San Juan Sacatepéquez and dictated both a summary of his gifts to the town's church over his lifetime and his wishes concerning the division of his considerable estate. The man was Miguel Perez Pirir, born in the 1550s and a son of the local Chajomá aristocracy. His life spanned the first half of our period. Through the analysis of his will, including his personal possessions, real estate, animals, the economic and social activities in which he engaged, and the way he divided his estate, we gain a valuable perspective on how some Cakchiquel adapted to their new situation.

The story does not end with this one episode, however. The old man recovered his health and lived another six years. During his last year he dictated three codicils, in which he recorded property already entrusted to his heirs and, in one instance, changed a son's inheritance. His son and principal heir, Domingo, also dictated a will on his deathbed in 1669, as did one of his adopted grandchildren in 1708. Through this series of almost miraculously preserved documents we are afforded a uniquely intimate, diachronic view of a family through the entire period of this study, a view not otherwise obtainable from the other documents of the time. Other wills, written between the 1590s and the early 1700s, demonstrate that the Pirir family, while exceptional in some respects, was by no means unique but was, in fact, representative of an entire stratum of Colonial Cakchiquel society.

Cakchiquel Kinship
Consanguines

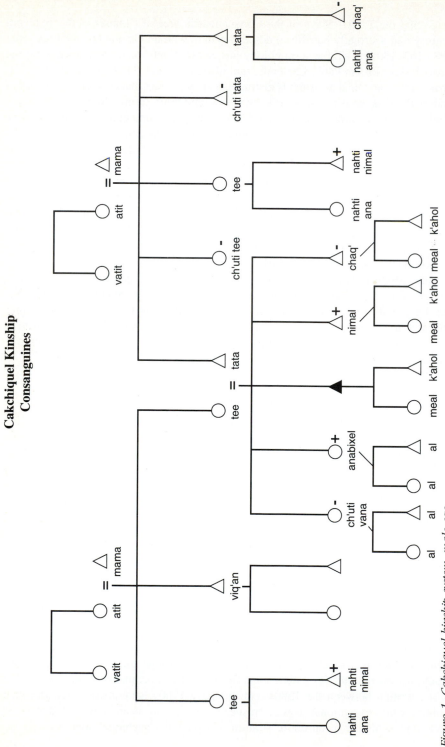

Figure 1. Cakchiquel kinship system, male ego.

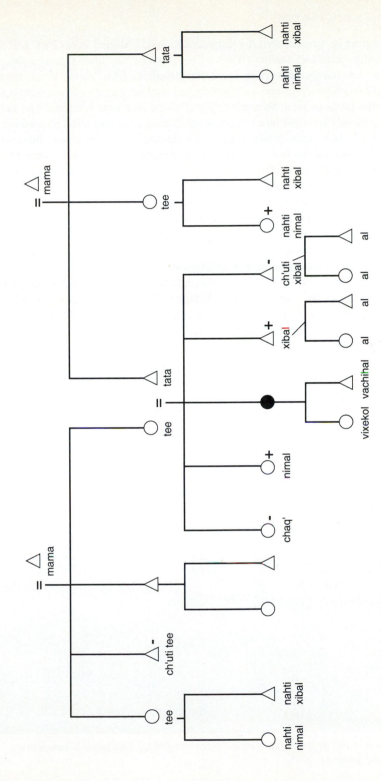

Figure 2. Cakchiquel kinship system, female ego.

By the time he first dictated his testament in 1642, Miguel Perez Pirir had long been a wealthy man and leading citizen of his town of San Juan Sacatepéquez. As aristocrats, his family appears to have possessed its own lands, in contrast to *macehuales* (commoners), who traditionally enjoyed only usufruct (use rights) with regard to the lands of their *chinamit* or *parcialidad* (see next section). The family holdings evidently centered on a tract of several hundred acres called Navorón in the tierra templada belt north of San Juan on the descent to the Motagua. Because he was probably one of the few survivors of his generation and family, don Miguel never seems to have been challenged in his possession of Navorón. He used this as a secure resource base to finance and support a wide range of both subsistence and market-oriented economic activities (see Chapter 4).

It would have been relatively easy for don Miguel to acquire additional tracts of land around San Juan during the years of relative depopulation in the later sixteenth century, as long as he avoided coming into competition with Spaniards. Yet, these same conditions would have made acquiring workers in the form of paid laborers very difficult. The fact that the Spanish demands for Indian labor had priority would have made this nearly impossible (see Chapter 7). Therefore, don Miguel, like others in his situation, came to rely on his children and grandchildren (especially males) to provide both the labor and supervision for his widely distributed holdings and activities. Ultimately, he created what was, in effect, a family corporation with

The Navorón area, in the tierra templada zone north of San Juan Sacatepéquez (photo by the author).

himself as head. As they matured, his sons were given responsibility for specific tracts and activities (for example, one son, Ambrosio, received training as a blacksmith).

Although it is tempting to classify the Pirires in the 1640s as a patrilineal extended family, it seems that, even though they were an economic unit headed by ninety-year-old don Miguel, they were not a single residential unit. Instead, his sons apparently lived on their main holdings, directing the efforts of their own families. Yet, like other Cakchiquel of the early seventeenth century, the Pirires were struggling against the general population trend of their time. By 1642, only two sons, Domingo and Ambrosio, appear to have had any living children. The other brothers either had never married, had never fathered any children, or, most likely, simply had no living descendants. Apparently cognizant of the uncertainties of individual survival and yet wishing to preserve his family's holdings, don Miguel left some of his larger tracts to *pairs* of brothers, especially Domingo and eldest brother Gerónimo (who at the time must have been in his sixties at least). The emphasis on joint landholding by pairs of brothers was even more pronounced in Domingo's will of 1669. He systematically entrusted lands, goods, and ritual obligations to pairs of his sons. Again, one is tempted to assume that such arrangements resulted in a series of fraternal joint families or *frereché*. However, the fact that each son also received at least one house in addition to the land argues against this interpretation.

Even though Domingo calculatedly apportioned the major tracts among pairs of his sons, he did not designate a successor as family head. Perhaps the eldest brother, Gaspar, now automatically assumed that role. Given the general conditions, however, it is not surprising that only the youngest son, Juan de la Cruz, was still alive in 1707 to head the group of Pirir men, mostly his nephews, as they jointly defended the Navorón tract before the audiencia against encroachment by squatters from the increasingly larger and harder-pressed town of San Juan.

The Queh family of Santiago Sacatepéquez and the Jocón family of San Juan were similar to the Pirires in organization, though on a less ambitious scale. Miguel Juan Queh died prematurely in 1662. He was thus roughly a contemporary of Domingo Pirir, though all his children were evidently minors at the time. In this case Miguel Juan apportioned a tract called Panybah among his older and younger brothers (Juan and Jacinto, respectively), his nephew, Lúcas (whom he referred to as *nuk'ahol*, "my son," in the document), the child of his deceased brother Gaspar and his wife and two daughters (presumably as dowries). Miguel Juan's elder brother, Juan, became the minors' guardian. They evidently thenceforth resided with him and he represented them before the audiencia, successfully requesting that their holdings be protected.

Thomás Jocón also died prematurely in 1708. He claimed to be the adopted son of Pedro Pirir, who by that time was already deceased. Adoption of orphans seems to have been another tactic to secure young hands in a time when the survival of one's own family was constantly in question and when, for the same reason, there were many candidates. By virtue of that relationship and his marriage to another of Pedro's adopted children, Melchora Bor, he claimed the right to the old Pirir tract named Pachalí. After Melchora died childless, Thomás remarried and had ten children with Catharina Sian. At the time of Thomás' death, his sons Domingo Ramos and Pablo were old enough to have the Pachalí tract left specifically to them. It is clear, however, that they held the land as trustees and jointly controlled it with their brothers as they matured, because the three survivors joined Pablo in a petition to the audiencia in successful defense of Pachalí in 1725.

With this background we gain some understanding of the logic behind the kinship system. Relative age was important, especially among males, as a way of both internally ordering the family corporation and structuring the interpersonal relationships among this primary kin group. In the all-too-likely event of a man's premature death, as in the Queh family, his immature children automatically became the responsibility of his brother(s), either real or distant (naht), who already classed terminologically his own children with those of the deceased. In the case of a father's death when his children were more mature, or in the absence of a male sibling, as in the Jocón family, the eldest son logically assumed leadership of the corporation. As his younger brothers matured, their nimal assigned them activities, but they retained joint control over their lands. The maternal uncle was a member of another corporation and was thus appropriately distinguished terminologically (viq'an). Sisters moved away to another corporation when they married, so their children could be classified together (al) without sex distinctions by their stay-at-home brothers. Given the corporate tendencies and the patrilineal bias, one would expect distinctions to be made between cross and parallel cousins, to differentiate between members of the group (especially paternal parallel cousins or a father's brother's children) and nonmembers (paternal and maternal cross cousins). Again, the seeming lack of such terms may be due to Spanish failure to detect them, or, given the depopulation suffered by the Cakchiquel, it may be that collateral relatives were assuming more importance in social life, with the sibling/parallel cousin terms extended to include cross cousins as well.

PARCIALIDADES

Family corporations were for only the wealthy and the very lucky, and most Colonial Cakchiquel were neither. Opportunities to create wealth required large, stable families to staff and manage diverse interests, but death capriciously whisked family and loved ones away. Adoption of orphans provided a partial solution, if the involved parties survived, but becoming wealthy also presupposed a resource base—land—which could be manipulated by an individual or family without interference by another party. Thus, for most Cakchiquel, wealth and its attendant status, if attained at all, were only fleeting experiences. For the vast majority, survival was still a collective venture, shared not just with family, but with members of another basic social unit of Cakchiquel society, called the parcialidad by the Spaniards.

In most cases the Colonial parcialidades were the direct descendants of a type of preconquest social unit which the Cakchiquel and Quiché termed chinamit. The word itself is Nahuatl in origin (chinamitl) and was sometimes used synonymously with calpulli in central Mexico. The Spaniards used a corruption of this latter term *(calpul)* interchangeably with parcialidad in referring to these units among the highland Maya in general. The preconquest Cakchiquel chinamit was, in fact, a highland Maya version of the central Mexican calpulli. As such, it was a key principle of organization, and chinamitales were vested with fundamental social, political, and economic functions. The chinamit was basically a territorial unit, ruled by an aristocratic core family whose head functioned like a small-scale *tecutli,* his central Mexican counterpart (see Berdan 1982:51–54). The head of the chinamit was aided by a council of elders and a small staff of messengers or criers, the latter making sure that all the chinamit's membership were informed of their leader's orders. Apart from the ruling family, the rest of a chinamit's population was essentially peasant-like in status and was burdened with a high degree of corporate control and numerous obligations (Hill 1984; Hill and Monaghan 1987).

Even in the sparse documentation available, it is clear that some Colonial parcialidad names recur and that at least some of these (the Tukuché and Cakchiquel proper) refer to larger amaq' or confederations of chinamitales. Evidently, the Spaniards divided some populations in the sixteenth century as they created towns, perhaps as a way of diminishing their potential for revolt.

As with the overall Cakchiquel population, we cannot know with certainty the size of preconquest chinamitales or amaq' groups. Nor do we know in all cases how many parcialidades formed a town. But, we do know the numbers and sizes of parcialidades in a few towns, and the data are presented in Tables 2 to 4. Colonial parcialidades normally ranged in size from 300 to 1000 or so people, and the Spaniards brought together from four to eight such units to form a town.

Whether originally a chinamit or an amaq', Colonial parcialidades retained a number of important preconquest corporate functions. Unfortunately, some of our best descriptions come from authors whose experience was not among the Cakchiquel but with their eastern and western neighbors, the Pokomám and Quiché, respectively. Still, such information as is available for the Cakchiquel indicates that they conform to the pattern of the other two groups.

TABLE 2   PUEBLOS AND PARCIALIDADES

Pueblos	Parcialidades	Average Population about 1690
Comalapa	7	550
Chimaltenango	4	1,000
San Juan Sacatepéquez	5[1]	540
San Pedro Sacatepéquez	6[2]	260
San Lucas Sacatepéquez	4[3]	300
Tecpán Guatemala	8[4]	350

[1]Earliest documentation lists only two parcialidades. Later eighteenth-century material strongly suggests five (*see* A3.16 Leg. 439 Exp. 8978, Año 1791).
[2]Sinacá parcialidad left in 1578 to form town of Xenacoj. Ya-Jonica and Chamalé parcialidades mentioned by 1644.
[3]Four "Calpules" reported in 1672 (see A1.11.2 Leg. 5775 Exp. 48513).
[4]*See* Hill (1989a).

TABLE 3   PARCIALIDADES AND POPULATIONS ABOUT 1562[1]

Comalapa	
Ikcomaqiz	506
Tukuché	311
Tacoxlea	588
Sinacá	434
Macá	336
Aqaqual Quinal	401
Cahuequj	341
San Juan Sacatepéquez	
Chajomá	765
Tepemiac	358
San Pedro Sacatepéquez	
Tepemiac	331
Cachiquile	576
Tukuché	122
Uspantecas	88
Sinacá	78
Chimaltenango	
(unnamed)	734
Cachiquile	429
Xahil	542
(unnamed)	392

[1]Basic data from Archivo General de Indias, Doc. Guatemala 45. *See also* Borg (1986). Figures do not include *reservados*.

In the 1630s the English priest Thomas Gage noted that among the Pokomám:

. . . they are in every town divided into tribes [parcialidades], which have one chief head. All that belong to that tribe do resort to him in any difficult matters, and he is bound to aid, protect, defend, counsel, and appear for the rest of his tribe before the officers of justice in any wrong that is like to be done to them (Gage 1958:221).

If anyone want a house to live in, or wishes to repair and thatch his house anew, notice is given to the heads of the tribes, who warn all the town to come to help with the work. Everyone has to bring a bundle of straw and other materials, so that in one day with the help of many they finish a house, without any charges more than of chocolate, which they minister in great cups as big as will hold above a pint (Gage 1958:222).

Amongst themselves, if any complaint be made against any Indian, they dare not meddle with him until they call all his kindred, and especially the head of that tribe [parcialidad] to which he belongs. If he and the rest together find him to deserve imprisonment or whipping or any other punishment, then the officers of justice, the alcaldes or mayors, and their bretheren the jurats [regidores] inflict upon him that punishment which all shall agree upon (Gage 1958:229).

Early in the Colonial period, parcialidades appear often to have been headed by their traditional aristocratic leaders, or *caciques* as they were commonly called by the Spaniards. The Spanish honorific title *don* was often added to the caciques' names. Thus, the Ikcomaqiz parcialidad of Comalapa was headed by don Juan Maldonado, and the Cahuequj parcialidad by don Martín Perez. Similarly, the Cachiquile parcialidad of San Pedro Sacatepéquez and the Chajomá parcialidad of

San Juan were led by don Alonso de Mendaño and don Juan, respectively (see Table 4). However, given the overriding fact of catastrophic and continuing population loss through disease, maintenance of lineal succession to the leadership position would have been highly problematic. In cases where entire aristocratic lines failed, "commoners" of high esteem assumed the executive roles. Unfortunately, we do not know how such men were selected. Perhaps it was through election, perhaps the parcialidad council made the selection. In any case, by the 1560s such individuals had already appeared and were called by a bewildering array of terms, including *principal, calpul,* and *chinamital,* all to the dismay of the confused ethnohistorian! In Comalapa there appears to have been some kind of internal hierarchy of offices within the parcialidad. Some of them had dual principales, while the Sinacá parcialidad had a principal (confusingly called don Diego Nimamac) and three individuals called "chinamitales" of the parcialidad. We do not know the functions of these offices. Among the Quiché of Chichicastenango in this century the "chinamtal" is a spokesman in marriage negotiations and a witness for oral contracts (Bunzel 1952:183). Perhaps a similar function had already developed among the Colonial Cakchiquel. In other Quiché towns, such as Sacapulas, the institution of a single executive was replaced by an executive council, the *ax waab',* whose

TABLE 4   PARCIALIDAD LEADERSHIP ABOUT 1560

Comalapa	
Ikcomaqiz	Don Juan Maldonado, cacique
Tukuché	Pedro Gonzales, principal y cacique
Tacoxlea	Baltasar Ly, principal (in place of don Miguel)
Sinacá	Don Diego Nimamac, principal
	Francisco Atzic Huhnac, chinamitl de parcialidad
	Diego Tzucuc, chinamitl de parcialidad
	Anton Ahin, chinamitl de parcialidad
Macá	Cristóbal Hernández, principal y cacique
	Francisco López, principal y cacique
Aqaqual Quinal	Juan Tzixin, principal
Cahuequj	Don Martín Perez, principal
	Francisco Yu, principal
San Pedro Sacatepéquez	
Cachiquile	Don Alonso de Mendaño, principal
Tukuché	Diego Coxlea, principal
Uspantecas	Juan Noc, principal
Sinacá	Francisco López, principal
Tepemiac	(no leader listed)
San Juan Sacatepéquez	
Chajomá	Don Juan, principal y cacique
Tepemiac	Miguel Lolmay, principal
Chimaltenango	
(unnamed)	Francisco Martín, alcalde
Cachiquile	Don Baltasar
	Diego Chumal, regidor
Xahil	Don Pedro Xahil
	Juan Perez Acuc, regidor
(unnamed)	Don Diego Chahon

members were often referred to as principales (Hill and Monaghan 1987:15–18). The principal and chinamitales of the Sinacá parcialidad may represent an early stage in the development of such an executive council.

Another, key function of Colonial parcialidades was their corporate landholding. Testimony taken in a land dispute of 1644 from Benito Gomez, a principal of San Juan Sacatepéquez, is clear on this point. As recorded by the presiding Spanish official:

> He stated that he knows the Indians of the calpul Yajonica, included in the town of San Juan Sacatepéquez and that he knew some of their forefathers since he first had use of reason (i.e. since he was a child). Since that time he has seen them peacefully and quietly possess the lands [in question], planting corn and chile and availing themselves of its fruits and game, without opposition from anyone, and he heard his parents and grandparents say that said calpul had thus possessed these lands since pagan times (i.e. since before the Spanish conquest).

Information gleaned from more fulsome documents pertaining to the Quiché area provide additional detail. Members enjoyed only usufruct to the land they worked, and to any pasturage or forest, though these rights could be passed on to descendants. Otherwise, the land reverted to the parcialidad, amongst whose members it was apparently divided. Parcialidad boundaries were defined by a system of markers, and encroachment was vigorously opposed in Spanish courts, if necessary, the costs of litigation being defrayed among the membership through contributions collected from each household (Hill and Monaghan 1987:64–73, 112–118, 126–132). Such corporate protection was necessary for all but the wealthiest individuals due to the costs of retaining Spanish legal counsel and filing the innumerable petitions and statements which any litigation sparked. As friar Ximénez observed at the beginning of the eighteenth century:

> . . . because if an Indian falls into the hands of [Spanish] justice the poor man is ruined from [the cost of] decrees, transcripts, and cajolery until the poor man is destroyed and the crime is left as it was, because the case can only be prosecuted while there is juice and, having squeezed him dry, they leave the poor man to die in jail. . . . (Ximénez, 1929–1931, I:105)

As we have seen, the corporate responsibility extended to individuals as well as land. Contributions (*nut,* or *cotzún* in Cakchiquel) were thus also collected as necessary to pay fines imposed on parcialidad members for minor offenses. Through its leadership it also had primary responsibility for social control, including corporal punishment (usually the lash, inflicted by the leader as the offender hung by his wrists from the rafters of the leader's house) (Hill 1989a:180, 183).

Parcialidades also had some regulatory function concerning marriage. Preconquest chinamitales were probably mostly endogamous, except for their aristocratic leadership. But, with the depopulation accompanying the conquest such units could no longer be socially self-sufficient. Under these conditions and with the new *pueblos* (towns) as sociopolitical entities created by the Spaniards (see below), parcialidad endogamy broke down (see Chapter 9). In its place the pueblo would eventually emerge as an endogamous, ethnolinguistically distinct social group.

PUEBLOS

Seen from this perspective, the towns created by the Spaniards were, for the most part, artificial collections of parcialidades. Towns were formed in the middle and late sixteenth century as a result of the Spanish policy of *congregación,* bringing together the many small, scattered settlements and remnant groups, the survivors of the pandemics which had so savagely decimated the native populations of all of Mesoamerica. The Spaniards' concerns were of a practical nature, and in this instance, the various interests groups' objectives coincided. With only limited personnel, both the royal administration and the religious orders, entrusted with the task of converting the Indians to Christianity, perceived the greater ease of civil and ecclesiastical administration should the many small settlements be combined into a few large ones. Missionary friars could do their job without nearly as much travel, while royal officials could more easily collect tribute and round up labor gangs for both private colonists and for public works. Finally, the internal security of the colony would also be enhanced since the reduced number of large towns would be easier to police (MacLeod 1973:120–125).

Yet the units of congregación were not individuals or families, but parcialidades. These indigenous groups thus thrown together did not necessarily have any history of association, and in some cases may even have been former enemies. Even with some previous alliances, parcialidades in the new town situation remained closed corporations to a significant degree. Two major social adjustments had to be made, an end to parcialidad endogamy and a means for parcialidades to coexist in the pueblo setting. These were not easily achieved and were undoubtedly the source of much friction in the newly formed pueblos. Spanish municipal organization provided a potential vehicle for integrating parcialidades of a single pueblo. Each town was officially administered by a *cabildo,* or town council, composed of two *alcaldes* and several *regidores,* whose number varied according to population, but was never more than six. The Spaniards intended that these offices should be filled by election from among the town's adult male population with new appointments to be made each January. The town *governador* was a Spanish appointee who also served a one-year term and who was responsible for tribute collection.

However, for parcialidades still jealous of their own lands and autonomy, this kind of town organization was unworkable as given. Spanish regulations were too imprecise with regard to how officeholders would be chosen, leaving parcialidades in doubt about their representation in the municipal government, which was, in theory, responsible for the administration of community funds and property. By regulation, this included a *caja de comunidad,* literally a community coffer in which the funds used to pay tribute and other town expenses were kept.

These moneys were raised in two ways. Tribute in particular was ideally assessed in the form of a head tax based on the number of tributarios enteros in a given town. Yet, there was always some shortfall. Official headcounts were infrequent, and in the long intervals people died, moved away, or their tributary status changed when they became reservados. The difference still had to be paid. It could be made up through some sort of collection among households, but this had limits because collections were also made by parcialidades and for a wide range of other purposes (see Chapter 4).

A widely used alternative was to create some income-producing community enterprise. This second method most commonly involved raising some kind of newly introduced livestock, especially cattle. Such activities were ideally suited to the conditions of the later sixteenth century, with its low populations and large, unoccupied areas between towns. Herding required little labor since the animals could be left to roam almost at will until needed for sale. The proceeds went into the caja and were used, among other things, to make up tribute shortfall, pay for town improvements, and subvent the costs of patronal fiestas.

The caja and the town enterprises were to be administered by the justices, the alcaldes and regidores, yet Spanish law contained no provision concerning the equal or proportional representation of a town's parcialidades in its municipal government. Lacking such protection, parcialidades were typically reluctant to form or remain in the new pueblos, let alone allow outsiders to oversee investments to which they, as corporate entities, had contributed. The processes through which the necessary compromises and adjustments were made in the Cakchiquel towns during the later sixteenth century are largely lost to us. However, we can get some impression of what happened among them by looking at an analogous, better documented case of town formation in Sacapulas.

TOWN FORMATION IN SACAPULAS

Though outside the Cakchiquel region, Sacapulas is not an inappropriate choice to illustrate the processes of town formation. There are some indications that the area was conquered and occupied for some time by the Cakchiquel when they were still auxiliaries of the Quiché. The claim of conquest comes from the "Annals of the Cakchiquels," the major sixteenth-century chronicle of the Xahil family, which ruled the Iximché polity (see Chapter 8). Evidence for an occupation is linguistic, the fact that the Sacapulas dialect of Maya shares a number of distinct features with Cakchiquel that it does not share with other highland Maya languages (DuBois 1981:34–56). However, even without any direct Cakchiquel connection, the Sacapulas people had the same preconquest sociopolitical organization, faced the same problems of town formation, and arrived at the same kind of town organization as the other, major highland Maya groups. Therefore, a brief review of its formative years is both illustrative and appropriate.

The town of Sacapulas was a product of the Spanish congregación program of the middle sixteenth century (Hill and Monaghan 1987:83–89). Building on earlier Franciscan efforts, Dominican missionaries succeeded in bringing together two amaq' groups, each composed of three chinamitales. These groups were all still headed by their traditional caciques in the 1570s (Ibid.:47–48). Though the two amaq' had shared a common boundary in the area, they do not seem to have been especially close allies before the conquest, and conflict soon arose when they were thrust together in the new pueblo. The situation was compounded by the fact that the town was founded on land belonging to one of the amaq', whose members referred to themselves as "natives" and to those of the other amaq' as "foreigners." By 1572 the foreign parcialidades were so dissatisfied with their situation that they petitioned the audiencia for relief.

They had four main requests. First, it seems that the Dominicans had urged the town to buy some brood mares whose offspring were to be sold to raise money for the caja and community expenses. Trouble began when the foreigners took some of the foals from the herd without notifying the natives. Because of the ensuing acrimony and accusations of betrayal, the foreigners asked for the audiencia's assistance in dividing the herd. But this was only the beginning. They next requested that the funds in the caja de comunidad be divided permanently between themselves and the natives. Third, they petitioned to be allowed to elect their own alcalde and regidores. Finally, they requested that they be allowed to remain in legal possession of their lands.

Inexplicably, the audiencia granted these requests, even though they amounted to creating a separate town for the foreigners. The native Sacapultecos responded to the news of the audiencia's decision by running horses through the fields of the foreigners, which lay adjacent to the town corrals. A few of the foreigners were even taken prisoner. Some of them were fined by the native-controlled cabildo, and others received corporal punishment. If the audiencia's ruling had been implemented, not only would the Dominicans' labors have been largely wasted, but the entire congregación program would have been endangered by the precedent of permitting small groups of parcialidades (the foreigners numbered less than 350 people in 1572) to set up their own correspondingly small pueblos. This was the very condition that congregación was intended to remedy! Although this larger implication may not have been grasped at the time, the Dominicans were spurred to action by both the discord that the ruling produced and the prospect of seeing their town melt away. Accordingly, they helped negotiate a six-point contract between the natives and the foreigners, with themselves as guarantors. This is a vitally important document, as it allows us to glimpse the concerns of the Maya themselves.

In the first provision of the contract, the natives agreed to pay the foreigners three foals each year as compensation for having to maintain fences around their milpas to prevent damage from the grazing horses. Second, both sides agreed to cooperate in maintaining the fences and corrals where the herd was kept. Third, they promised not to antagonize each other further by encroaching on each other's land or fishing places. Punishment for trespassers would include confiscation of tools and fines for any damages. Fourth, both sides promised not to take horses from the community herd unilaterally. Fifth, they agreed that there would be but one coffer for community funds but three keys would be required to open it; two of these would be held by the native alcaldes and the other by the alcalde representing the foreigners. Still not really trusting each other to handle money unsupervised, they further stipulated that each group would collect the funds for the patronal fiesta of Santo Domingo separately among their respective members. Finally, they agreed that the town justices and principales of both groups should be impartial in their administration of the town, without regard to the parcialidad membership of its residents.

The audiencia ratified the contract with only two modifications. With its small population, Sacapulas only rated two alcaldes and two regidores, so each side would elect one of each. Also, the audiencia ordered that the horse herd be divided annually, with a subsequent clarification that each side receive a share proportional to its initial investment in it. In practice during the later sixteenth century, it seems that the two alcalde positions were filled by the caciques of parcialidades belonging to each of the two amaq'. The Spanish-appointed governor was also a member of the traditional aristocracy. As far as we know, the terms of the agreement were observed without incident until 1645. At that time the foreign parcialidades petitioned the audiencia to issue an order to maintain the "custom" of electing an equal number of justices to the cabildo. They also requested relief from trespass on their lands by natives. Given the formal nature of the 1572 agreement, the audiencia granted the foreigners' requests. Apparently this was the only major violation of the contract, since there is no record of further litigation between the two parties over such matters in the large documentary record of this town.

THE SEVENTEENTH CENTURY

The Cakchiquel towns must have gone through similar disputes revolving around the issues of parcialidad autonomy and representation in the cabildo, as well as the administration of town assets, since they ultimately reached very similar accommodations. As town organization matured in the seventeenth century, the parcialidad leaders remained the true authority in the pueblos, while the formal offices of alcalde, regidor, and governor became essentially fronts, whose occupants would be drawn representatively on a rotating basis from among the town's component parcialidades (see Chapter 8). Spanish requirements were met, while at the same time the true administration of local affairs was handled by traditional figures of authority.

As noted by Friar Ximénez for the Quiché of the late seventeenth and early eighteenth centuries:

> In this same manner they govern themselves today, because although they have your Magesty's Alcaldes and Gobernadores in many places, in having a dispute with someone who has transgressed they call the heads of their chinamitales and there before them is presented the evidence against the defendant, all verbally, and having proven the case, proceeding to the execution of punishment without documents, decrees, or the entanglements of scribes and counsellors. . . .
>
> For the things and works in which they compete with their towns the Alcaldes are again not absolute but must call the principales [the heads of all the parcialidades] and all together they confer on the matter. . . . [T]hey determine what means are necessary and determine what each one of the town must give and each calpul [parcialidad] head collects his share, himself giving first his own part, and the same for the Alcaldes, such that all contribute equally, except the very poor . . . and each one [of the calpul heads] makes a note of those who have not contributed and the reason, and in this way they see to all their things. . . .
>
> It is a thing that not even the greatest intelligences could order better, the offices of Alcaldes with all of the others down to the lowest go by turns among all the Calpules, all

equally bearing the honor or the work, with no one being excused, because before the new year all these heads [of Calpules] and the justices [alcaldes] of the place get together and name [people to these positions] without anyone being aggrieved, down to the one who carries water and firewood for the *mesón* [official travellers' lodgings] and to those who sweep the plaza, with such order and concert that it is a marvel, and no Calpul bears more than its share because its head defends it. . . . (Ximénez 1929–1931, I:104–105)

Around 1770, Archbishop Cortés y Larraz briefly but clearly confirmed the same pattern specifically for the Cakchiquel town of Comalapa, noting the true power brokers in town affairs:

The calpules, which in other places are called by other names [the heads of the parcialidades], are the ones who direct and dispose of everything, there being no other voice in the towns but theirs. In this [town] there are five or seven [the latter is the true figure] and these have all the others [of the town] at their disposition (Cortés y Larraz 1958, II:91).

The importance of this distinction between a town's officially recognized authorities and its true leadership will become apparent when we examine relationships between Cakchiquel communities and Spanish demands in Chapter 8. For the moment it is enough to note that the social universe of the seventeenth-century Cakchiquel was a complex blend of traditional social groups, imported institutions, and modifying innovations. As a result, individuals found themselves entangled with an array of groups—family (whether corporate or not), parcialidad, and town. Although these groups provided both some security and a sense of identity, they also made many stern, often conflicting demands on people's time, effort, allegiance, and money.

BIBLIOGRAPHIC NOTE

The basic model of Colonial-period Central American population dynamics was formulated by MacLeod (1973). Others have attempted to examine population trends in specific subregions, including Lutz (1976, 1982), Lovell (1982, 1985), Veblen (1982), and Hill and Monaghan (1987). The reconstruction of Colonial Cakchiquel kinship is based on the late seventeenth century Coto (1983) and Guzmán (1984) dictionaries. *See* Hill (1984) and Hill and Monaghan (1987) for a detailed discussion of chinamitales and their postconquest reorganization as parcialidades.

4 / Land

In the agriculturally based society of the Colonial Cakchiquel, land was literally life, and control over land was about the only means at their disposal for ensuring life. Land was thus a crucial commodity and one which became increasingly scarce as the Colonial period progressed. Competition for land was everpresent, either with Spaniards or with other Cakchiquel, and the competition became fiercer and more desperate as time passed. As in so many other aspects of Colonial Cakchiquel culture, the principles and practices of landholding involved a complex combination of preconquest usages, officially sanctioned and recognized Spanish introductions, and new practices innovated by the Cakchiquel themselves in the Colonial situation.

We know little about preconquest landholding practices. The Spaniards had little motivation to bother themselves with trying to learn about native principles regarding land since Spanish law would (ideally) be used in settling whatever disputes might arise. As we shall see, things did not work out that simply and the Spaniards ultimately were forced to acquaint themselves somewhat with Maya forms of land tenure, thereby providing us with some glimpses of the preconquest system.

PRINCIPLES OF LAND TENURE

As can best be reconstructed, traditional Cakchiquel land tenure took two main forms, which corresponded to the two main social strata: the aristocracy and the commoners. As in other parts of highland Mesoamerica, Cakchiquel aristocrats appear to have had the ability both to own land as individuals or as part of a family patrimony, and to pass such ownership on through inheritance to their descendants. Presumably, such individually held lands could be let, sold, or traded without interference from any third party, though we have no direct evidence on this point (Hill and Monaghan 1987:126–132).

Commoners, on the other hand, do not appear to have owned land. Rather, they seem to have enjoyed usufruct to the land they cultivated as individuals or families, with ultimate control vested in the corporate chinamit (see Chapter 3). Although usufruct to specific tracts could be passed on to descendants, commoners as individuals were apparently not free to alienate their plots from the rest of the chinamit holdings. The leadership of this group would have decided all questions of land use by members, including reapportioning land left unoccupied by the death of a man without male heirs. Periodic reapportioning of land among members may also have occurred, as it did among calpullis in some parts of central Mexico, but direct evidence is again lacking (Berdan 1982:55–68).

Disputes among members and between chinamitales were minimized to an extent by the erection of systems of boundary markers along the perimeters of each individual's and each group's holdings. At the chinamit level, boundary markers were often reinforced by the placement of settlements in defensible positions on or near their frontiers with other such groups. Open hostilities may also have been an option for a chinamit trying to defend its boundaries, but among the Cakchiquel and other highland Maya people, these units were organized into confederations (amaq') that were engaged in incessant warfare with the Quiché, Pokóm, and Pipil peoples, as well as with each other. In such circumstances, some form of mediation must have existed at the amaq' level to defuse potentially disruptive disputes among the component chinamitales and thus maintain a united front against outsiders.

These forms of land tenure endured well into the Colonial period but were complicated by official Spanish policies and the introduction of Spanish concepts and laws concerning municipal property, which were based on a long tradition of communitarian property in Castile (Vassberg 1984:5–56). Although dating back perhaps as far as pre-Roman times, forms of communal land ownership received formal sanction during the lengthy reconquest of the Iberian peninsula from the Moors, which culminated in the fall of Granada to King Ferdinand and Queen Isabella in 1492, the same year as Columbus' first voyage of discovery. In accordance with practices developed during this reconquest, all lands taken by force of arms technically belonged to the crown and were thus termed *tierras realengas* (royal lands). Yet generations of Spanish monarchs had been anxious to populate their newly won territories with loyal subjects, and therefore gave generous grants of land to commoner-settlers willing to form towns. Over time, a complex variety of forms of "municipal property" emerged (Ibid., 20).

Municipal property included the *propios* and *tierras concejiles,* which belonged to the municipality and were ususally rented out as a way of generating income for community expenses. These holdings contrasted with an array of commons available for the free use of town residents. Among these were the *ejido,* a piece of land which could serve a variety of purposes and was usually located on the outskirts of town, but not typically planted. *Dehesas* were enclosed tracts that usually served as pasture, though they might also be at least partly cultivated. *Cotos* were another type of enclosed tract which could be entirely cultivated, while *prados* and *entrepanes* were high- and low-quality pastures, respectively. A final form of commons was the *monte,* generally wooded uplands, which provided fuel and lumber as well as pasture.

In theory, any resident could use any otherwise unoccupied tract in the municipal holdings and could continue to do so as long as he plowed and planted each year. Even unused royal lands could be brought under cultivation through the reconquest right of *presura,* which allowed for the free use of any unoccupied lands. The key principle guiding Spanish practice regarding effective land control was thus use, and Spanish towns with no other formal instrument for the occupation of the lands on which their citizens depended could always claim "possession from time immemorial, which was usually accepted by Castilian courts" (Ibid., 20).

Therefore, there was a large body of law and custom in Spain based on the principle of community ownership of land. Individual access for commoners was limited to usufruct only so long as a tract continued under cultivation. Thus, in certain important respects, Maya and Spanish principles of landholding were surprisingly similar. Yet the Spanish imposition of even much-streamlined regulations regarding landholding by indigenous New World peoples created a great deal of uncertainty for Mesoamerican Indians in general and the Cakchiquel in particular.

Spanish regulations concerning landholding were embodied in the monumental *Recopilición de Leyes de los reinos de las Indias* (or *Laws of the Indies*), which attempted to prescribe standards and procedures for every imaginable circumstance. Notwithstanding this attempt to formulate a universal law code, the contradictions and ambiguities regarding land in the *Laws of the Indies* guaranteed both misunderstanding and conflict. As in the reconquest of the Iberian peninsula, all New World lands won by Spanish arms were technically tierras realengas, though these were far too vast to be reserved to royal use alone. Again similar to reconquest practice, the crown was also anxious to populate its New World holdings with loyal Spaniards. It was therefore inclined to grant land for the formation of towns and to individuals, either for services rendered to the crown or through sale at a nominal price through the practice of *composición,* whereby the crown graciously consented to sell some of its tierras realengas.

At the same time, the crown was also concerned with protecting the interests of its Indian subjects. Along with the policy of forming Indian towns through congregación (see Chapter 3), crown policy was to grant such communities an ejido of one square league (approximately seventeen square kilometers), measured from the front steps of the town church, which typically dominated the central plaza of the rectilinear, Spanish-designed pueblos. At the same time, Spanish law specifically stated that the Indians were to remain in possession of whatever lands they had previously enjoyed, despite their resettlement in the new towns. Technically, a royal title should have been extended to each Indian community, securing its control of the ejido. However, given the extreme population reduction caused by the conquest and accompanying diseases, Spanish officials in the Guatemala highlands saw little need for such formalities. There was initially such an excess of land that there was no apparent necessity to assign specific tracts or inventory the holdings of indigenous individuals or groups. Also, the absence of formal titles to the lands of Indian communities would make it much easier for Spaniards to claim and gain legal ownership to valuable tracts of farmland near the Colonial capital through composición.

Even without avarice on the part of the early colonists, Spanish land law, while seemingly surprisingly just, was exceedingly vague as to its application and administration. Lands could be granted to individual Spaniards or to form Spanish towns only if it could be demonstrated that they were unused and therefore open for claims. Yet, how could such a determination be made, especially in the absence of any systematic census of Indian holdings? With reduced Cakchiquel populations and a long fallow cycle in which land might be taken out of production for several years, a given tract might indeed look vacant and unused. In practice, many of the early Spanish claims to tracts in the Sacatepéquez area just north of the Colonial capital were accepted almost without reference to the possibility of prior claims by Cakchiquels. Perhaps during the late sixteenth century, when many of these claims were made, the Cakchiquel populations of the Sacatepéquez towns were so reduced that even grants of several *caballerías* (one caballería equals approximately 111 acres) to each of the many Spanish applicants did not impair the Indians' ability to subsist.

However, by the seventeenth century, the situation had changed. The Cakchiquel became much more concerned with protecting their land and more adept at doing so. As indicated previously, Spanish law and custom recognized prior use of land as a valid claim, and the Spanish administration was obligated to protect Cakchiquel holdings. Yet, how could claims of prior occupation be established? One form of evidence acceptable to Spanish law was the testimony of eyewitnesses from preconquest or early postconquest times who were knowledgeable about different groups' landholdings. However, by the seventeenth century such individuals hardly existed. The Cakchiquel soon developed a more permanent class of evidence, which they typically referred to using the Spanish term *títulos*. Technically there could be only one valid título, or title, to a piece of property, one granted by the crown or its representatives. Yet Spanish practice admitted virtually any written instrument as evidence of prior ownership, and the Cakchiquel were quick to realize the power of documents in cases before the audiencia. To the Cakchiquel, títulos soon came to denote any papers which proved ownership, or at least prior occupancy or use. Such Cakchiquel títulos could therefore take a variety of forms.

At the amaq' and chinamit levels títulos were often transcriptions in Cakchiquel (using Spanish characters; see Chapter 8) of such groups' traditional histories, often including a list of the group's preconquest boundary markers. Because these markers could still be identified by the Colonial-period descendants of the documents' authors, investigating Spanish officials could be accurately guided along the entire periphery of a group's holdings and intrusive claims could be readily identified. To the extent that the claims of chinamitales and parcialidades now resettled into towns were recognized by the audiencia, these groups gained de facto legal status, which reinforced both their importance as sociopolitical entities and the authority of the leadership as custodians of their traditional territory's integrity. Individuals or families could back up any claims they might have by presenting *testamentos* or *cédulas* (informal bills of sale), also written in Cakchiquel. The Pirir family, for example, presented don Miguel's testamento to gain a restraining order *(despacho de ámparo)* for their large holding at Navorón. In his will, don Miguel was careful to note those tracts he had acquired through purchase and for which he had a receipt from the previous owner. Other rich Indians employed the same devices.

LANDHOLDING STRATEGIES

In practice, and regardless of social rank, the problem faced by all Colonial Cakchiquel was to acquire or maintain access to sufficient land to support themselves and meet their social and tributary responsibilities. They employed a variety of potential strategies, the use of which depended on the individual's social station, wealth, population trends in his area, his degree of exposure to Spanish principles regarding landholding, and his ability to navigate successfully among the at-times conflicting native and imported principles.

The rich Indian, head of a family corporation, or the direct descendant of preconquest aristocrats (often all one and the same) had the greatest variety of options at his (or, more rarely, her) disposal and could ultimately achieve the greatest security for himself and his dependents. Such an individual would have been much more likely to have owned private tracts and would by definition have been wealthy enough to retain Spanish counsel to present and guide his petition before the audiencia, which was the only means of securing his holdings. The seventeenth-century Cakchiquel seem only rarely to have sought a royal title to their lands, though we do not know the reason for this. Perhaps they were unfamiliar with the possibility of composición, or they may have been unwilling to purchase their own lands from the invaders.

Whatever the reason, the Cakchiquel usually requested a *despacho de ámparo* as protection for their lands. This writ functioned essentially like a restraining order, protecting the party to which it had been granted from summary expropriation by a third party. Such a document did not confer ownership of land, but it did not require composición either. It could prove an adequate defense against claims by other parties (both Indian and Spaniard) because they would need both the funds to pay for their petition to the audiencia and some proof that their claim had precedence over that of the individual holding the ámparo. Once a request for an ámparo had been made, the petitioner normally had to validate his claim to an investigating Spanish official. A rich Indian was much more likely to have written testamentos witnessed by the local authorities that he could present, as well as the testimony of witnesses. A wealthy Indian was also much more likely to have purchased land and to have had the purchase agreement or cédula written down by the town scribe before witnesses. All these documents were títulos to the Cakchiquel and were accepted by the audiencia as proof of prior use, if not ownership, of land. If granted, the ámparo itself became a título in the minds of the recipients and would be duly presented in any future litigation.

Poor or commoner Cakchiquel (again, usually one and the same) typically could not employ the strategies used by the wealthy. By definition, they were less likely to have purchased the land as individuals or as families and less likely to have gone to the expense of having such unofficial transactions formalized in writing by the town scribe, let alone retain Spanish counsel. Similarly, a small estate and few heirs would normally preclude the need for a written testamento. Instead, the average Cakchiquel probably secured access to land through his usufruct right to a portion of the territory controlled by his chinamit/parcialidad.

By pooling its members' resources, a parcialidad could make an effective case for a writ of ámparo. Through various forms of collections from among members (usually called *nut* or *cotzún* in Cakchiquel and *derrama* in Spanish), a parcialidad could raise the funds necessary for retaining counsel to represent its case before the Spanish authorities. As traditional, corporate groups, parcialidades might well have a título in the form of a written history and listing of boundary markers to demonstrate their possession of a tract "from time immemorial." Testimony from aged witnesses could also be presented, which could at least place the group's possession in some chronological context. As noted above, if a parcialidad gained an ámparo for its land, its corporate existence was substantially reinforced. Such a group might even be able to afford to purchase its lands via composición and receive a royal title, though this seems to have been more common in the succeeding eighteenth century.

A town might also act as a corporate unit with regard to landholding, especially if its component parcialidades had been associated before the conquest. Outside threats, either from Spaniards, rich Indians, or other communities, could also result in a collective defense by an entire town. Like parcialidades, towns could rely on collections made from among residents to retain counsel and defray any other expenses connected with the case, such as boundary surveys and the transcription of their títulos for presentation to the audiencia. However, towns had an additional tactic at their disposal: the local justices could claim a scarcity of lands for the residents to work for their own support and to meet their tribute obligations. Such claims might also be made by individuals and groups, but a plea of this sort from a town's justices had to be addressed by the Spanish authorities in some fashion because any threat to the prompt and full collection of tribute was viewed with alarm and because Spanish law required that Indian communities have sufficient lands for their residents' support.

A final type of Colonial Cakchiquel landholding consisted of lands dedicated to the support of saints' cults. For the most part, these lands appear to have been endowments given by wealthy individuals, and either their direct production or rents derived from them were used to defray the costs of the fiesta celebrating the day of the saint to whom it was dedicated. Once so assigned, such tracts appear to have been removed from the unofficial Cakchiquel real estate market. They also were safe from Spanish usurpation because the *Laws of the Indies* specifically recognized such gifts to the church. Under this statute, royal permission was, ideally, necessary and jurisdiction over the tract was to be vested in church officials. These specifications do not seem to have been observed in practice, though the rights of *patronazgo* were. These included not only the notoriety and enhanced social status of the donor, but also the continued control over the tract and the ability to name successors to its guardianship. In this way, landed endowments of saints' cults were as much a means of securing land as they were acts of piety and public demonstrations of wealth. A brief review of some actual cases presented before the audiencia will illustrate some of the ways in which these different strategies were employed.

THE PIRIR FAMILY

The activities of the corporate Pirir family span the seventeenth century (Hill 1989b). Almost certainly a descendant of local preconquest Cakchiquel aristocrats, patriarch don Miguel (who was born around 1550) seems to have begun his career with a clear advantage over most of his contempories, the ownership, or at least control, of several hundred acres at a place called Navorón, just north of San Juan Sacatepéquez. As one of the few survivors of the pandemics that decimated his generation, and with a secure land base, don Miguel was able to amass many additional tracts in the Sacatepéquez area, often through purchase. These holdings seem not to have been challenged either by Spaniards or other Indians during his lifetime, probably owing to the low population of the times. Nevertheless, while on what he believed to be his deathbed in 1642, don Miguel went to some effort to dictate a lengthy testamento, witnessed by the town justices and others, in which he divided his considerable estate, assigning specific tracts to different sons or pairs of sons and to the support of seven different saints' cults. Boundaries or neighbors were usually at least mentioned, and in some cases were specified at length. The absence of any contradiction from the justices concerning the lands apportioned by don Miguel or their boundaries indicated their tacit acceptance of his ownership, a potent piece of evidence should the need ever arise to defend any of the holdings.

The existence of the testamento allowed Domingo, don Miguel's son and successor as family head, to gain a royal despacho de ámparo for the main Navorón holding in 1655. Domingo, in turn, dictated his testamento from his deathbed in 1669, in which he also carefully noted the property bequeathed to each son or pair of sons, again including the boundaries or neighbors of each tract. His testamento was also witnessed by the town's justices, again indicating their acceptance of his ownership. All three of these documents, the two testamentos and the ámparo, were carefully preserved by the Pirir descendants and were formally presented as títulos before the audiencia in a dispute with the town of San Juan Sacatepéquez in 1707.

Although slightly beyond our time period, a review of this early-eighteenth-century dispute is worthwhile since it illustrates several of the different tactics for maintaining control of land in action and also typifies the conflict between private and corporate ownership which characterized the late seventeenth century. As already noted, Cakchiquel population was recovering by this time, resulting in serious pressure on landholdings. Symptomatic of this trend was the attempt of thirty-nine Indians of San Juan Sacatepéquez to encroach on the Pirir land at Navorón late in 1707. Juan de la Cruz, Domingo's only surviving son, was at this time head of the family corporation and quickly retained Spanish counsel to petition the audiencia for a writ of ámparo, based on the royal ámparo granted Domingo in 1655. The audiencia granted this petition in December of 1707.

Two months passed before the squatters retaliated. The reason for the delay is not known but may have been due to their difficulty in amassing the funds necessary to retain their own counsel. Through him, they requested a redress of their grievances and defended their encroachment, citing a dispute in 1675 in which the town of San Juan successfully defeated a Spanish landowner's attempt to usurp two caballerías of land along the Río Pixcaya. The town received an ámparo for this tract, part of which they had long ago designated as common land and open to use by any of its residents in a *convenio,* or covenant, written in Cakchiquel in 1607. The rest was reserved for the support of the church and the cofradía of Nuestra Señora del Rosario. Their counsel also argued that the royal ámparo granted

Domingo Pirir in 1655 was invalid since it failed to mention the boundaries of the holding. He therefore petitioned that the Pirir ámparo be at least modified to recognize the lands his clients occupied. On the same day, Juan de la Cruz filed a petition of his own in which he explained how the men of his corporate family held the land together, with each working his own portion. He again complained about the squatters and asked that the audiencia order their eviction.

Formal investigation of the case by a Spanish official did not begin until May of 1708 when both the Pirires and the community of San Juan were ordered to present all relevant documents in their possession for review. As noted above, the Pirires presented the testamentos of don Miguel and Domingo, the royal ámparo of 1655, and a list of the saints' cults which they supported. These constituted strong evidence of uncontested prior possession of the Navorón tract, since no dissent had been forthcoming from the town justices who witnessed either document, and the royal ámparo was official recognition of this fact. For their part, the community leaders presented their town's títulos, which represented a wide spectrum of documents. Included were a mid-sixteenth-century map noting the boundaries of their preconquest holdings, a short description of the location of the main boundary markers, a brief translation of their traditional history, a copy of the ámparo they received as a result of the 1675 dispute, and a copy of the 1607 agreement.

The disputed land was duly inspected by the presiding official, who prepared a report containing either the originals or copies of all the above documents for his superiors. Yet, before he left town, the justices and the Pirires came to inform him of an agreement they had reached. The Pirires would give up a small part of their Navorón tract, and in exchange the justices promised that no further demands would be made on the Pirires' holdings. We cannot know how or why this agreement was struck, but several factors may have been at work. One may have been that both sides had strong cases based on the documents they had presented and some of the document types were similar. Thus, if the ámparo of either the Pirires or the town were overturned by the audiencia, how secure was the ámparo of the winning party? How well might their ámparo protect them the next time a dispute arose? These Cakchiquel were shrewd enough to see the consequences should the documents of either side be found deficient. The result would have been that all the documents that the community and its wealthy and commoner members alike, relied upon to ensure control of land would henceforth be suspect. Rather than set such a potentially damaging precedent, the parties involved reached a compromise which avoided the question of which side's documents constituted the stronger case.

Another factor may have been a feeling of community. As residents of the same town as the squatters, the Pirires were coparticipants in a range of institutions and obligations. They supported the same church and observed the same patronal fiesta. They all took their turns as officials in the town government. They were all part of the same unit of tribute payment to the Spaniards. Thus, in a real sense, they all shared the same fate, a fact which may well have been impressed upon them by the town justices and principales. The result was an accord which, as far as we can tell, was adhered to. Perhaps more important, they avoided a direct challenge of the legitimacy of any class of títulos.

CALPUL YA JONICA

The calpul or parcialidad Ya Jonica was one of several which belonged to the eastern Chajomá amaq' and which the Spaniards brought together as part of their congregación program to form the town of San Pedro Sacatepéquez. There seems to have been no concern with formally securing any of their traditional landholdings in the sixteenth or early seventeenth centuries, but by 1644 the group's leaders initiated a legal process aimed to get not just Spanish recognition of their claims but also formal title. In mid-July of that year seven of the group's principales petitioned the audiencia to measure and erect boundary markers on a tract of land called El Carrizal, which they claimed belonged to their parcialidad by virtue of possession and use since before the conquest. Part of the land was used for milpas, while the rest served as pasture and pens for draft animals (probably mules) and cattle. The Ya Jonica people stated that they wished to buy the tract and acquire royal title through composición.

As was normal in such proceedings, their initial petition was drafted by a Spanish scribe, who also signed the document on behalf of his nonliterate clients. The *fiscal* of the audiencia (like a state's attorney with the added responsibility of protecting the Indians' interests) recommended that the Ya Jonica people's request be granted and that a Spanish official be assigned to the case. Accordingly, a party consisting of an investigating judge, *defensor* (an attorney to represent the rights of all Indians involved), and a surveyor set out for San Pedro five days later. Once there, the judge also named an interpreter (in this instance an Indian who spoke both Spanish and Cakchiquel, which was unusual) and then proceeded to notify the town justices and those of neighboring San Juan and San Raimundo of the reason for his arrival. Each of the three towns would be required to send representatives to attend the proceedings. Their main function was to inspect the lands in question and to affirm that they did not fall within the territory claimed by their respective towns.

This was a formal affair called a *vista de ojos* (visual inspection), followed by a measurement of the tract's periphery and the erection of boundary markers, usually in the form of stone cairns supporting wooden crosses. The following day testimony was taken from persons deemed knowledgeable and acceptable to all parties. In this case, three Spaniards and two Indians made statements. The Spaniards were all *labradores* (farmers) in the area and all affirmed that for as long as they could remember, the lands had belonged to the Ya Jonica, who used them for milpas and for snaring deer (see Chapter 5). They also claimed to have heard old Indians say that the tract had always belonged to the Ya Jonica.

Because the land was to be sold, some idea of its value needed to be established, so, as was usual in such proceedings, the Spanish witnesses were asked to make an estimate. They all agreed that the area destined for use as stock pens was worth twenty-five *tostones* (*see* Chapter 5), and the surrounding caballería could be valued at no more than eight tostones, as it was useless for milpa, being all rocky hills and ravines and lacking water. The two Indian witnesses confirmed that the tract fell within the Ya Jonica group's traditional boundaries, and one of them explained the communal landholding practiced by the parcialidad (this was septuagenarian Benito Gomez, whose testimony was cited in Chapter 2).

With proceedings in San Pedro concluded, the presiding official deposited his report with the audiencia, and in a matter-of-fact way the fiscal recommended that the composición be granted, providing in the normal manner that the Ya Jonica calpul pay all the costs of the process. In this instance, the total came to forty-four *pesos* (eighty-eight tostones), with the bulk of it (over twenty-seven pesos) going to pay the salaries of the supervising official, defensor, surveyor, and interpreter. This sum, though small compared to those paid in the eighteenth century, was still beyond the means of all but the richest Cakchiquel, but by pooling resources the Ya Jonica were able to gain royal title to a tract, which enabled them to diversify their economic base by stock breeding.

INDIANS OF XENACOJ VERSUS THE TOWN OF SAN MARTÍN JILOTEPÉQUE

Another conflict over land rights illustrates how the criterion of use could conflict with evidence of "immemorial possession" provided by a town's título. In this case, sloppy Spanish administration, combined with several Cakchiquel individuals who understood how to manipulate the system, resulted in litigation which dragged on for almost forty years before a definitive settlement was reached.

The town of Santo Domingo Xenacoj was founded in the late sixteenth century at the instigation of Dominican friar Benito de Villacañas, who persuaded the members of the Sinacá parcialidad to occupy the area, which was about to be claimed by a Spaniard (Remesal 1966:II:178). The tactic proved successful in thwarting Spanish claims, but the town was built on a knoll in very rugged country and its residents suffered from a chronic shortage of tillable land. As a result, residents had to seek land far from town, even appealing for the use of unoccupied areas in other towns' holdings. Such was the case with Domingo Hernández Quel and his brother Pedro, who apparently approached the justices of San Martín Jilotepéque in 1631, requesting to lease or rent *(arrendar)* some land along their town's side of the Río Pixcaya. Permission was granted, though no document was drawn up, probably because the area controlled by San Martín was so vast and its population was still small enough that population pressure was not yet a factor.

Over the next ten years, the brothers built up their tract, pasturing cattle and planting sugarcane. Whether they came sincerely to regard the land as theirs or only sought to cheat their benefactors, they obtained an ámparo in 1641, the contents of which were made known to the San Martín people as a matter of procedure. At the time they acquiesced, but by 1643 some of their own residents had begun to pioneer the area, apparently encroaching on the Quels' holding. Both sides complained, Domingo and Pedro citing their ámparo and the San Martín people insisting that the brothers be evicted since the lands had only been rented to them. At the time, the audiencia judged that the Quels' ámparo constituted the stronger claim and, until a final decision could be reached, they should remain in possession. In November of 1643, an official was sent to conduct a vista de ojos and to supervise the erection of boundary markers.

The official conscientiously carried out his orders, even over the protests of the San Martín justices. The four-caballería tract soon came to be known as the *estancia* (ranch) of San Miguel, and its possession by the Quel brothers went unchallenged until March of 1645. The audiencia still had not issued a ruling, probably because the San Martín people still had not presented their case. In any event, the San Martín Indians again entered the area, killing some of the Quels' cattle, and prepared to build houses and plant milpas. In responding to the Quels' appeal for relief, the audiencia again found their ámparo to be the stronger case, and the same official was ordered to investigate. He was instructed to inspect the boundary markers, and if they had been dismantled by the San Martín people, he was to have new ones erected. He was further empowered to evict anyone who may have entered the tract. The orders were carried out in May, and as a result, the San Martín people were evicted and ordered not to return until the audiencia had decided the case.

The Quel brothers requested another ámparo for the same tract in 1649, which was duly granted. Shortly thereafter, however, in April of 1651, they sold the tract to a Spanish officer for 300 pesos. The surviving sale contract was a formal affair, drawn up by a royal official, in which the brothers certified that the lands had been marked and measured and purchased from the crown and titled via composición. It is impossible to determine if they were lying, if they actually believed that the ámparos granted them constituted official title, or if this was simply inserted into the text at the request of the buyer as a means of making his purchase more secure. Regardless, they went through the formalities of obtaining the audiencia's permission to sell the land, though no one checked to see if there were any pending disputes involving it. This was a crucial and administratively unforgivable oversight and would ultimately cause the succeeding purchasers of the tract to lose much of their investment.

The new Spanish owner held on to the land for only two years before he sold it to a group of at least eight Xenacoj Indians in 1653 for 400 pesos. This was an enormous sum for that time and place. Keep in mind that the Ya Jonica parcialidad paid only four pesos for a caballería of land only a few years before and only 44 pesos for the entire composición. Even considering that the four caballerías purchased by the group from Xenacoj may have been better quality land with some river frontage, such prices could only have been justified if the purchasers thought that they were buying securely titled property. In fact, a formal bill of sale also accompanied this transaction, and in 1677 the members of this group received formal, legal possession (posesión jurídica). Thus, under Spanish law, their claim to ownership, backed up as it was by a long trail of documents, could scarcely have been stronger. Unfortunately for them, subsequent events would prove that it was not strong enough.

Despite their eviction in 1645, the San Martín people had never left the area entirely and had even created a small ranch dedicated to the support of their cofradía of Nuestra Señora del Rosario. By this tactic they effectively blocked any further expansion of the Xenacoj people's holdings, since, as noted above, lands dedicated to the support of saints' cults were generally protected by Spanish law. Yet it was not until 1680 that the San Martín people felt strong enough to act. In June of that year they retained the services of a Spanish procurador and through him presented a petition to the audiencia in which they claimed that all the land along the north and west banks of the Río Pixcaya belonged to their town. They cited the presence of the ranch as proof of possession and presented a transcription of their mid-sixteenth-century título, which contained a brief history of the Chajomá branch of the Cakchiquel (of which they were part) and a list of boundary markers (Crespo 1956:13–15). They requested that the audiencia receive testimony regarding their claims and that they be granted an ámparo for their holdings.

Accordingly, a Spanish official was sent to investigate. Eight different Spanish and mestizo (individuals of mixed Spanish-Indian ancestry) witnesses confirmed the San Martín people's story. While the investigation was underway, the Xenacoj group submitted their own petition containing the ámparos they had previously obtained, noting that the one of 1645 had specified the eviction of the San Martín people, and the two bills of sale, from Quel to the Spaniard, and from him to themselves. The San Martín people relied on the legal acumen of their *procurador* to respond effectively to the Xenacoj group. He noted first of all that his clients had the prior claim, as demonstrated by their sixteenth-century título, and that all Xenacoj lands lay on the south side of the Río Pixcaya. He next attacked the validity of the Xenacoj group's documents. These, he argued, were illegitimate since, although the four caballerías had been measured and boundaries sited, it had never been established that the lands were indeed realengas and thus open to claim. This oversight invalidated all subsequent documents of ownership, including the two bills of sale. He also noted that there was no record of the lands having been purchased from the crown via composición, and he appealed the injustice of the two vistas de ojos, which had been implemented over the objections of his clients, without their own claims being investigated. Finally, he suggested that his clients' claims should be given priority in any case, since theirs involved common land for an entire town, while their opponents represented only private interests. He closed by requesting the eviction of the Xenacoj group and an ámparo for his clients.

These were powerful arguments which ultimately won the case. The procurador for the Xenacoj people could only argue that the sixteenth-century título was not a legal document, just a simple paper without substantiation that only contained a list of boundary markers written by the San Martín people themselves. His clients, on the other hand, could point to almost fifty years of occupation by non-San Martín people, including nearly thirty years of their own. The case dragged on due to procedural matters, especially a search for the documents connected with the ámparos granted in the 1640s, for which the Xenacoj group were required to pay the enormous sum of fifty pesos. However, in May of 1681 the audiencia finally decided to revoke the ámparo granted the Quel brothers in 1644, awarding possession to the San Martín people. The Xenacoj group lost its initial investment of four hundred pesos, but the audiencia did stipulate that the San Martín people reimburse them for the fifty-peso document search fee as well as for any houses or other improvements they had made on the land. This ultimately amounted to 150 pesos, though it must have been little comfort to the group of Xenacoj people, who had seen their initial investment, their many years of labor, and their future security vanish, in spite of what they surely must have felt to be unassailable títulos. For their part, the San Martín people prudently had their procurador request duplicates of all documentation connected with the dispute. These became part of the town's títulos and were duly presented as evidence in 1722 in a boundary dispute on their western border with the town of Comalapa and in 1751, when the town finally got around to purchasing all their remaining lands from the Crown via composición.

DIEGO PEREZ XPANTZAY AND THE POROMÁ PARCIALIDAD

The most complex example from the end of the seventeenth century is reminiscent of that between the Pirires and San Juan Sacatepéquez in 1707 in that it too involved population pressure and conflict between a wealthy descendant of the preconquest aristocracy and a larger social unit to which he belonged. However, in this case, that larger unit was a parcialidad, the Poromá, which had been one of the prominent chinamitales of the Iximché polity.

As in the Pirir dispute of 1707, this case began with a complaint from a landowner, this time late in 1689, that his holdings were being usurped. The plaintiff was Diego Perez Xpantzay, his Maya surname indicating that he was a descendant of one of the most prominent Cakchiquel families. However, in this instance, he claimed rights of possession based on inheritance not from a male, paternal relative but from his mother and her line. His deceased mother was Francisca Yeol (probably a corruption of Lolmay), the daughter of the former cacique Francisco Hernández Yeol (again probably Lolmay and who was listed as an ahau [lord; member of the indigenous aristocracy] in 1524; Recinos 1957:129). As such, she had inherited a tract of land from her father, which she later exchanged with her brother for two of his. A convenio (covenant) had been drawn up by the town scribe and witnessed by the local priest, alcaldes, and others in 1635. She left the tracts to her son, Diego, in a clause of her testamento.

Diego, his sons, and four other men with the Yeol surname (apparently maternal kinsmen) had enjoyed the uncontested use of the tracts in what seems to have been a complex, corporate family arrangement until the beginnings of a dispute he claimed was maliciously started by what turned out later to be fellow members of his own Poromá parcialidad. Diego accused them of illegally making collections among the townspeople to raise the funds for a litigation to dispossess him of the land. He presented his mother's testamento and a copy of the exchange agreement, which proved his story and his long possession of the tract. Accordingly, in his initial complaint of November 11, 1689, he requested an order of ámparo for his holdings and this was duly granted him.

For their part, the other party, composed of men with such diverse surnames as Cobox, Porom, Cum, and Gomez, claimed that, on the contrary, it was Diego Perez who was the usurper. In their petition to the audiencia, these men claimed to represent others of their group and asserted that their ancestors had possessed a tract called Xanquiba or Quixanquiba since time immemorial. This tract had itself been in litigation for some time. Unfortunately, their títulos had been lost for a time, although when they were later recovered, the group of Poromá men presented them before the town justices. To end the dispute, the justices had the town scribe draw up a convenio in which the Poromá agreed to pay twenty-three pesos to other claimants, including three pesos to the mother of Diego Perez Xpantzay. The governor of the town also demanded six pesos for himself as "costs." In return, the Poromá people believed that they now owned a portion of the tract claimed by Diego by virtue of inheritance.

However, the Poromá complaint went beyond this. They also claimed that they were many people and that they did not have enough land and that, notwithstanding the earlier convenio, the governor now wished to take that part of their tract which had belonged to Francisca Yeol in order to give it to her son, Diego. The governor did this, they claimed, only to gain the favor of Diego, who was a rich Indian. They closed their petition by requesting a writ of ámparo for their land, an order that Diego and the governor cease troubling them, and another order that the governor return the six pesos they had paid him for the now-worthless convenio.

The audiencia did not like to be bothered by such petty, local land disputes and, therefore, often tried to delegate the responsibility for investigating and settling such cases to local authorities and even to local private Spanish subjects. In this instance, the audiencia instructed the local priest to inform himself about the affair and report back. In his brief report, the priest stated that, despite their claims, no one was trying to take the Poromá land and that they would be content if Diego would simply exhibit the títulos from his ancestors and give them copies for safekeeping.

Almost simultaneously with the priest's report, the Poromá submitted another petition, again claiming that Diego was attempting to take their land. For that purpose they claimed that, as a rich Indian, he had the governor in his pocket and had so taken the lands of many other poor Indians. Further, he had divided the parcialidad by recruiting the four Yeol men, who the Poromá claimed were their fellow chinamitales, to take his side in the dispute. They also presented their own títulos, which they claimed would substantiate their claims of possession. On the basis of this information, they requested a ruling in their favor. All the documents were sent to the *asesor,* the audiencia's legal advisor, who recommended that Diego be ordered to present copies of his títulos to the Poromá as the priest had indicated and that an ámparo be issued to them. The audiencia issued orders to that effect, including the provision of a two-hundred-peso fine for violation of the ámparo.

However, by granting both parties ámparos, the audiencia had done nothing to resolve the dispute. Miguel Galindo, a Spanish resident of the Tecpán area, reported on the proceedings in the town hall when he attempted to notify the town justices and the Poromá of the content of Diego's ámparo. The Poromá representatives listened patiently to the contents of the order, as translated for them by Galindo, and promised to obey, but said that they too had an ámparo for their lands in the same case. Diego was summoned to the scene, where Galindo summarily ordered the justices to resolve the dispute by deciding what each party should possess according to their respective ámparos. They all huddled for a while but could reach no agreement. The Poromá stated that they would be content if Diego renounced his claim on their lands, while he responded that his títulos proved that the lands were legitimately his. These positions were essentially the same when, two days later, an official representative of the audiencia arrived in Tecpán, though now the Poromá claimed that the lands in question were commons and that Diego had paid the justices and heads of the other parcialidades to say that the lands were his.

Another letter to the audiencia from the local priest, written on November 19, added little new information. He stated that Diego had made a true relation of the facts to the audiencia and certified that he was a solid citizen, good supporter of the church, charitable to the poor, and past holder of offices in the municipal government. He also claimed that it was common knowledge that his opponents (by which he seems to have meant only those individuals whose names appeared in the petitions) were well known for their intrigues and litigiousness and were destroying the town with their constant collections of money, all to be spent in divisive litigations. The priest closed by saying that the dispute would not be resolved until a competent judge was sent to settle matters by evaluating each party's documents, viewing the contested area, and assigning the land accordingly.

That did not happen until December, when Francisco de Albizuri arrived in Tecpán to carry out his commission of conducting an inquest concerning the disputed lands. Through Miguel Galindo, who again acted as interpreter, Diego stated that he had already paid the Poromá forty-six tostones for the expenses they had incurred in litigating this dispute and thought that the matter had been settled. On the basis of this statement and the documents Diego had previously presented, Albizuri gave him official possession of the land on December 9. However, in his moment of victory, Diego was generous. Because the tract was large, because he claimed that those of the Poromá chinamit were always loved and regarded by him as brothers, regardless of the trouble they had caused him, and because he desired peace, he offered the following deal. If the Poromá returned his forty-six tostones and promised never to bother him or his descendants again, he would give them half the land in question as commons for the parcialidad. They agreed, and a convenio was drawn up in which Albizuri required it be further stipulated that the agreement would have the same force as a decision passed by a competent Spanish official, with both parties renouncing all other claims and rights of appeal. The dividing line would be the road running to the town of Semetabaj, with lands on the right hand going to the Poromá. Copies were made and signed by all parties and witnessed by the town justices.

Such an agreement should have ended things, especially given the renunciation of all further claims and rights cleverly inserted by Albizuri. Yet, such was not the case. Imprecise boundaries and, perhaps, some dishonesty on the part of the Poromá resulted in considerable acrimony when it came to clearing and planting, giving rise to new troubles. However, because the Poromá had already signed away their ability to bring further action before the audiencia, they cleverly opted to bring their new complaint before the Corregidor del Valle de Guatemala, the chief administrator of the subdivision of the Spanish Kingdom of Guatemala to which Tecpán belonged. This official had no knowledge of the prior dispute between the Poromá and Diego Perez Xpantzay, nor of the convenio that was supposed to have ended it. Thus, he was prepared to consider the Poromá petition late in September of 1690.

The crux of the complaint was that they had cleared some land in preparation for planting, incurring expenses in addition to their own toil of 117 tostones for *taqueguales* (hired laborers) who felled more than 1320 trees. They claimed that after the work was done, Diego, as a rich Indian, had bought off the local officials and had the Poromá evicted from half the land which had been cleared. Given that Diego was rich, the Poromá people wanted him to reimburse them for their work and costs. Diego and the town justices were ordered before the corregidor and, after some negotiations and forgiveness of old debts, Diego was ordered to pay a total of eighty-eight tostones to eight Poromá men. Diego did not have the money with him, so the corregidor ordered the justices to ensure that the payments were made.

At the same time, the Poromá men addressed a petition to the Receptor de las Condenaciones de penas de la Cámara de Gastos (a Spanish official of the audiencia in charge of collecting fines imposed by that body) claiming that Diego had moved one of the boundary markers, thereby stealing a large piece of land from them. Another official was ordered to investigate the charges and arrived in Tecpán on September 14. Diego notified him of the agreement of the previous December and complained that the Poromá men had cleared and planted wheat in his land and were now demanding payment in cash. It was clear to the official that justice was on Diego's side, since his land had been used without his permission. He therefore ordered the Poromá men to pay Diego rent for the land they had planted according to the Indian custom of determining the number of *mecates* planted (a mecate equals about ten acres), the value of which would be judged by the town justices. The next day, the official inspected the boundary markers and found that one had indeed been moved. He ordered it to be replaced in the presence of the justices but did not establish who had moved the marker or when.

A week later, Diego filed a petition with the audiencia in which he complained that, despite the various ámparos and the convenio, the group of Poromá men continued to make trouble for him. He explained that they had presented themselves before the corregidor without telling him about the convenio and how all the lands had been adjudicated in his favor but that he, as an act of kindness to his fellow parcialidad members, had given them half for their common use. Now, he asserted, they had appeared before the corregidor, claiming ignorance of how the dispute had been settled and demanding payment for the lands they had cleared. Diego requested that the audiencia inform the corregidor of the earlier agreement.

The asesor reviewed the case after obtaining the record of the Poromá demands for payment before the corregidor. In a scathing opinion to the audiencia he confirmed Diego's right to the entire tract and excoriated the Poromá men for appearing before the corregidor. As punishment, he recommended that they be required to return to Diego any money they had collected from him and that he not be required to pay them the forty-six tostones specified in the convenio. Further, they should lose without compensation the crops they had planted in Diego's land, be content with the half which Diego had ceded to them, and cause him no further trouble, under pain of fifty lashes. The opinion was endorsed by the president of the audiencia and the sentence issued on September 26. Through procuradores, both parties requested copies of all the documents pertaining to the case in late October, the Poromá with an eye to an appeal, Diego looking to amass additional títulos for a possible further defense. In late November the Poromá retained new Spanish counsel, but he made no appearance before the audiencia until late in March of

1691. Given the behavior of the Poromá men, and the convenio of 1689 in which they agreed to give up further litigation, the audiencia summarily disallowed any further motions concerning the case.

CONCLUSIONS

It is hoped the preceding, detailed examinations of disputes have illustrated the extent to which choices among alternatives were a necessary part of securing land. Although there were principles, and even laws, regarding land tenure, these were often ambiguous in practice, especially given the intensely competitive environment of the later seventeenth century. Compounding matters was the Spaniards' failure to conduct anything like a systematic survey of all the lands claimed by towns and parcialidades, as the major corporate entities, let alone those claimed by individuals. Without such records, it was often impossible to evaluate different claims to the same land, or even to establish if a tract was claimed at all. The records of such surveys which the Spanish authorities did conduct (usually only as part of the investigative process when disputes actually arose or at the request of a party requesting composición) were usually imprecise, and with the passage of time, the death of witnesses, and the loss of títulos, disputes easily reemerged later. For these reasons it is impossible to dispose of the topic of land tenure simply by stating that the Cakchiquel observed this or that custom. Instead, landholdings were always tenuous, and the Cakchiquel, as individuals or as groups, availed themselves of every possible device to gain or maintain possession. We turn next to the varied uses to which the land was put.

BIBLIOGRAPHIC NOTE

Vassberg (1984) presents a lucid discussion of Spanish landholding principles from the reconquest through the seventeenth century. The Pirir documents and records of the 1707 litigation are contained in Archivo General de Centro America (AGCA) document A3.15 Leg.2787 Exp. 40301. Record of the composición in favor of the Ya Jonica calpul is in AGCA document A1 Leg.5942 Exp.52000. The case of the Xenacoj Indians versus San Martín Jilotepéque is recorded in AGCA document A1 Leg.6013 Exp.52978. Diego Perez Xpantzay's problems with the Poromá parcialidad are enumerated in AGCA document A1 Leg.6063 Exp.53970 and A1 Leg.6064 Exp.53971.

5 / Material Life

In terms of their material existence, the Cakchiquel, like all other participants in Mesoamerican civilization, were the beneficiaries of several millennia of technological developments, resulting in a distinct and remarkably stable way of life. For the vast majority of Colonial Cakchiquel, subsistence continued to revolve around the ancient triumvirate of vegetable foods, maize beans, and squash, supplemented by a cornucopia of lesser cultigens, the domesticated turkey, and an immense variety of wild plants and animals. Especially at the peasant household level, this way of life changed little as a result of the conquest, and for many years thereafter the Spaniards remained dependent on locally produced goods for their survival. Yet, even by the seventeenth century, the Kingdom of Guatemala had not become rich like Mexico or Peru, so imported alternatives to indigenous goods never became all that common. However, there were additions to the Cakchiquels' technological inventory from the Old World via Spain, and some of these were revolutionary in terms of their impact on traditional patterns of production, distribution, and consumption. Whereas most Cakchiquel simply adopted some of these introductions where ecologically or economically feasible or politically necessary, some individuals grasped the opportunities presented by new crops, animals, and technologies and were adventurous enough to take advantage of them as the means of obtaining or securing enhanced socioeconomic status in their communities.

CROPS AND DIET

As the accompanying table illustrates, domesticated plants in particular had been developed to a high degree by generations of indigenous Mesoamericans, with the major staples all adapted to some degree to the full range of tierra caliente, templada, and fría environments (see Table 1). Secondary domesticates such as chiles, avocadoes, and tomatoes are more restricted in their distribution, while most fruits and fibers grow best or only in tierra caliente. Spanish plant introductions to the Cakchiquel were relatively few in number but were still significant because of the quantities required by the Spaniards (especially of wheat) and because most of them were tierra fría crops, thus adding to the economic importance of a zone which had only limited uses before the conquest. The more significant introductions from the Cakchiquel viewpoint were the domesticated animals. In a subsistence regime in which turkeys constituted the only domesticated meat source, chickens and, es-

TABLE 1   CROPS AND ANIMALS OF THE COLONIAL CAKCHIQUEL

| | INDIGENOUS FOOD PLANTS | | |
	Tierra Caliente	Tierra Templada	Tierra Fría
Staples	maize———————————————————————————		
	curcubits———————————————————————		
	climbing beans————————————————————		
	ground beans—————————————————————		
	chiles—————————————————————		
			potatoes
Important secondary plants	tomatoes		
	tomatillo———————————————————————		
	sweet potato		
	jícama————————————————————————		
	sweet manioc		
	chain—————————————————————————		
		amaranth	
		guisquil	
Important fruits	avocadoes——————————————————————		
	zapotes——————		
	pitahayas————————————————————————		
	cacao		
Other plant foods	plátanos		
	pineapples		
	papayas		
	anonas		
	peanuts		
Fibers	cotton		
	maguey		
	INDIGENOUS DOMESTICATED ANIMALS		
	turkey		
	dog		
	INTRODUCED FOOD PLANTS		
	sugarcane		wheat
			chick peas
			broad beans
			apples
			peaches
			pears
			quince
	INTRODUCED DOMESTICATED ANIMALS		
Draft	horses		
	mules		
	donkeys		
	oxen		
Food	sheep		
	goats		
	cattle		
	chickens		

pecially, dried beef, or *tasajo,* were important new sources of animal protein. But, as we shall see, the significance of all of these animals involved far more than just their potential for labor or the diet.

As best we can reconstruct it from Spanish sources, Colonial Cakchiquel cuisine was inherently healthful but seems to have suffered in terms of the variety of dishes by comparison to central Mexican cooking of the same period. As it had in the past, corn continued to be the base for most meals, prepared as steamed tamales of several different kinds, as griddle-baked tortillas of different sizes and thicknesses, or as pozol or atole, the drinkable, boiled gruel. Another beverage, *saka,* was made of ground, toasted corn. Boiled beans might be eaten separately or could be included in tamales, either whole *(xep)* or as a paste *(toom).* Spanish friars reported the existence of stews ("guisados") made with either meat, beans, or vegetables, to which corn "masa" (the raw material for tamales or tortillas), corn flour, or ground squash could be added. Also noted was a pacaya stew thickened with a flour made from dried squash.

The Cakchiquel enlivened this basically bland diet with a wide variety of fruits, which seem to have been eaten raw, and with a variety of sauces made from chiles. Unfortunately, the Spanish friars seem only to have recorded the most basic or generic terms for these, much in the same way that the Nahuatl term *molli* (Hispanicized into "mole") denoted "chili sauce" in general. However, as we know from the writings of the sixteenth-century Franciscan Bernardino de Sahagun, there was an immense variety of such mollis to delight the palates of central Mexicans both before and after the conquest. Thus, *riquil* (chile sauce), *ruquin xcoya* (chile ground with tomatoes), and *yahum iq* (bruised chile in water) may only represent the tip of a culinary iceberg, though one which does not appear to have survived the Colonial period.

The Cakchiquel also prepared a variety of drinks. Some, as we have seen, were based on corn. Another, *aak',* was evidently based on chian seed *(Salvia hispanica).* Most highly developed were beverages based on cacao, the bean from which chocolate is made. *Pulim* seems to have been a simple infusion or decoction made from crushed or ground cacao alone, while *q'utuh* was a thick, frothed drink made from a paste consisting of a combination of finely ground cacao beans, the naturally bitter taste of which was enhanced or softened through the addition of ground chile, vanilla, *achiote* (annatto) and, possibly, honey from domesticated bees raised in the tierra templada zones. The frothing was achieved by pouring the liquid quickly back and forth between two gourd cups, in which it was customarily served, or by twirling rapidly between the hands a special molinet, or hand mill, the effect of which was similar to a blender. A good q'utuh was judged by the fact that the bubbles held their shape and did not burst. *Quiy* was an intoxicant, some of the ingredients of which are described below.

If the Colonial dictionaries do provide some idea as to the range of foods and dishes, they do not tell us who consumed them or how frequently and on what occasions. Some insights into these matters are provided by the English priest Thomas Gage, who lived among the Pokomám neighbors of the Cakchiquel in the 1630s.

In their diet the poorer sort are limited many times to a dish of frijoles . . . either black or white boiled with chile, and if they can have this, they are well satisfied. With these beans they also make dumplings [probably xep], first boiling the bean a little, and mingling it with a mass of maize, as we do mingle currants in our cakes. Then they boil again the frijoles with the dumpling of maize mass, and so eat it hot, or keep it cold. This and all whatsoever else they eat, they either eat it with green biting chile, or else they dip it in water and salt, wherein is bruised some of that chile. But if their means will not reach to frijoles, their ordinary fare and diet is their tortillas. These they eat hot from an earthen pan, whereon they are soon baked with one turning over the fire, and they eat them alone either with chile or salt, and dipping them in water and salt with a little bruised chile.

When their maize is green and tender, they boil some of those whole stalks or clusters, whereon the maize groweth with the leaf about, and so casting a little salt about it, they eat it. . . . Also of this green and tender maize they make a furmenty [probably posol], boiling the maize in some of the milk which they have first taken out of it by bruising it. The poorest Indian never lacks this diet, and is well satisfied as long as his belly is thoroughly filled.

Even the poorest that live in towns where meat is sold will do their best when they come from work on Saturday night to buy a half-real or real worth of fresh meat to eat on the Lord's day. Some will buy a good deal at once, and keep it long by dressing it into tasajos, which are bundles of flesh, rolled up and tied fast. This they do when, for example, they have sliced off from the bone of a leg of beef all the flesh, cutting it in long thin pieces like a line, or rope. They then take this flesh and salt it . . ., and hang it up like a line from post to post, or from tree to tree, to dry in the wind for a whole week, and after roll it up in small bundles, which become as hard as stone, and as they need it they wash it, boil it and eat it.

. . . Nay this tasajo is a great commodity, and hath made many a Spaniard rich. They carry a mule or two laden with these tasajos in small parcels and bundles to those towns where no flesh at all is sold, and there they exchange them for other commodities among the Indians, receiving peradventure for one tasajo or bundle (which cost them but the half part of a farthing) as much cacao as in other places they sell for a real or sixpence. The richer sort of people will fare better, for if there be fish or flesh to be had, they will have it, and eat most greedily of it, and will not spare their fowls and turkeys from their own bellies. (Gage 1958:222–223)

Regarding the importance of wild game in the diet, Gage made the following observations:

The Indians will also now and then get a wild deer, shooting it with their bows and arrows. When they have killed it, they let it lie in the wood in some whole or bottom covered with leaves for the space of about a week, until it stinks and begins to be full of worms; then they bring it home, cut it into joints, and parboil it with an herb which groweth there somewhat like our tansy, which they say sweeteneth it again, and maketh the flesh tender, and as white as a piece of turkey. Next they hand up the parboiled joints in the smoke for a while, and then boil it again, and then they eat it, usually dressed with red Indian pepper.

These Indians that have little to do at home, and are not employed in the weekly service under the Spaniards [repartimiento; see Chapter 7], will look carefully for hedgehogs [porcupines], which are just like unto ours, though certainly ours are not meat for any Christian. They are full of pricks and bristles like ours, and are found in woods and fields, living in holes. . . . Of these the Indians eat much, the flesh being as white and sweet as a rabbit, and fat as is a January hen kept up and fatted in a coop. . . .

Another kind of meat they feed much on is called iguana; of these some are found in waters, others upon the land. . . . The sight of one is enough to affright one. Yet, when they are dressed and stewed in broth with a little spice, they make a dainty broth, and eat also as white as a rabbit. (Gage 1958:223–224)

In addition to bows and arrows, the Cakchiquel also took deer by means of snares and lassos. Miguel Perez Pirir even bequeathed a mountain hunting preserve to his son, Domingo, in order that the grandsons have a place to take deer in this way (Hill 1989b).

Regarding beverages, Gage wrote:

The Indians are generally much given to drinking, and if they have nothing else, they drink of their poor and simple chocolate, without sugar or many compounds, or of atole, until their bellies be ready to burst. But if they can get any drink that will make them mad drunk, they will not give it over as long as a drop is left or a penny remains in their purse to purchase it. Among themselves they make drinks far stronger than wine. These they confection in those great jars that come from Spain. They put in them a little water, and fill up the jar with some molasses or juice of sugar-cane, or some honey to sweeten it. Then, to strengthen it, they put in roots and leaves of tobacco, with other kinds of roots which grow there and which they know to be strong in operation. Nay, to my knowledge, in some places they have put in a live toad, and closed up the jar for a fort-night or a month, till all that they have put in be thoroughly steeped, the toad consumed, and the drink well strengthened. Then they open it, and call their friends to drink it. Commonly they hold their drinking bouts at night, lest the priest in the town should have notice of them, and they never leave off until they be mad and raging drunk.

This drink they call *chicha* [probably *quiy*]. It stinketh most filthily, and certainly is the cause of many Indians' death, especially where they use the toad's poison with it. (Gage 1958:225)

The toads in question were probably members of an indigenous species *(Bufo marinus)*, which have a poison gland that secretes the compound known as bufotenin. Although definitely poisonous in sufficient quantity (and, hence the cause of the deaths attributed to chicha by Gage), smaller doses have a distinct hallucinogenic effect. The "other kinds of roots" may well have been varieties of mushrooms that also had hallucinogenic properties (see Chapter 6).

In terms of eating, it is clear that most Cakchiquel dishes (in common with Mesoamerican cooking generally) were "finger foods" and that utensils to convey food to the mouth were largely unnecessary. Regardless of wealth or rank, meals were taken seated on the floor, by or near the fire so that tortillas could be had fresh from the griddle. In a wealthy household there would be more earthenware bowls and platters so that each person could have their own portion, while among poorer families, diners would share a common bowl. In either case, the main corn dish, whether tortillas or tamales, was held or broken in the fingers and then dipped into some sauce before it was popped in the mouth. If meat were served as some kind of stew, it was scooped up with a piece of tortilla and the whole package chewed together. Gruels like posol were usually simply drunk, though spoons made from small gourds cut in half lengthwise *(paq'ah)* were also used. Probably like today, adult men who shouldered the primary subsistence burden were served first or had first choice, with women and children splitting the remains.

HOUSES, DOMESTIC EQUIPMENT, AND HOUSE LIFE

Food preparation was based on a simple but time-tested and efficient assemblage of utensils, without which no Cakchiquel household could function. Corn was soaked in a solution of lime and water to separate the kernels from their coverings. The water was then strained out through a large clay colander *(xchaul* or *xohbal g'o)* prior to grinding the corn. Cacao, dried squash, and other seeds also needed grinding prior to use for many dishes, and this was accomplished with a quern and muller (better known throughout Mesoamerica as *metate* and *mano,* or *ka* and *queebal* in Cakchiquel). These were made of hard, volcanic stone roughed into shape with stone (later iron) tools and gradually smoothed over years of use. Cooking also required some specialized equipment, primarily in the form of pottery, one of the most ancient Mesoamerican crafts. However, by the seventeenth century, pottery were reduced for the most part to utilitarian shapes, since the elite and the cult which required elaborate, artistic vessels, had almost passed from the scene. Tortillas were cooked on a clay griddle, or *comal (xot),* and tamales were steamed in a special neckless jar, or *tamalero (bohoy soco).* Pots *(bohoy, sele)* in various sizes were used both for cooking and storage, with especially large vessels *(vayz)* used to prepare food for large gatherings such as weddings. All of these items were considered the property and province of women, and grinding stones and pots (as well as weaving equipment) were sometimes buried along with their mistress.

There was considerable variation in late preconquest house types, almost certainly related to status differences. Apart from the palaces of the rulers, even the most elaborate houses were relatively small, single-story affairs, rarely over three and a half meters wide by eight meters long. Such a dwelling rested on a stone foundation platform several courses high, depending on the topography of the building sight, but was high enough to require a stepping stone to gain entrance. On this were built base walls two or three feet high of adobe bricks. Above this was a log frame superstructure topped by a pole and thatch roof. Upper walls were of wattle and daub (woven cane, cornstalks, and/or saplings covered with mud plaster and, perhaps, whitewashed with lime). Inside, plastered masonry benches covered with rush mats lined the walls and were used both for sitting and sleeping. Opposite the doorway and midway along the back wall there was a small, household shrine or altar, and a mud-plastered hearth might occupy the floor on one or both sides. This was clearly the top end of Maya housing, with a clear gradient of less ambitious and formal dwellings below it (Hill 1982; Fauvet-Berthelot 1986).

Unfortunately, we have no examples of Colonial Cakchiquel houses and only the briefest descriptions of them and the activities carried out in them. Thomas Gage painted a characteristically bleak picture of the housing of the Pokomám neighbors of the Cakchiquel in the 1630s.

Their houses are but poor thatched cottages, without any upper rooms, but commonly only one or two rooms below. They dress their meat in the middle of one, and they make a compass for fire with two or three stones, without any chimney to convey the smoke away. This spreadeth itself about the room and filleth the thatch and rafters so with soot that all the room seemeth to be a chimney. The next room, where sometimes are four or five beds according to the family, is also not free from blackness. The poorer sort have but one room, where they eat, dress their meat, and sleep. Few there are that set any locks on their doors, for they fear no robbing nor stealing, neither have they in their houses much to lose, earthen pots, and pans, and dishes, and cups to drink their chocolate being the chief commodities in their house. There is scarce any house which hath not also in the yard a stew [sweat bath], wherein they bathe themselves with hot water, which is their chief physic when they feel themselves distempered (Gage 1958:221).

Despite Gage's statements, it is clear that a family of any means occupied not just a house but a compound, formed by several structures. Primary among these was the main dwelling, which, like its preconquest counterparts, could have been of pole and thatch, adobe, or even stone construction, depending on the local geology, climate, and the wealth of the householder. True, houses remained one story and were limited to two rooms at the most, but across the front might be an extension of the roof, resting on wood posts to form a covered porch. While poorer people or more modest houses relied on thatch roofs that needed periodic replacement, richer families invested in the more durable tile roofing introduced by the Spaniards. Another structure might be given over to storing foodstuffs or, if the owner was a merchant, goods. A simply constructed, open-walled ramada-like structure might also be built in which activities like weaving or pottery making took place. A wealthy Indian would likely maintain a small but well-constructed and well-appointed chapel as a separate building in his compound, in which he would keep the image of the saint(s) whose fiesta he sponsored each year (called *guachibales,* these individually or family-funded saints' cults are discussed in Chapter 6). This was also the structure in which the other, most valuable goods were stored: wooden coffers with iron locks contained the best clothing and, perhaps, expensive feathered dance costumes. Metal agricultural tools, neither sacred nor especially valuable to us but crucial to efficient Colonial Cakchiquel agriculture, were also kept here. Similarly, important guests, including Spaniards, would be received and even lodged, if necessary, in this eclectic chapel. As per Gage, the other indispensable element of a residence was the sweat bath *(tuh),* usually in the form of a low, rough masonry structure which could easily be warmed by passing in stones which had been kept in a fire outside until hot (the therapeutic value assigned by the Cakchiquel to the sweat bath is discussed in Chapter 6).

Despite significant wealth differences among the seventeenth-century Cakchiquel, there seem to have been only modest differences in house furnishings. Wealthier households may have had more pots, or may have been able to replace broken ones more readily, but the vessels themselves were not materially different from what a poor family owned. Reed mats (which deteriorate fairly quickly in a tropical environment) could be replaced more frequently in a well-to-do household, but the mats themselves would be little different from those of other families. On the other hand, poorer families slept on the ground on their mats, covering themselves with their *tilmas* and using their rolled-up clothes, or even a stone, as a pillow. Rich Indians had simple bedframes of boards or cane with a thick mat as a mattress and a sheet *(telq'em)*, covered with a true blanket. Still, a pillow was nothing but a piece of wood covered with the folded clothing of the sleeper.

DRESS

Weaving was the other womanly domain par excellence. As ancient as pottery, weaving was done with a backstrap loom, with one end of the set-up attached around the seated weaver's waist and the other attached to any handy tree or post. This technology limited the width of the resulting fabrics to between about twenty-four and thirty inches. By Colonial times the main medium was cotton, but one source asserts that, before the conquest, such cloth could only be worn by members of the aristocracy and their retainers, while commoners had to make do with coarse maguey fiber garments.

The highland Maya in general and the Cakchiquels in particular are justly world-famous for their weaving and also for the distinct, community-specific costumes that permit one who is familiar with their textile code to know readily the town of the wearer's origin. Yet, as we shall see later, these community-specific costumes seem to be an eighteenth-century development. During our period, clothing was both more traditional and more eclectic, simpler and more complex. In the seventeenth century the social rank of the wearer still dictated the style and type of clothing worn. For commoner men, the basic garments remained the ancient Mesoamerican loincloth, or *maxtlatl (vex)*, and mantle (tilma), worn knotted over one shoulder (*see* Figure 5-1). A cloth (*sut* or *tzut*) might be wrapped around the head, which was normally shaven, or replaced by a cheap, Spanish-style felt hat. Commoners usually went barefoot, but might wear hemp or leather sandals for long trips. In cold country and in public, women wore a long, shift-like blouse, or *huipil (pot)*, over a long skirt *(uk)* (*see* Figure 5-2). In hot country and when working at home, women spared some wear and tear on their garments as well as keeping cooler by discarding the huipil, a practice that scandalized Spanish friars but was probably agreeable enough to everyone else. The hair was braided with strips of colored cloth, worn up out of the way with the ends gathered at the front like a halo.

The clothing of wealthy or noble Indians was both richer and included more imported Spanish elements (*see* Figures 5-3 and 5-4). Womens' clothing was not so different in form as it was in execution, especially the extent to which colors were incorporated into the textiles. Among the techniques employed were weaving and embroidering, especially in a yoke around the neck opening, both with colored thread (red and blue being specifically mentioned) and with the bright feathers of tropical birds. Spanish style shoes might be worn, with broad, colorful ribbons as shoestrings. Ears were pierced as in preconquest times, but not the lower lip, and Spanish-style drop earrings replaced the gold, jade, or obsidian plugs of earlier days. Metal bracelets were also worn, as were necklaces made up of brass hawk-bells, silver Spanish coins, and glass beads. The wealthy male's clothing differed even more from that of his plebeian counterpart. Traditional elements included

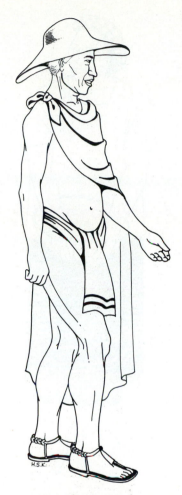

Figure 3 Hypothetical reconstruction of seventeenth-century male commoner dress.

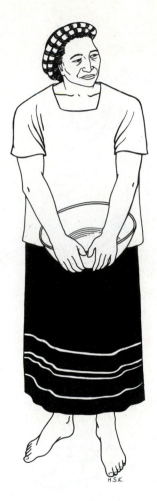

Figure 4 Hypothetical reconstruction of seventeenth-century female commoner dress.

tailored shirts, cloaks, and knee-length pants secured with a sash, all woven or embroidered with colored cotton or even silk threads and edged with twists and tassels. Alternatively, imported lace might be used as a border for the trousers and cape. Spanish-style shoes might replace sandals, but the Indians only rarely wore hose with the former, preferring to leave the calves uncovered. Ruffled lace neck collars were also eschewed, though a doublet might cover the shirt. Before the conquest, men of noble rank pierced their ears, nasal septum, and lower lip for the insertion of plugs of precious metals and stones. This practice had been discontinued under Spanish pressure, but the ensemble was topped off with a broad-brimmed Spanish felt hat, with a plume of tropical bird feathers. Of course, such elaborate clothing need not have been worn every day, although it probably was by some status-conscious Cakchiquel; it was much more likely that richer Indians had more and better clothing than their poor counterparts and could afford special suits of fine clothing (stored in the coffers mentioned earlier) for public, festive, or ritual occasions.

IMPORTED TECHNOLOGIES

To this point, the material realities of Colonial Cakchiquel life seem little different from those of their preconquest ancestors. Yet two realms of Spanish technology had been introduced and, through their acceptance, had revolutionized both production and distribution and made for a distinct Colonial economy. In terms of production, the introduction of iron-working technology was the most significant development. Before the conquest, the highland Maya had only limited metallurgy, which was applied to gold and some of its alloys primarily for the production of ornaments that served as symbols of elite status. Thus, the main agricultural tools at the time of the conquest were simple wooden hoes (patam, xoc) with oak blades. Stone hoe blades are also known archeologically (Feldman 1985:30). The main cutting tool was an obsidian blade, which, while incomparably sharp, is inherently fragile and dulls quickly. Both these technologies continued into the Colonial period (obsidian-tipped arrows for hunting and lancets for bleeding being used well into the eighteenth century). But it is clear that, whenever possible, the Cakchiquel preferred to exchange these implements for iron counterparts or replacements.

Yet the Kingdom of Guatemala contained no iron deposits or smelters, so all iron had to be imported, either as finished products ready for use, or in some other form that could be recycled or modified. At the same time, the seventeenth century was a period during which Spain was increasingly unable to supply her colonies, even with this indispensable commodity (MacLeod 1973:196). Accordingly, iron was a fairly scarce and, hence, valuable material. This explains why iron agricultural tools were stored in the chapel buildings along with the other valuables; they were valuable and the basis of a more intensive and productive form of agriculture. This scarcity of iron also meant that the knowledge and skill to transform and recycle iron were valuable commodities themselves, and this in turn explains why Miguel Perez Pirir set one of his sons to learn blacksmithing from two Pokomám

Figure 5 Hypothetical reconstruction of seventeenth-century aristocratic male dress.

Figure 6 Hypothetical reconstruction of seventeenth-century aristocratic female dress.

smiths from Mixco, who the old man engaged for the then enormous sum of 100 *tostones* per year. It also explains why such care was taken in the Indian wills of the period to enumerate and fairly divide such tools among heirs (*see* Chapter 9 and Hill 1989).

With iron axes, machetes, and saws land could be much more quickly cleared and the wood processed into beams and boards, which could be sold to Spaniards or used in local construction and joinery, made easier and more elaborate by iron saws, planes, augers, and the like. Gage was very impressed with the Indians' mastery of such tools and other related technologies.

> . . . in most of their towns there are some that profess such trades as are practiced among Spaniards. There are amongst them smiths, tailors, carpenters, masons, shoemakers, and the like. It was my fortune to set upon a hard and difficult building in a church of Mixco, where I desired to make a very broad and capacious vault over the chapel. . . . Yet for this work I sought none but Indians, some of the town, some from other places, and they made it so complete that the best and skillfullest workmen among the Spaniards had enough to wonder at it. So are most of their churches vaulted on the top, and all by Indians.
>
> In my time they built a new cloister in the town of Amatitlán, which they finished with many arches of stone both in the lower walks and in the upper galleries, with as much perfection as the best cloister of Guatemala built by the Spaniard. (Gage 1958:230)

With the iron hoe, the highland Maya developed an intensive form of horticulture, still in use today, called "hoe plowing" (MacBryde 1945:17). Such hoes are not the small, lightweight implements used by weekend gardeners to cultivate around their flowerbeds, but are heavy, broad-bladed agricultural tools, hafted on quite stout poles, and wielded with considerable effort. As a result, the soil is very nearly as thoroughly worked as with a plow, yet seeds are planted by hand and the three main crops of corn, beans, and squash are typically planted together. There is something of a symbiotic relationship between corn and climbing beans, with the cornstalks providing trellises for the bean plants to climb, while the beans (like all legumes) put nitrogen necessary for good corn growth into the soil. Through contour furrowing, the predominantly steep hillside terrain of the region, too rugged for the plow, could be brought under intensive cultivation. By planting crops with different growth habits together (tall corn, bushy beans, and ground-running squash) the Indians could lessen erosion due to the intense rains that characterize the tropical wet season. Today, good volcanic soils will return good yields for five years, but their use can be stretched out as long as fifteen or twenty, while alluvial bottomland can be planted annually for fifteen years, after which beans alone might be planted every other or every third year. So intense is this use, with crop rotation and short fallow periods, that lands once cleared may never be allowed to revert to natural forest cover (MacBryde 1945:17–19).

On level terrain the Spanish-introduced Mediterranean scratch plow, or ard, drawn by oxen, could be employed. In the seventeenth century this technology seems to have been applied to the cultivation of wheat for Spanish consumption, so only those Indians engaged in commercial agriculture might be expected to have owned or employed it.

The other crucial technology made available to the Colonial Cakchiquel was that connected with livestock. We have already seen how the Cakchiquel incorporated tasajo into their diet, but the use of animals in the draft and pack roles was probably even more important because it revolutionized (in the right hands) both production and distribution. Oxen were perhaps the least important draft animals since the rudimentary road system of Colonial Guatemala precluded the use of oxcarts anywhere except the immediate vicinity of the capital. For the same reason, horsedrawn transport was similarly restricted. Mules, however, could have been designed with the Colonial Maya highlands in mind.

PRODUCTION AND DISTRIBUTION

Having glimpsed some of the key commodities and other components of Colonial Cakchiquel economic life, we now turn to how they integrated these elements in systems of production and distribution. Along the way, we shall better understand the impact of technological introductions from Spain.

The household was the basic production unit of the period, but due to the ever-present danger of disease, it was an ephemeral entity, the membership of which both varied from household to household and could change over time. Most Colonial Cakchiquel households were small and could effectively exploit only one environmental zone. Given the low populations of the time and the fact that the major food plants were adapted to all three major zones, a small household could be an effective subsistence unit and even participate in the region's market economy, as have generations of Maya peasants recorded ethnohistorically and ethnographically.

Much more could be accomplished with a larger family spanning three or four generations, especially if its members were distributed among different environmental zones and engaged in a variety of activities. Such units did, in fact, develop among the Colonial Cakchiquel and their neighbors and are referred to here as *family corporations*. These were not simply extended families whose members all lived together and occupied themselves with identical subsistence activities. Rather, they involved a series of related (usually but not necessarily patrilineally) households, located in different environmental zones and engaged in a variety of complementary economic pursuits. As we shall see, this form of organization was crucial for diversifying productive activities, participating significantly in the opportunities offered by the market economy of the Spanish capital, and attaining or maintaining higher social status.

As noted in Chapter 4, the parcialidad was the social group through which most Cakchiquel gained access to land. However, it is unclear to what extent it was a production unit during Colonial times. A few references to the Quiché and Pokóm indicate some specialized production by members of preconquest and early Colonial parcialidades, though there is no evidence of pooled labor or production (Hill 1984:311–312). Rather, the impression is one of families with access to specialized technology or raw materials by virtue of parcialidad membership, but working as individual households. Though parcialidad territory could extend over more than one environmental zone, there is no evidence that distribution of products from them took place within this group.

As noted earlier, pueblos were artificial Spanish creations, but there was some specialized production at this level in the seventeenth century, and information pertaining to the Pokóm suggests that this was already in place by the late sixteenth century. For example, it is clear that at least one town specializing in pottery making either sprang up or continued from preconquest times in the territories of each of the former major indigenous polities. Thus, the town of Santa Apolonia developed as a dependency of Tecpán and supplied the entire region of the former Iximché polity with pottery. San Raimundo seems to have performed a similar role within the old Chajomá territory, though wares from the nearby Pokomám town of Mixco and its dependency, Chinautla (together serving the area of the old western Pokomám polity), found their way in as they undoubtedly did before the conquest. The pattern was repeated among the Quiché, with San Pedro Jocopilas supplying the Nima Quiché, to their west Santa María Chiquimula supplying the Tamub, and Rabinal supplying the towns of that former polity. Of course, via trade and markets, pots could pass through political and even ethnic boundaries as they do today (Reina and Hill 1978), so people were not limited to vessels from the nearest pottery-making town. Thus, the assemblage of any household might contain a mix of vessels from different towns, and perhaps even some Spanish-made wares from the capital. However, as with parcialidades, the pattern of production seems still to have been based on individual households whose members (females in the case of pottery) had access to clay(s) and pottery-making technology by virtue of their community membership.

Given the diversity of environments, raw materials, and even technologies, a complex interdependency developed among Indians in the different climatic zones. The absence of distributive mechanisms within parcialidades or towns made transportation and markets a crucial means of ensuring that goods got where they were needed. Trade, including large-scale, long-distance trade, had been part of Mesoamerican civilization for many centuries before the Spanish conquest and was based on human bearers using tumplines to support packframes laden with goods. After the conquest, the same need to get products from one place to another was still there, but the bearers were not; populations were too reduced to supply the bearers for large human packtrains or to provision them. Mule trains, however, were another matter. Mules can carry more than twice the load of even the best human porter, they require no provisioning but can graze while on the road, they can safely negotiate even the worst trail over the roughest terrain, and one muleteer easily can control a number of animals.

The Spaniards had almost no interest in this internal, Indian trade. They were concerned instead with the export to world markets of high-value commodities like cacao and, later, indigo. Spain's inability to provide sufficient quantities of finished goods, or even raw materials, to her colonies meant that, aside from the occasional Spaniard and his few mules laden with tasajo or, illegally, wine and other spirits, there was no Spanish participation in this internal trade. However, the Cakchiquel and other highland Maya were quick to realize the possibilities of animal transport and master the techniques of both train management and mule breeding, probably acquiring this knowledge initially while serving as muleteers on the large, Spanish-run trains which made their way from the Pacific coast cacao fields up to Mexico and from the Caribbean and Pacific ports up to the capital at Santiago. Mules and horses never completely replaced the packframe, especially for the small-scale, itinerant merchants who lacked the capital to buy an animal. Yet, for those with the resources, pack animals did afford a new means for moving goods in bulk, not only from Indian town to Indian town in different zones but from the Indian countryside to the Spanish capital in the lucrative trade which supplied its residents.

Markets are an ancient and enduring feature of Mesoamerican life whereby the products of diverse environmental and ecological zones find their ways to consumers. Before the conquest, major markets were held in or adjacent to the capitals of the main polities and lesser markets in the centers of dependent chinamit or amaq' groups, merchants paying a "gift" to the local lord in return for permission to do business. With the conquest and formation of new towns under the congregación program, markets came to occupy the town square or plaza once or twice weekly and even the smallest town had some kind of market. Fairs coincided with the patronal fiesta of each town, attracting people from neighboring towns and itinerant merchants with packframes and animals laden with goods from other regions. There were also a few regional markets in towns that, because of their location, served to integrate larger areas containing many towns and even serve as transshipment points for goods from different regions. There were at least two of these in seventeenth-century Cakchiquel territory: Chimaltenango and Sololá. To the east in Pokomám country, the town of Petapa served a similar function. The two Cakchiquel towns attained regional market status as a result of their locations near the Continental Divide, which made them logical places for goods from around the central and northern highlands to be exchanged for goods from the Pacific coast and Motagua valley. Chimaltenango had served this function since before the conquest, when it was called Bocó. Sololá was only founded after the conquest, like most of the other Lake Atitlán towns, and may have assumed much of the importance once held by Tecpán, the town from which most of its residents had been brought. The Cakchiquel probably also did some trading at Petapa, which integrated the towns of the Valley of Guatemala. It lay near the intersection of the main roads from the highlands to both the Pacific and Caribbean coasts, so much interregional and even international trade passed its way.

While we have no detailed description of these seventeenth-century fairs and regional markets, they must have been exciting affairs, as they are today. Market-day activity begins well before dawn as people living any distance from town stir themselves, have a quick breakfast of posol, and head off down their respective trails to town, perhaps lighting their way with smoky torches made from strips of resinous *ocote* (fatwood). Itinerant merchants had probably arrived the night before, camping in the plaza or on the edge of town. Perhaps some lodged with families with whom some ongoing arrangement had been made. Perhaps people of the same preconquest chinamit, split up by the Spaniards (like the Xahil or Tukuché), still recognized some affiliation and hosted each other when in their respective towns.

At any rate, vendors begin setting up early, and by the time the sun has risen, the town plaza and its side streets are bustling with activity. To the uninitiated, all seems chaos, with buyers pressing by each other, each on his or her own schedule of purchases. But, on closer inspection, one sees that there is order here despite the crowds and cramped conditions. Goods are grouped together and their locations institutionalized so both buyers and sellers know just where to go. In one section all the pottery vendors line up. These may include the potters themselves (if from a nearby town), with their week's production fresh from firing arrayed before them, their husbands, or merchants from different towns who have larger stocks packed on mules. Metates and manos, leather goods, reed mats, and cordage all have their own sections where buyers and sellers may compare quality and price. Another section is for fruits brought up from tierra caliente, another for salted coastal fish. Other areas are given over to the sale of different kinds of vegetables: onions, chiles, tomatoes, squash, along with sections where sacks of corn and different kinds of beans are sold. Even salt vendors have their own section where highlanders from Comalapa, trading the salt they have made and brought up from the Pacific coast, perhaps rub shoulders with their linguistic cousins from the Chixoy river town of Sacapulas. Animal sales are usually conducted away from the crowded plaza, but pigs, goats, sheep, cattle, chickens, turkeys, horses, and mules all change hands. Through all the sights and colors, sounds of haggling and crying babies, textures and smells of fresh fruits, vegetables, and dung, there permeates the smell of oak fires, heating the pots of posol, tamales, beans, and chocolate and the griddles of tortillas belonging to the food vendors who supply the crowd.

Before the conquest, most market transactions involved barter, the exchange of goods for goods. True money, in the sense of a medium of exchange the quality and quantity of which are controlled by a central authority, did not exist. The closest thing the preconquest Cakchiquel had to a common medium of exchange was the cacao bean. These continued in use after the conquest and well into the seventeenth century as small change, used to purchase items up to twenty beans in value. Beyond this point, Spanish coin was used and it constituted a third revolutionary introduction from that country. Initially, money was forced on the Cakchiquel because it was first used as the medium for the many kinds of tribute to which the newly conquered people were now subject (MacLeod 1973:142). Spanish Colonial money was based on coinage, with the silver *peso* as the basic unit. Guatemala produced little silver and was, therefore, dependent on the mint established in Mexico and, later, in Peru. The peso was too large a unit for most Indian transactions, however, so *tostones* (one-half peso coins) and *reales* (one-eighth peso coins) were most commonly used. Yet, such general-purpose money meant that all goods and services were now convertible to a single medium of value and exchange. Also, unlike most other commodities the Cakchiquel possessed, money could be stored without deteriorating (unlike agricultural produce) and was compact and portable enough (unlike land) to be kept safe at all times. Money could even beget more money, through loans at interest and the rental of goods acquired with money, at fixed rates of payment.

The Cakchiquel quickly grasped all of these possibilities and by the seventeenth century had developed their own money-management techniques. Both Indian-run institutions and individual Indians made loans. At the time of his death in 1662 Miguel Juan Queh had outstanding loans totaling well over three hundred tostones. Religious sodalities (*cofradías, see* Chapter 6) made loans and sometimes forced distributions of their working capital, one peso to each family in town, from whom they demanded a real in interest. In both cases, interest rates worked out to 12.5 percent and were evidently the same throughout much of the highlands. Both Queh and the Pirir family also owned and rented the elaborate costumes used in the dances which accompanied important ritual events (*see* Chapter 6). As Gage explains:

> These Indians get much money by letting out great tufts of feathers, which the Indians use in their dances upon the feasts of the dedication of their towns. For some of the great tufts may have at least three score long feathers of divers colors. And for every feather they charge half a real, besides what price they set to every feather if any should chance to be lost (Gage 1958:210).

In addition to the feathers, dance costumes of rich, imported fabrics such as velvet, damask, and wool serge, along with other accoutrements, were rented. As we have already seen, the Cakchiquel also rented land, though often the renter came to see his payments as constituting purchase. Presumably, other goods and services were also available, such as oxen, plows, pack animals, and specialized crafts such as weaving, carpentry, joinery, masonry, and blacksmithing.

THE PIRIR FAMILY: A SEVENTEENTH-CENTURY SUCCESS STORY

The conquest and colonialism were burdens which weighed heavily on the vast majority of Cakchiquel, yet some individuals and families were able to adapt so successfully to the new order and its attendant economic opportunities that they became wealthy by local standards and were thus able to attain or perpetuate elite social status in their communities. As noted above, family corporations, engaged in diversified commercial agriculture and related activities, were the key to this type of success. Populations were too small and the man/land ratio too favorable in the early and middle years of the seventeenth century for wage labor to have developed. Why should one Indian work for another if he could have land of his own (or at least for his own use through his parcialidad) just by clearing it? Besides, the Spaniards already made heavy demands on Indian labor through institutions like *repartimiento* (see Chapter 7). Under these circumstances, large families were the only means of ensuring enough hands to staff large, diverse operations. Still, given the continuing impact of Old World diseases on the Indian population, successful family corporations were as much the result of good luck as they were of good planning.

Our best-documented example of such an organization is the Pirir family of San Juan Sacatepéquez, headed in the 1640s by nonagenarian Miguel Perez Pirir. A good deal of don Miguel's success was due to the fact that he began life with a significant advantage over most of his fellows: his personal ownership of the four-hundred- to six-hundred-acre tract called Navorón, located in the tierra templada belt on the descent into the Motagua valley. This was evidently an inheritance from his aristocratic preconquest forebears. But don Miguel was not content just with this one holding or with traditional Maya agriculture. His concern over maintaining some semblance of his family's elite social status impelled him to innovate. Over the years he acquired additional tracts in the San Juan area, representing the full range of tierra fría, templada, and caliente environments. At the height of his holdings in the 1640s, don Miguel oversaw well over thirty descendants and their spouses, spanning four generations.

Whatever traditional agriculture they may have engaged in, it is clear that commercial agriculture and related activities oriented toward the Spanish capital at nearby Santiago was the main income producer. The Pirires grew wheat in their tierra fría fields, plowed with teams of oxen, and had their own threshing place. They cultivated sugarcane in the tierra caliente of the Motagua basin and kept a hundred beehives. Their livestock holdings were impressive, with forty-eight head of cattle, twelve yokes of oxen, seventy-five horses, and seventeen mules and asses. Evidently, they kept much of this livestock under the supervision of eldest son Gerónimo at the Navorón tract, which they had by this time converted to an *estancia,* or ranch. The Pirires were clearly breeding animals for both food (cattle) and for draft/transport (horses, mules, and oxen). Along with these enterprises, don Miguel also operated two forges staffed by smiths from Mixco, who also trained one of his sons in the craft.

Thus, the Pirir family was a well-integrated corporation. They grew and raised products for an urban market on their own lands, using their own oxen for plowing. They grazed their cattle on their own pastures, where they also raised and kept the horses and mules needed to transport their produce to the capital. Scarce iron was recycled and made into the necessary implements at their own forges. Nearly the entire operation was staffed exclusively by family members and was thus self-contained, and they were well on their way to full self-sufficiency as one son learned blacksmithing.

The Pirires were not only producing goods, they were also renting equipment and selling services to others—the forge and blacksmithing, oxen and plows, and probably pack animals and transportation. With steady revenue from both the sale of commodities in the capital and the provision of equipment and services to other Indians and with a large, stable work force, don Miguel could acquire additional tracts on the unofficial land market as they became available, thus further enhancing his family's productive potential. He also had plenty of cash on hand to support lavishly the church and the saints' cult, both important ways of maintaining social prestige (*see* Chapter 6).

Although don Miguel was clearly exceptionally successful for his time and place, he was by no means unique. The Colonial chroniclers mention other wealthy individuals, families, and even towns. In all cases, their success seems to have rested on a similar combination of diversified, market-oriented agricultural and transport enterprises. On his trip, Gage found that:

> I would needs go by the way to one of the biggest towns in that country, called Chimaltenango, standing in an open valley three leagues from the city [of Santiago], and consisting of a thousand housekeepers and rich Indians who trade much about the country. In this town in my time there was one Indian who alone had bestowed upon the church five thousand ducats [pesos]. (Gage 1958:172)

In the Pokomám town of Mixco in Fuentes' time, the Rey family was famous for its wealth and generosity. The patriarch, Sebastián Rey was still remembered in the town for his many gifts to the church, including its expensive bells, necessarily imported all the way from Spain. He had left his children fine fortunes also, such as that maintained by his son, Mathías Rey. But even they were not unique. Fuentes stated that there were other rich families in the town who maintained themselves through the combination of corn and wheat farming, mule trains, and lime ovens (used to prepare the lime plaster which covered the interior and exterior walls of all Spanish buildings of any consequence) (Fuentes y Guzmán 1969–1972, I:383).

These are admittedly scanty data, but along with references to differences in dress, diet, housing, and ritual obligations, it is clear that an entire class of wealthy Indians existed in the seventeenth century and that these people owed their success to the combination of large families working together and their ability to innovatively incorporate Spanish crops, animals, technology, and money economy into a single commercial enterprise.

Individuals like don Miguel would easily be recognized in our own society as hardheaded executives and risk-taking entrepreneurs, as many of their descendants remain today. But it would be wrong to think of such Colonial Cakchiquels simply as businessmen concerned only with material gain and social prestige. These were no doubt important considerations, and the Cakchiquel are as capable of economically "rational" thought as any other people. Yet these Maya viewed the world in ways very different from us, and the seemingly strange forces and beings of their universe and techniques they used to mediate with them and find their own ways were as much a part of a man like don Miguel as his business acumen. It is to this world of beings, powers, and rituals that we now turn.

BIBLIOGRAPHIC NOTE

Feldman (1985) provides an exhaustive compilation of highland Maya goods, production areas, and distribution, with a special focus on eastern Guatemala. Unfortunately, he has drawn his data indiscriminately from sources separated widely in dates of composition. As a result, it is difficult to detect changing patterns of production and consumption in his work. Nevertheless, it remains a useful compendium of data and references. MacBryde's works (1933, 1947) are classic treatments of early twentieth century production and distribution. Reina and Hill (1978) specifically discuss highland Maya pottery production, distribution, and consumption.

6 / Belief and Ritual

The Spanish conquest and subsequent missionary activities by Spanish friars meant that many of the traditional public cults could not continue as such. Unfortunately, our understanding of exactly what did happen has been limited by the fact that all of our sources on Colonial Cakchiquel belief and ritual were penned by Spaniards who had their own interpretations that have little relationship to our present understanding of belief, ritual, or cultural change. Accordingly, a reconstruction of Colonial Cakchiquel religion as a *system* of beliefs and practices is not possible. Most of our information on these subjects consists of little more than hints and clues that can only be interpreted by reference either to other, better-documented Mesoamerican peoples (such as those of central Mexico) or to present-day practices as recorded ethnographically.

So far as we can tell given the remote time and the sources, Cakchiquel belief, like that of other Mesoamerican peoples and unlike that of the Spaniards, was not a closed ideological system. New "gods" in particular posed no problem for the Cakchiquel since they were accustomed to a multiplicity of supernatural beings that were all manifestations or transformations of a single divinity. If the new supernaturals offered aid or protection, they could be assimilated into the pantheon and even worshiped without abandoning or contradicting older beliefs. The incorporation was made all the more simple by some distinct parallels between Cakchiquel and Catholic practice. Confession was a widespread practice in preconquest Mesoamerica, though, as we shall see, its function was rather different there than in Catholicism. The importance of burnt offerings, especially incense, was another superficial similarity. Supernatural patrons were also prominent in both belief systems.

The Spaniards credited the ease of their initial conversion of the Indians in the sixteenth century to their own efforts and divine aid rather than to the Indians' perception of the similarities between their own and the new faith. The friars thus expected that the Indians would thenceforth be exemplary Christians. Only a little more time would be necessary to wean them completely from their heathen ways. But the Cakchiquel saw no contradiction between worship of the Catholic pantheon and their own, nor could they see any reason to give up such an indispensable tool as calendrical divination. When, by the seventeenth century, it became evident to the friars and other Spaniards that traditional practices were not being abandoned but were instead being carried out either surreptitiously or under the guise of Catholic rites, the entire missionary program was called into question and some excuse for the seeming failure had to be found. The clerics tended to blame the Indians' own intransigence and stupidity, the latter leading to their easily being deceived by the devil into perpetuating what was, ultimately, his worship. Seventeenth-century secular officials such as Fuentes y Guzmán and outside observers such as Gage thought that the friars themselves were in large part to blame owing to their venality, lack of proficiency in the Indian languages, and, hence, their less than rigorous indoctrination of the Indians. The accuracy of these assertions need not detain us. The important point is that Colonial Cakchiquel belief and rituals exhibited many strong, basic continuities with the preconquest past while, at the same time, incorporating some Spanish elements which seemed to parallel their own practices.

TIME

As we saw in Chapter 1, the Cakchiquel concept of cyclical time was central to their understanding of the universe and its dynamics. In the most general sense, what had happened in the past eventually would happen regularly again in the future. Time itself was composed of a variety of cycles, the units of which had their own potentials for human affairs at all levels of organization. Man could do little or nothing to influence destiny since his own nature was largely conditioned by the very same units of time. Still, the idea that the future would be an immutable repetition of the past meant that it was possible to know of, prepare for, and perhaps even take advantage of time to come; especially if calendrical records were maintained to keep track of the cycles' and units' potentials. Of course, Mesoamerican peoples had been doing just that for many centuries before the Spanish conquest, and the Cakchiquel were full participants in this tradition. So fundamental were their beliefs concerning time that the Cakchiquel maintained their calendars and techniques of calendrical divination throughout the Colonial period, and in some places, down to the present.

At the time of the conquest, the Cakchiquel utilized three separate calendars: the *cholol q'ih,* or 260-day divinatory calendar or "day count"; the 365-day solar calendar; and the so-called Iximché calendar, based on a 400-day "year," which had been instituted for the political purpose of keeping track of the time which had passed since the Tukuché revolt of 1493. All three continued in use down through at least the early seventeenth century, though the Iximché calendar only appears to have been used by the descendants of the Xahil family in the document which has come to be known as the "Annals of the Cakchiquels" (*see* Chapter 8).

All of these calendars are based on the pan-Mesoamerican vigesimal (by twenties) system of counting, resulting in basic units or "months" of twenty days each. The solar calendar regulated the pace of earthly life. It was composed of eighteen twenty-day months, each containing four five-day "weeks." A final five-day period preceded the new year and was considered to be a dangerous time. By this calendar agricultural activities such as clearing, planting, and harvesting were scheduled following the rhythms of the tropical highland year. The Colonial Cakchiquels may also have continued to schedule major public ceremonies according to this calendar, though the sources are not explicit on this point. The Iximché calendar was a form of "long count" concerned with counting days since a specific historical event rather than keeping track of celestial or cosmic cycles. Accordingly, it was "purely" vigesimal, composed of twenty twenty-day months, resulting in a nonsolar, 400-day "year." Twenty of these "years," in turn, constituted a *may*.

As opposed to political or even celestial events, the *cholol q'ih* tracked divine, cosmic forces which directly conditioned humans' fates. This "day count" was based on a series of twenty day names which cycled with a series of numbers from one to thirteen. Thus, each day in the count was denoted by both a name and a number, each with special potential for human activity, with the total combinations equaling 260 days. For divinatory purposes the days were grouped into thirteen twenty-day periods which also had unique potentials. The solar and divinatory calendars cycled independently of each other but synchronized in terms of starting days once every fifty-two years. This period is referred to as a "calendar round" by Mesoamericanists and was known to the Aztecs as *xiumopilli,* or "the tying up of years." The Cakchiquel called it *huna,* which, confusingly, was the same term used for the 400-day Iximché year.

THE SELF

Like other Mesoamerican peoples, the Colonial Cakchiquel retained a view of a universe in which the cosmos, human activities, and physical and mental well-being were all intimately connected. The self was thus not in any way disconnected from the rest of the universe but was intimately connected to it. Individuals' actions could have cosmic ramifications which could also manifest themselves in the body and mind.

The units of cosmic time tracked in the *cholol q'ih* initially manifested their potentials for human affairs via the divine force imparted to each individual by the sun (day) under which he or she was born, or the sun under which this force was ritually fixed in him or her. The Cakchiquel called this force *natub,* which the seventeenth-century Spanish friars translated as "shadow," "shade," "reflection," and "consciousness," exactly parallel to the much better-documented ancient Mexican concept of the *tonalli.* Both words referred to a divine force, the nature of which was determined by the potential of the day in question. Like the ancient Mexicans, the Colonial Cakchiquel believed that this force determined an individual's temperament or disposition. The interplay among the natub, the individual's own actions in life, and the other life forces which inhabited the body (discussed later) determined each person's fate, but the natub was the crucial first element. Furthermore, they believed that some wild animal was born at the same moment as every human and that thenceforth they shared the same fate. This was the *tona.* If the animal were to die (say at the hand of a hunter), his human counterpart would soon follow and vice versa (*see* Chapter 9). All the other days of the *cholol q'ih* had variable potentials for the individual depending on the sun under which he had received his natub, and these could be foretold by a calendar specialist, or *ah q'ih,* who kept track of such matters in calendar books, *ahilabal q'ih* (equivalent to the *tonalamatl* of central Mexico).

Like the tonalli, the natub could evidently leave the body for relatively short periods of time with no ill effects. Indeed, some dreams and most hallucinatory experiences were interpreted as journeys of the natub while out of the body. However, longer absences of the natub were harmful and disease was the consequence. Loss of the natub could occur in a variety of ways. A sudden shock or fright might dislodge or jar the natub from the body, and in its disoriented state the natub might not be able to find its way back. This cause of disease, commonly called by the Spanish term *susto* ("fright"), is still widespread in Mesoamerica. The natub might also leave the body because of some imbalance with the other bodily forces or its power be lessened owing to impure (especially sexual) or impious behavior. As a force associated with the sun, the natub was a "hot" force in the hot-cold dichotomy common to Mesoamerican peoples, and overexposure to the "cold" could cause it to weaken. The result was, again, illness. Artificial forms of heat such as the sweat-bath were used as a means of strengthening the natub, thereby curing the illness. The ancestors could also damage or call away the natub as punishment. Finally, through sorcery, the natub could be assaulted while in the body or captured while outside it.

Though techniques existed for the recovery of the natub, they depended to a great extent on the proper diagnosis of the cause of the loss or damage. This, along with the timing of ceremonies intended to cure, was one of the major functions of divination. Whereas the natub was centered in the head, its power, like that of the other bodily forces, was diffused throughout the physique, evidently by means of the blood. Therefore, any impediment to the blood flow was considered a threat to health since it could result in an uneven distribution of, or imbalance in, bodily forces, which might cause the natub to leave. Accordingly, bleeding was an important treatment.

Like the ancient Mexicans, the Colonial Cakchiquel believed in the existence of two other divine forces which occupied the body and together made life possible. The force known to the Mexicans as the *teyolia* focused in the heart and was responsible for many cognitive functions, including memory, understanding, will, and imagination. Although no corresponding Cakchiquel term has been identified, it is clear from the Colonial dictionaries that these Maya had a very similar belief because for them the heart was also the seat of the very same functions. As Coto noted in his seventeenth-century dictionary entry for "heart" *(q'ux):*

> They attribute to it all the sensations of the powers of memory, understanding, and will. They use this word, *q'ux,* for the soul of the person and for the vital spirit of all life. From this word, *q'ux,* is formed the verb *tin q'uxlaah,* to think, to reason, to imagine, etc. (Coto 1983:113)

The third force was called *ihiyotl* by the Mexicans. It was believed to dwell in the liver and was thought to be responsible for desires and other strong passions. Among its most salient qualities were its luminescence as a dense gas or vapor, its odor (usually understood to be foul), its importance as a source of energy, and the idea that it could be released or transferred as or via breath. We find just the same characteristics associated with the Cakchiquel word *uxla*. It also was likened to "soul," "vapor," "smell," and "breath" in the Colonial dictionaries, and the word is still used among some Quiché speakers to refer to the spirits of the ancestors (Tedlock 1982:41). Although normally firmly fixed in the body, emanations of the uxla could occur as a result of unrestrained passions, especially those of envy and illicit sex. These were potentially dangerous to people, animals, and things close to the offender. Yet, in the absence of such a transgression, the uxla of most Cakchiquel was not dangerous, but, indeed, necessary for the healthy balance of bodily forces.

However, certain individuals, called *nagual,* could project their uxla at will into another covering or even into another person. Nagual belief was and is widespread in Mesoamerica. The Spaniards took it to be the worst form of witchcraft because they understood from Europe that the ability to transform was something gained only by selling one's soul to the Devil. For the Cakchiquel and other Mesoamericans, such projection or transformation of a bodily force was simply a manifestation of power which, by itself, was neither good nor evil. Such power could, however, be put to socially helpful or harmful purposes by individuals.

Unfortunately, we know little else about Cakchiquel naguales. Preconquest rulers supposedly had the ability to project their uxla, though it is not clear from where this ability came. In central Mexico it was the product of a combination of factors. These included the "sun" under which an individual was born, acquired knowledge, and the observance of fasts and other bodily mortifications such as bloodletting. Although the ability to project the uxla could be used for positive purposes, the fact that it was something hard to detect and control meant that the nagual was at least potentially a dangerous person, especially when he chose to combine this ability with sorcery.

Though he partook of the divine through his possession of the forces associated with the brain, heart, and liver, the Cakchiquel believed that, in general, man himself was limited in terms of perception, knowledge, and understanding. According to the more completely recorded beliefs of their former associates, the Quiché, this was the product of divine second thoughts after the creation of the first humans, born out of fear that humans would equate themselves and their deeds with those of the creator if they were too perfect. Accordingly, man was remade:

> And their eyes were chipped
>   By the Heart of Heaven.
> They were blinded like the clouding of the surface of a mirror.
> Their eyes were all blinded.
> They could only see nearby then,
>   However clear things might be,
> And thus they lost their understanding,
>   And all the wisdom of the four [original] men
> At the start,
>   At the beginning. (Edmonson 1971:153)

Fortunately, humankind was not entirely limited to its own meager resources. Certain individuals could temporarily free themselves (or one or more of their bodily forces) from human constraints and travel through space and time to learn about the future, the past, and the will of supernatural beings. Other specialists kept track of the passage of time and through their calendar books knew the potentials for the different periods and cycles of time for human affairs. Finally, rarely, a supernatural being might deign to visit a mere mortal to impart some crucial information or bestow the gift of divinatory power.

BEINGS

Nowhere is our understanding of Colonial Cakchiquel belief more incomplete than on the subject of the supernatural beings that inhabited their universe. The Spaniards understood that all indigenous supernaturals were simply manifestations of the Devil and that the poor Indians had been deceived into worshiping one or another of them. Consequently, Spanish writings shed little light on this aspect of Cakchiquel belief. Friars and civil officials alike concerned themselves with stamping out indigenous beliefs and with introducing Catholicism. The Indians themselves had taken most of their traditional religion underground to avoid Spanish persecution. Apart from the calendar books, there do not seem to have been any indigenous writings of a strictly religious nature. While we know that the preconquest Cakchiquel believed in a variety of "gods" (at least some of which were local manifestations of pan-Mesoamerican belief), we cannot easily determine which of these may have survived the conquest and early missionary efforts. At the same time, the Cakchiquel were not simply passive recipients of a new religion. Instead, they actively interpreted what the friars taught them and blended elements of the new cult with traditional practices. The Spaniards attributed such assimilation to Indian stupidity, backsliding, and superstition rather than to a creative attempt to create order out of the contradictory premises and demands of two distinct belief systems.

As best reconstructed in its most general terms, the immediate preconquest pantheon included mainly patron deities of the individual chinamitales and the ancestral spirits, though there was also a variety of lesser spirits which inhabited springs, rivers, and ponds (the *xulu*), or trees. Worship of the patron deities of the leading chinamitales, such as Tohil of the Cavek among the Quiché, may have assumed something of the status of a "national" cult, though it seems clear that all of them were manifestations of a single godhead. The images of these deities were assigned to their respective groups in the remote past at the legendary Tollán, the place of mythical origin for most Mesoamerican peoples. Carried on the backs of priests, the power of the god as manifested in the image protected the group on the long journey to the land they would ultimately settle, perhaps after some conflict with the indigenous inhabitants in which the chinamit received the supernatural assistance of its patron. Once settled, the patron of each chinamit went to live in a mountain in each group's territory, from which it continued to provide protection and the blessing of rain, while its image remained in the group's temple pyramid, itself a model mountain. In return, the patron demanded to be fed with foods only humans could supply from this world: incense and blood.

The preconquest Cakchiquel were probably at least as much concerned with their ancestors as with the patronal deities, though to some extent the two classes of beings may have been merged. All the major conquest-period Cakchiquel documents (such as the *Annals of the Cakchiquels*, *see* Chapter 8) exhibit almost an obsession with ancestors and descent. Since most of these documents were produced by and for aristocrats anxious to maintain their elite status under Spanish colonial rule, we might be tempted simply to attribute this concern with ancestors to a fairly predictable attempt to maintain social exclusivity through pedigree. While this was undoubtedly part of what such documents were intended to accomplish, there was much more to the veneration of ancestors than this. Through the use of the indigenous writing before the conquest, leaders of preeminent chinamitales traced their descent back to the legendary founders of their groups. This was done not only to legitimize their authority but also to establish themselves as possessors of the same supernatural powers those ancestors had. The concept of the ruler as a semidivine "man-god," possessing some "divine fire" (and, hence, supernatural abilities such as the power to transform or project his uxla into another shape), is a widespread Mesoamerican belief (López Austin 1973). By using their powers on behalf of their group (especially in warfare), the rulers were nearly as much responsible for its success as the patronal god. And this power was so great that it did not end or dissipate with the man-god's death. The natub in particular could be preserved by keeping it in an image or receptacle of some form, and it could continue to afford protection to the group. Among the Cakchiquel, as with most other Maya, veneration of these illustrious rulers and preservation of their powers was a cult of its own. Rulers' physical and spiritual remains were interred in or near temple pyramids in which the images of the patronal gods were kept and which resembled the volcano/mountains in which the patronal gods lived. The two were thus at least symbolically equated, and their basic protective functions were probably identical.

Although veneration of ancestral rulers may have been an obsession for their aristocratic descendants and may have formed part of each chinamit's or larger polity's cult practice, the ancestors of the common people were important to them as well. Whatever land a family worked was a legacy of the ancestors who first settled, cleared, and cultivated it. Since commoners were illiterate, however, remembrance of specific ancestors faded after a few generations. Accordingly, the ancestors took on a nonindividual or collective identity. Their spirits, though necessarily weaker than those of the rulers, also remained close by in the mountain of the patronal god, from which they could observe, protect, and, if necessary, punish their descendants.

Against these beliefs came the Spanish friars, especially the Dominicans and Franciscans, who used devotions to the saints as a means of both indoctrinating the Cakchiquel and supporting their own curacies. When towns were formed in the sixteenth century under the congregación program, each was assigned a patron saint, as in Spain. Parcialidades, especially when they represented continuity from preconquest chinamitales, also received patrons. Even individuals and families could adopt saints as their personal patrons. In all cases the relationship with the saints was clear to the Cakchiquel; in exchange for veneration, offerings of incense and candles, and celebration of the saint's day, the patron would aid the group dedicated to him. How much does this differ from the pattern of preconquest patron gods? Over time, the saints *became* the patron gods, losing their foreign origins and acquiring the status of founders and protectors of the towns and parcialidades, as they remain among most highland Maya today.

Still, the question remains as to why the Cakchiquel and other Indians should have accepted these alien supernaturals with such fervor as they evidently did. Gage was of the opinion that the Indians interpreted at least some saints as having tonas or nagual power (he thoroughly confused the two) because of the animals commonly associated with their depiction:

> For this reason [the belief in tonas and naguals], as I came to understand from some of them, they yield unto the Popish religion, especially to the worshipping of saints' images, because they look upon them as much like unto their forefathers' idols; and secondly, because they see some of them painted with beasts—Jerome with a lion, Anthony with an ass, and other wild beasts, Dominic with a dog, Blas with a hog, Mark with a bull, and John with an eagle—they are more confirmed in their delusions, and think verily those saints were of their opinion, and that those beasts were their familiar spirits [tonas], and that they also were transformed into those shapes when they lived [nagual], and when they died, their beast [tona] died too. (Gage 1958:234)

Because of their original and continuing superficial orthodoxy, the cult of the saints was the most public, visible, and, therefore, best-documented type of Colonial Cakchiquel ritual organization. These took two main forms in the seventeenth century, depending on the wealth of the sponsors. A *guachibal* was a private (family) cult dedicated to the veneration of a particular saint. These were usually created by wealthy, landowning Indians who commissioned a carving of the saint's image, undertook the perpetual support of the saint's day celebration, and maintained a chapel at their homes in which the image was kept along with other valuable goods, such as the feathered dance costumes used in celebrations. Such sponsorship was evidently an important means of establishing and maintaining high social status among the Colonial Cakchiquel. For example, Miguel Perez Pirir founded four guachibales during his lifetime, dedicated to San Jacinto, Santa Cruz, San Gabriel, and San Antonio, whose images cost from 100 to 260 tostones each. Beyond this was the yearly cost of the saint's day observance, consisting of a mass (for which the resident priest or friar had to be paid), a procession in which the image was paraded on a litter decorated with fabulously expensive feathers, dancing (which again involved costly feathered costumes), and a feast for family and friends. Even the Spaniards were impressed with the splendor and expense. Fuentes waxed particularly eloquent:

> The Indians of these towns are, as we said, devout and much given to the worship of the church and the veneration of the saints. . . . Just the various, colorful feathers with which they adorn the rich litters of their guachibales (each one seemingly a copious and variegated jungle [of feathers]), are so costly that they reach many thousands of pesos, there not being a day of the year without the guachibal of this or that saint, celebrated by our Mother Church, that they do not celebrate with a procession, sermon, and mass of greater or lesser fee, according to the solemnity of the day this guachibal is: having in their residences a place and house apart with not insignificant adornments and elegant with aromatic smoke and variegated flowers where the image of the saint that each family celebrates is set up.

> . . . and thus one sees that those who serve these sacred cults with the expenses from their own funds are considered the most noble and excellent caciques [leaders] of their towns; being in each calpul or lineage of principal men four or five guachibales distributed among those with the most assured funds and during their lives they are held in greater esteem than others. (Fuentes y Guzmán 1969–1972, I:331–332)

In some cases the cost of the celebration was met through rental of feathers and feathered dance costumes. These were evidently so rare and valuable that they produced considerable income for their owners. Miguel Perez Pirir owned such a costume, which he left to his main heir, Domingo, as a means of supporting the four guachibales left to him. Gage provides additional details:

> These Indians get much money by letting out great tufts of feathers, which the Indians use in their dances upon the feasts of the dedication of their towns. For some of these great tufts may have at least three score long feathers of divers colors, and for every feather they charge half a real, besides what price they set to every feather if any should chance to be lost. (Gage 1958:210).

Fuentes mentioned other Indians who became wealthy through the rental of complete costumes, including clothing of velvet and damasks of varied colors with hose to match and small bells (Fuentes y Guzmán 1969–1972, II:43–44)

Fuentes also stated that the obligation to support a guachibal was passed as part of the founder's estate. As noted above, Miguel Perez Pirir entrusted his four guachibales in the 1640s to his primary heir, his son Domingo, along with feather dance costumes, which could be rented out as a means of supporting the cults. Domingo, in turn, passed on each of the four guachibales to pairs of his own sons in the late 1660s.

> Thus from the fathers it passes like an inheritance to the sons and, in this way, it passes from one generation to the next without the devout piety of the family which began it ever failing, because it continues by inheritance with the possession of the lands, houses, and other goods which remain at the death of the elders, seeing it not only as an obligation but as a rich ornament and precious jewel in the inheritance. (Fuentes y Guzmán 1969–1972, III:331)

The other type of saint's cult was the *cofradía* (sometimes also called *patanibal,* or "burdensome thing" in Cakchiquel, *see* Chapter 9). These might receive donations and other support from wealthy Cakchiquel; Miguel Perez Pirir, for example, left a tract of land worth two hundred pesos to the San Juan Sacatepéquez cofradía of Nuestra Señora in the 1640s.

Still, in the seventeenth century, cofradías seem to have been composed primarily of commoners who held only usufruct to the lands they cultivated and who thus had insufficient resources individually to fund the saint's day celebration. But, by pooling their resources and through gifts from wealthy patrons, cofradías became endowed institutions. Instead of meeting the expenses of the saints' day celebrations out of their own pockets, the *cofrades* (members) acted as stewards of the endowment. If the endowment were in the form of agricultural land (as in the case of the Pirir gift above), the cofrades would arrange to rent it out, usually for a fixed fee, or plant it themselves, with the produce to be sold. Endowments could also consist of animals kept on cofradía-owned *estancias* (ranches). Cattle and horses were apparently the most common stock animals. In such cases, the cofrades would have to divide among themselves the work of caring for the animals, with a certain number of animals to be sold off each year. Finally, cofradía endowments could consist entirely of cash, with the cofrades acting as money managers. In a society lacking banks, loans totaling in the hundreds of pesos could be made to Spaniards as well as other Indians. Sometimes, forced "loans" were made. These involved apportioning the cofradía's capital, usually one peso per household in a town or parcialidad. Recipients would be required to repay the principal plus one real, or twelve and a half percent interest. Fuentes y Guzmán specifically mentioned three cofradías (San Crespín, San Miguel, and Concepción) in the Quiché town of San Miguel Totonicapán with principal in the amounts of 20,000, 12,000, and 8000 pesos, respectively; all of it was lent out at the one-for-eight rate (Fuentes y Guzmán 1969–1972, III:14).

The most important cofradías were probably those responsible for the veneration of the town and parcialidad patrons, and there could be anywhere from two to ten of these in a town. Their fiestas were essentially longer, large-scale versions of the guachibal celebrations. The mass, performed by a Spanish friar, was seemingly the least important component of the fiesta, observers being much more struck by the Indian-administered events, especially the dances.

Unfortunately, dancing is yet another topic for which we have only the scantest information. Dances were an important part of ritual observance throughout pre-conquest Mesoamerica, but their functions among the Cakchiquel are not clearly delineated (see Figure 6–1). Still, the information we do have suggests that this traditional expression of devotion was simply extended to the saints. Fuentes wrote:

> In these patronal town fiestas they dance adorned with rich and precious feathers, a variety of coins, mirrors, and chalchiguites [beads of jade or another green stone], carrying on themselves an immense weight of these adornments, being in this as in everything else indefatigable, because they dance in the church yards continuously the entire day and from one day to the next up to eight days, which is how long one of these town fiestas should last.
>
> They enact their dances around the one who plays the tepunaguastle [wooden drum made from a hollowed tree trunk] . . . [which] is played with the blows of some little wooden rods covered at the ends with ule [rubber]. . . .
>
> They dance singing the praises of the saint which they celebrate, but in the prohibited dances they used to sing the histories and deeds of their ancestors and false gods. (Fuentes y Guzmán 1969–1972, I:216–217)

Yet, Fuentes harbored concerns that the dances were perhaps too close to preconquest pagan practice. At the end of a passage describing the origins of such idolatry he wrote:

> Such they solemnized or celebrated these acts of sacrifice and thus also do they celebrate today the festivities of the saints called guachibales; dancing around with the tenacity which we shall see [referring to the previous passage], adorned with the same regalia

which they used in that deluded time [before the conquest]: but their songs have been reduced to the praise of the saints, relating and representing their miraculous histories, composed by their ministers [friars]. (Fuentes y Guzmán 1969–1972, I:77)

Gage penned a longer, more detailed account of dances among the Pokomám, eastern neighbors of the Cakchiquel, whose practices in the 1630s seem to have been nearly identical:

The Indians of the town have their meeting at night for two or three months beforehand, and prepare for such dances as are most commonly used amongst them, and in these meetings they drink both chocolate and chicha [the intoxicating beverage described in Chapter 5]. For every kind of dance they have several houses appointed [as places to practice], and masters of that dance, who teach the rest that they may be perfected in it against the saint's day. . . . And when the feast cometh, they act publicly for the space of eight days what privately they had practiced before. They are that day well apparelled with silks, fine linnen, ribbons, and feathers according to the dance. They begin this in the church before the saint, or in the churchyard, and thence all the octave, or eight days, they go dancing from house to house, where they have chocolate or some heady drink or chicha given to them.

The chief dance among them is called *toncontin.* . . . This dance is thus performed. The Indians that dance it are commonly thirty or forty, if it be a great town, fewer if it be a small town. They are clothed in white, for their doublets, linnen drawers, and *ayates,* or towels, which hang almost to the ground on the one side, are white. Their drawers and ayates are wrought with some works of silk, or with birds, or bordered with some lace. Others procure doublets and drawers and ayates of silk, all of which are hired for that purpose.

On their backs they hang long tufts of feathers of all colors, which are fastened with glue into a little frame made for the purpose and gilded on the outside. They tie this frame around their shoulders with ribbons, so that it does not fall or slacken with the motion of their bodies. Upon their heads they wear another smaller tuft of feathers either in their hats or in some gilded or painted headpiece or helmet. In their hands they also carry a fan of feathers, and most of them will use on their feet feathers also bound together like short wings of birds. Some wear shoes; some do not. And thus from top to toe they are almost covered with curious and colored feathers.

Their music and tune to this dance is only what is made with a hollow stock of a tree, rounded and well pared within. It is very smooth and shining . . . with two or three long clefts [slits] on the upper side and some holes at the end. They call it *tepanahuaztli.* On this stock, which is placed upon a stool or form in the middle of the Indians, the master of the dance beats with two sticks, with ends covered with wool and wrapped in leather smeared with pitch. . . . Thus they dance in compass and circle around that instrument, one following another sometimes straight, sometimes turning about, sometimes turning half way, sometimes bending their bodies and with the feathers in their hands almost touching the ground, and singing the life of their saint, or some other. All this dancing is but a kind of walking round, which they will continue two or three whole hours together in one place, and thence go and perform at some other house.

The chief [governor?] and principals [parcialidad heads?] only of the town dance this toncontin. It was the old dance which they used before they knew Christianity, except that instead of singing the saints' lives, they sang the praises of their heathen gods.

They have another much used dance [which, from Gage's description, would seem to be the one the Cakchiquel called *xq'ul,* which appears to have been a celebration of

Figure 7 Hypothetical reconstruction of seventeenth-century dance costume.

warfare and nagual transformation; see below], which is a kind of hunting of some wild beast which formerly in time of heathenism was to be sacrificed to their gods, but now to be offered to the saint. This dance hath much variety of tunes, with a small tepanahuaztli, and many shells of tortoises, or instead of them, with pots covered with leather, on which they strike as on tepanahuaztli, and with the sound of pipes [flutes]. . . .

These dancers are all clothed like beasts, with painted skins of lions, tigers, or wolves [coyotes], and on their heads such headpieces as may represent the head of such beasts. Others wear painted heads of eagles or fowls of rapine [hawks, etc.], and in their hands they have painted staves, bills [halberds], swords, and axes, wherewith they threaten to kill the beast they are hunting. Others, instead of hunting after a beast, hunt after a man, as beasts in a wilderness should hunt a man to kill him. The man thus hunted must be very nimble and agile, as one flying for his life, and striking here and there in defense at the beasts, but at last they catch him and make a prey of him. As the toncontin consists mostly of walking and turning and leisurely bending their bodies, so this dance consists wholly in action, running around in a circle, and leaping and striking with those tools and instruments which they have in their hand. (Gage 1958:243–245)

Gage and some other sources mention additional dances that were obviously Spanish creations designed to aid in the indoctrination of the Indians. These included such themes as the death of St. John the Baptist, the martyrdom of St. Peter, and the story of Noah. Although Gage reported that these performances intrigued the Indians, it does not seem that they generated anything like their interest in the traditional dances.

XAHOBAL CHE (THE TREE DANCE, OR *VOLADORES*)

Probably the most important of these dances, and certainly the most spectacular, was the one called *xahobal che*, or Tree Dance. This was the Colonial Cakchiquel version of the widespread Mesoamerican rite, better known by its Spanish name, the *Baile de los Voladores*. Still performed in some parts of Mesoamerica, it was a crucial rite in every Cakchiquel town as its performance at the time of the patronal fiesta helped ensure the continuing, predictable dynamics of the cosmos.

As recorded by Fuentes, preparations for the rite began "20 to 30 days before its performance" (probably the former figure, which would correspond to a Cakchiquel "month"). The first task was to prepare the eighty- to ninety-foot pole that gave the ceremony its Cakchiquel name. Probably (as recorded ethnographically among some Quiché speakers; *see* Bunzel 1952:425) this was itself a ritual event extending over several days, involving apologies for the damage caused by cutting the tree and prayers that it not break when felled. On a subsequent day, many people would assemble for the enormous task of carrying the pole, now stripped of all branches and bark, from the woods to town where it would be ritually planted in the plaza. Prominent throughout all these preparations and the actual ceremony is the man representing a monkey, who, like the other main participants, has trained for many years, perhaps even from childhood. Among the Quiché, the monkey impersonator climbs the pole before it is cut down, jumping at the last moment to another tree as a real monkey might. He also cavorts about the tree as it is trimmed and stripped and rides on it into town. Finally, the monkey impersonator rides on the top of the pole as it is raised and set into a deep hole specially dug for the purpose.

With the pole raised, the revolving frame, or *tornillo,* was affixed. This was a hollowed-out timber which fit over a point cut on the top of the pole, allowing it to turn. To this timber they nailed the four pieces which held the rolled-up ropes of the four bird impersonators who would "fly" (and for which the Spaniards named the rite the voladores, or "fliers").

Prior to the actual flights came a procession into the town plaza, led by a large troupe of dancers, accompanied by musicians playing the tepunaguastle, flutes, and conch trumpets. Then the actors in the flight ritual made their appearance. As performed in the seventeenth century, there were nine principals: the monkey, four bird impersonators, and their four assistants. Fuentes was especially impressed by their costumes:

> The voladores dress themselves with much pomp and extreme ostentation, with the representation of birds in richly feathered wings and masks representing the birds they imitate, with many strands of greenstones, coins and bells, and with noisy and sonorous rattles in their hands. The other four servants also dress and adorn themselves with richly colored and ostentatious vestments of velvet, damalk, and gold cloth, with many diverse feathers and sashes of various colors, and many small bells worn as bracelets and chokers (Fuentes y Guzmán 1969–1972, I:345).

The monkey climbed the pole first, using rope lashed around it as a ladder. He probably danced on the tiny surface of the tornillo as do his counterparts in other parts of Mesoamerica, saluting and invoking the four cardinal directions. On a practical level, he was responsible for gathering up the fliers' ropes and arranging them so that they played out easily and did not tangle. Next to ascend were the four bird impersonators, followed by their assistants. It was the responsibility of the latter to tie the fliers securely to their ropes. After some acrobatics on the tornillo, the fliers hurled themselves from their perches. As they did, the tornillo began to turn and the ropes played out. When they had flown about halfway down, their assistants also sprang into the air to grab the ropes of their respective fliers, descending dexterously and sometimes holding on with just one hand. If performed properly and without incident, impersonators and assistants landed gracefully on the ground after thirteen revolutions.

Yet, things could go disastrously wrong. Winds could upset the fliers (whose hands and feet were free of the ropes) or keep them aloft and spinning for long periods while the assistants could only hold on. Ropes might foul, leading to collisions among the fliers, perhaps even causing an assistant to lose his grip and fall. Landings also called for perfect timing and coordination lest collisions occur at that crucial moment. Injuries were not unusual and deaths not unknown. Still, once each flight was over, the performers returned to the top of the pole again and again all afternoon. All the while the monkey impersonator continued his acrobatics on top of the tiny, turning tornillo.

To the Spaniards who witnessed it, the Dance of the Voladores was simply an enchanting spectacle, an acrobatic display. Yet, to the Cakchiquel it was clearly much more. Though no period account provides much of an explanation of what it meant to the Indians or of its purpose, the symbols are common enough throughout Mesoamerica to enable us to tease out some of the meaning. The pole itself symbolized the central axis of the universe, which in this instance bound together the underworld, the earth, and the heavens. The four perches of the tornillo represent the cardinal directions of the earth's surface. Thus, the pole and tornillo depict, in a very abstract form, the structure of the Mesoamerican cosmos. But there was more than just structure to this rite, there was process as well. Apparently, the birds impersonated were eagles (another name for this ceremony was *xahbal cot,* or "Eagle Dance"). In Mesoamerican symbolism, the eagle represents the sun, itself a metaphor for time. Thus, the flying of the eagles represents the passage of time, and their movement around the cardinal directions symbolizes the passage of the seasons. The four fliers revolving thirteen times on their way to the ground yield the number 52, calendrically significant as the number of years in the Mesoamerican "century" and as one-fifth of the 260-day *cholol q'ih* divinatory calendar. Perhaps the repeated flights mentioned by Fuentes actually numbered five, thus portraying one full cycle of cosmic time. Whatever the case, what the ancient Mesoamericans and their Colonial descendants achieved with this performance was the schematic representation of both cosmic structure and cosmic process, the space-time continuum of their universe.

Why did they do this? We cannot tell for sure but it seems likely that, by operationalizing this model of their universe, they hoped to induce the ongoing, regular, and predictable passage of time and the seasons so necessary for successful agriculture and continued existence. Perhaps there was even an element of divination involved, with uneventful, successful flights portending a normal, predictable year. As we saw in Chapter 1 and shall see in Chapter 7, this public maintenance of the structure of their universe and, especially, the cyclical nature of time was also essential to the way in which the Cakchiquel adapted emotionally to the reality of Spanish domination.

RITUAL PRACTITIONERS

Another subject of which we are largely ignorant is the range and functions of the different Cakchiquel practitioners. Clearly, Spanish Catholicism was only a part of the total world of Colonial Cakchiquel belief and ritual. The Spanish friars recorded in their dictionaries a variety of terms used to denote such individuals, but they usually rendered them in Spanish simply as "diviner," "sorcerer," or "wizard" and assumed that they were all equally minions of the devil, who preyed upon the ignorance and superstition of the common folk. Fortunately, an early eighteenth-century document describing the religious organization of some neighboring Quiché towns affords a glimpse at what appears to have been a hierarchy of ritual specialists. From that document combined with the sparse dictionary information, we can at least partially reconstruct the recruitment, advancement, and functions of these people.

Individuals seem to have had only limited efficacy in approaching the beings and forces of the Colonial Cakchiquel universe. Whereas supernaturals might contact individuals via dreams or visions, ordinary humans could do little to initiate such contact. Simple prayer, as introduced by the friars, seems to have been an alien concept to a people whose relationships with traditional supernaturals seem always to have involved some kind of offering as an indispensable accompaniment to a request. Candles and incense were acceptable as offerings to members of both the Catholic and indigenous pantheons. Candles in particular were capable of transmitting the content of confessions to different supernaturals in order that the sins might be forgiven. But the Cakchiquel felt that an offering and request to any supernatural was more appropriately made by a specialist intermediary or a group (like a cofradía, which still employed the services of a friar or priest) than by a lone individual. Still, individuals who, perhaps, could not afford the services of a ritual practitioner or who feared being discovered by the friars for having employed them could attempt to interact on their own behalf with the supernaturals.

> Those who had nothing with which to pay the ah cunes [see below], or who were afraid of being discovered with them, bought a candle and before it, having lighted it in the hand of the infirm one, they told all their sins. And afterward the infirm one would say to his wife: "Daughter, take my sins before God; take the candle that carries them." (Margil 1704 in Dupiech-Cavaleri and Ruz 1988:247)

Ritual practice centered on divination and curing, with the two closely intertwined. Individuals born under certain "suns" of the 260-day calendar were thought to have divinatory potential, but initial recruitment depended on some evidence of clairvoyance, evidently the result of some kind of dream. Today, among some Quiché speakers, this awakening is attributed to having been struck by the axe of the diminutive red supernatural, Saki Coxol, which imparted power in the form of lightning to the blood of the recipient, enabling him to "understand" or "receive messages from the external natural and supernatural world" (Tedlock 1986:134–135). The Cakchiquel called such clairvoyants *sakvachinel,* based on the word "to dream." Dreams could be portents of the future in their own right and some individuals might go no further than this as diviners. (Today, Quiché diviners interpret the movements of the lightning imparted to them in their bodies' blood. This form of divination, called pulsing, can be performed in response to specific questions, with sensations in different parts of the body providing the answers.) Others began the lengthy formal training in order to understand the potentials of both earthly and cosmic time and to be able to intercede successfully with the supernatural beings.

The first rung on this career ladder seems to have been the status of *ah cun.* As a trainee, he apparently had limited formal divinatory skill. Instead, he was concerned with diagnosing and curing illnesses affecting the natub, and he seems to have relied to a great extent on information provided by his patients (probably corroborated by the movements of the lightning in his own blood) in arriving at his diagnoses (see Chapter 9). To increase blood flow and remove stagnant blood he employed herbal remedies and bleeding (the Colonial dictionaries include the term *ah toq'ola* as "bleeder," literally, "he who stabs"). Depending on the cause of the danger to the natub, confession (which was an indigenous Mesoamerican practice that had obvious similarities to Catholicism) and the burning of copal incense (presumably on auspicious days of the calendar) might be employed as a way to appease angry supernaturals. There does not seem to have been any particular limit on the number of ah cunes; friar Antonio Margil's early eighteenth-century report claims that there were some six hundred such practitioners divided among the ten communities he investigated. The ah cunes thus seem to have constituted a pool of candidates from which each parcialidad drew its diviner or *ah tzité* ("he of the divining seeds").

As his title indicates, the ah tzité had received additional instruction. He trained the ah cunes and had himself learned from an *ah q'ih* to divine by casting and counting red tzité seeds and quartz crystals, representing the days of the 260-day calendar. Fuentes recorded only the simplest form of divination, which, perhaps, anyone could perform:

> The most common among them [ways of casting lots] is a count of kernels of corn, which they count by pairs, and if an uneven number does not result from their count the divination is uncertain, and taking up another handful of corn they repeat their count up to three times, and if they all come out even, they say the day is not appropriate for divination; but if it comes out odd, they say that the lost object [the subject of the divination] is in such-and-such place. (Fuentes y Guzmán 1969–1972, III:273)

Studies of contemporary highland Maya diviners demonstrate that use of the tzité seeds is much more complex and sophisticated than Fuentes' description would indicate (*see* Colby and Colby 1981, Tedlock 1982). Indeed, during the seventeenth century the process was evidently so intricate that some of these practitioners possessed a kind of manual or book *(tzité q'am vuh)* in which they could look up the meanings of their lots. (Among contemporary Quiché diviners who use this technique, the lightning in the blood is still important in interpreting the seeds since its pulsing can cue the diviner to some aspect of the question that he has been asked to investigate or clarify an ambiguous reading.)

The ah tzité also confessed others of his parcialidad and made offerings of copal incense to placate supernaturals for the damage caused by the construction of houses and the opening of new fields. Through casting and counting the tzité seeds as days of the divinatory calendar, he was likewise responsible for the selection of auspicious days for such activities as well as for parcialidad offerings to the supernaturals (which were intended to avoid or alleviate disease, famine, and drought), rites which he also directed. Some evidently also learned the specialized technique of scrying, divining by means of gazing into the reflective or semireflective surface of polished stone or water. This technique seems to have been especially useful for diagnosing cases of soul loss (i.e., loss of the natub), since the reflection of an individual whose natub had left him was much less brilliant than that of one in whom it was firmly in place.

At the top of the hierarchy, each town or group of towns seems to have had its calendar priest, or *ah q'ih* ("he of the sun [day]"). This was the practitioner who trained the ah tzité. He possessed the *ahilabal q'ih,* the book for determining individuals' fates according to the potential of their natub, corresponding to their birth dates. Accordingly, he officiated at the name-giving ceremony by which the natub was fixed in the infant and was consulted to determine whether or not the natub of a potential spouse was compatible with that of the would-be partner (*see* Chapter 9). Through his training and great experience, he could, in addition, interpret omens and dreams. The ah q'ih also possessed the *q'amutz,* the book containing the days, months, and years as tracked by the solar calendar. He was thus the one to determine auspicious days for scheduling community rituals. Yet, the ah q'ih seems not necessarily to have given up pulsing, scrying, dreaming, bleeding, confessing, casting lots with the tzité seeds, or curing when he assumed this status; nor did he evidently give up private practice to assume this much more public, priestly role. He could apparently continue to consult with private clients, though perhaps his services were too expensive for all but the wealthiest Cakchiquel to afford.

SORCERY

In contrast to all of the above practitioners, who basically functioned for the benefit of their society, the *ah itz* was a sorcerer, someone who used magical techniques in attempts to kill others out of envy or to avenge some insult. Our best Colonial-period information on this subject is contained in the record of a Spanish investigation in 1715 into the death of a San Miguel Totonicapán Indian, Martín García Belesuy (Hill 1988). Though from a Quiché town and just outside our time period, there is every reason to suspect that the beliefs and practices described in this record were also common among the Cakchiquel a few years earlier. As recorded in this one case, the technique of sorcery involved introducing foreign substances into the victim's body, either magically or by getting him unsuspectingly to ingest food or drink containing them. Once in place, these substances could only be removed magically, a task which required another kind of specialist called an *elesay itz* (remover of sorcery) in Cakchiquel. Bleeding, sweat baths, and herbal cures would have no effect. Yet, treatment was also a test of strength between sorcerer and remover, and a powerful sorcerer could frustrate the attempts of a weaker remover. Accordingly, both patient and remover could try to buy off the sorcerer with money or goods, if they could determine his identity.

Martín's trouble began one evening when he visited the house of one Bartolomé Tíu in his capacity as one of the past cofrades of the Cofradía de las Animas. The visit was evidently a formal one to pass on the leadership of the cofradía to Tíu. Accordingly, he served chocolate to his guests. Upon drinking his, Martín found three maggots in the bottom of his cup. He said nothing to his host at the time, but three days later he suffered some kind of internal hemorrhage, resulting in bloody diarrhea.

Martín was extremely debilitated by this and suspected that it was sorcery on the part of Tíu, who had used the chocolate drink as a medium through which foreign substances had been introduced magically into his body. Martín sent his brother, Antonio, to ask that Tíu come and cure him, presumably in return for a healthy fee or other consideration. Tíu took offense at the accusation that he intentionally had done Martín harm; he consistently maintained that the maggots had fallen accidently into the chocolate, which had been placed beneath some meat hung in the kitchen before serving. Still, he agreed to help and went to Martín's house, where he gave him a drink made of twenty-five burned and finely ground cacao beans mixed with corn gruel. This had only limited success, stopping the bleeding for only two days.

In an attempt to find a permanent cure, Martín enlisted a reputable curer and reputed enemy of Tíu, Antonio Socop, probably an ah cun, the previously described diviner trainee concerned with diagnosing and curing illnesses affecting the natub. Who better to combat sorcery than an enemy of the sorcerer? Martín sent meat five times to Socop, along with his requests for treatment. The latter finally agreed but said he must first go to the church and burn candles before the image of Our Lady and ask permission to cure from the Holy Sacrament (as a manifestation of Christ) and the Blessed Souls (of the ancestors). Martín was too weak to go with Socop, so he sent his brother Antonio again. The pair went to the church at four in the morning, yet, despite taking the precaution of locking the door behind them so they would not be discovered, someone, who they seemingly thought to be Tíu, appeared in the doorway. Before disappearing, the figure broke wind loudly before them, releasing an emanation of his uxla that rendered the candles they had brought unlightable. Upon returning to Martín's house, Socop apologized but said that Tíu's sorcery was too strong for him to fight.

Tíu's aid was enlisted again several days later. This time, they took a sweat bath together and Tíu bled Martín's head using special lancets. These were procedures better suited to treating a "normal" illness (such as an imbalance among bodily forces) than to combating the effects of sorcery. When Martín's condition worsened, Tíu was again accused of sorcery. He deflected the charges by claiming that his lancets had been stolen by someone prior to their use on Martín. Only two had been recovered at the time of the treatment, and Tíu suspected that Socop had treated them in some way so that they would harm Martín and cast suspicion on himself. He vowed revenge and, indeed, Socop died shortly afterward from undetermined causes, without benefit of the last rites.

In desperation, Martín sent Antonio for yet another curer, one Diego Hernández Cot. He agreed and held a consultation with his patient in which he asked if Martín had eaten or drunk anything which might have made him ill and if he had any enemies. Martín told him about Tíu and the chocolate. Diego said he would attempt a cure but was somewhat afraid to do so because of a recent experience. It seems that while he was at the house of Martín's other brother, Domingo, a dog had soiled his chair. The excrement appeared to have the shape of a face with eyes and ears which Diego thought might be Tíu. Diego was worried, because if Tíu could manifest himself in this way (perhaps he thought that the dog was Tíu's nagual), he must have great powers indeed and could well be capable of thwarting any cure. Still, Diego had agreed to try and asked for two reales to buy olive oil for Martín to drink as a diagnostic test. The family was instructed to observe carefully the contents of Martín's next bowel movement. The oil worked quickly (though it cannot have done much for Martín's condition) and Diego determined that it contained some kind of toad secretion, indicating the presence of a toad within Martín's body, which was the cause of the illness.

He told the family to collect garlic, chiles, and tobacco, which he mixed together in a small gourd cup. This he placed against Martín's stomach mouth down, as one would a cupping glass for bleeding. However, rather than cutting into him, Diego used magic and simply removed the gourd, taking from it a small toad, which he ordered burned. Then, he lifted his face up toward the loft of the house and addressed Tíu (who, of course, was not physically present), asking him why he had made this poor man so sick. If he were doing it for money or for some other thing which he envied, he had only to ask for it and it would be given to him. Diego continued to treat Martín, applying the cup to other parts of his body to extract the objects magically put there by Tíu. Diego had determined that there were thirteen such objects and promised to get them all. He extracted strands of corn silk from his patient's head, two beetles and two lengths of cord from one ear, and a tadpole from the other. More corn silk, a fly, and four lengths of cord were taken from two places on his chest, and a substance like the sediment from corn beer was removed from his breast. Even Martín's brother could not believe what he was seeing and gave Diego another empty cup. Unperturbed, he went back to work extracting the sediment.

All of these things were burned with the exception of the tadpole, which disappeared just after another entreaty to Tíu. Diego explained that it had returned to Tíu, its master. Still, Martín's condition worsened. On the first of March in 1715, he called the Indian officials of his town to hear his deathbed accusation of Tíu. He died shortly afterward, but the officials forwarded his statement to the Spanish authorities, who conducted the lengthy investigation which produced the record of this case. The authorities were skeptical about the accusation of sorcery and could produce no hard evidence to support a murder charge against Tíu. However, both he and Diego were found guilty of "practices harmful to the service of Our Lord God" and were sentenced to fifty lashes each and the public humiliation of being paraded through town on mules with a trumpeter and crier to tell everyone of their "crimes."

THE CULT OF SAN PASCUAL

Individual illnesses were familiar enough to the Cakchiquel since before the Spanish conquest and were explainable in a variety of ways, as were failed attempts to cure. But epidemics and pandemics on the scale and with the severity of those caused by introduced diseases, unknown before the conquest and against which traditional remedies seemed useless, were a new phenomenon. How could these be understood? How could the Cakchiquel attempt to deal emotionally or psychologically with such catastrophes? What protection or control could be found to avoid them? In at least one instance in the seventeenth century, we can document an answer to these questions. The form of their response was a crisis cult, a common reaction to widespread calamity, but the content was a uniquely Colonial Cakchiquel blend of traditional Maya and introduced Spanish beliefs and practices.

About 1650 an epidemic began in the Guatemalan highlands that was especially vicious to the Cakchiquel towns around the capital of Santiago. The Cakchiquel called it *cumatz,* using the Mexican (Nahuatl) word for snake, since they felt that the symptoms (probably those of typhus) were analogous to the movements of a snake in the victim's body. Fuentes reported:

> . . . because it being as they relate it an extremely sharp and pricking pain in the stomach, with vehement cramps which branch out in the manner of spasms, with numbness in the limbs, nerves, and joints, to which with torturous speed runs the sharpest pain: and from its mode of curving and undulating as it runs through the body, they gave it the name Cumatz, which means snake; and remaining in the stomach, one feels this humor return and re-return from one part to another incessantly, always accompanying that pain, with indescribable torment and anguish for the miserable patient, with high malicious fever and implacable thirst . . . incurable in all those who fall victim to it. (Fuentes y Guzmán 1969–1972, III:274)

The Cakchiquel evidently viewed this as a "cold" disease (caused by an imbalance of "cold" over "hot" in the body; *see* Chapter 9), since many of them attempted to treat it through long baths in the hot springs of San Antonio Aguascalientes. It was of no avail, however, and the disease ran rampant, leaving the towns, in Fuentes' words, "in a state of desertion" (Fuentes y Guzmán, 1969–1972, III:273). Among those who fell victim to the disease was a prominent Indian of San Antonio. He declined as did all the others, had received the last rites, and was on the point of death when he had a vision of a beautiful man, dressed in the style of a friar but in shining garments, covered with light. The sight of this personage gave the Indian sufficient strength to raise himself up and ask in Cakchiquel; "Who are you, the Great Lord?" The man replied with a question of his own and asked why the Indians did not celebrate the fiesta of San Pascual Bailón as they did for the other saints. The Indian responded that he had never known of or even heard the name of such a saint. He said he thought that the other Indians had no knowledge of him either, though he must surely be a great lord. The personage stated that he was San Pascual Bailón and that he would be grateful and intercede for the Indians in their illnesses if they would call on him, celebrate his fiesta, and make statues and portraits of him to keep with them always. God wanted him to be the Indians' patron, he said, and through his intercession they would be free of the disease afflicting them and liberated from death.

The Indian was both astonished and cheered by these words and promised immediately to become his devotee. But he also said he feared that the rest of his people might not believe him should he tell them of his vision and just call him crazy. In response, the saint told him to say: "That it is a certainty that San Pascual Bailón offers to be your patron and advocate, and that if you invoke him and keep his portrait he will liberate you from death. To show that you are my messenger, you will die in nine days and from this day the pestilence will cease and no other Indian will die" (Fuentes y Guzmán 1969–1972, III:275). The saint then disappeared.

The Indian called his fellow comrades to him to hear of his vision and also to send for the town vicar. The latter found himself in a difficult position as he examined the Indian on the content of his vision. Although he might personally have doubted that the saint had appeared to the Indian, it would be difficult to judge publicly that he had not, lest he deny either the ability of the saints to make themselves known miraculously to mortals or the ability of Indians to have such experiences (making them second-class citizens in the church). Accordingly, the next day he sang a mass and exhorted the San Antonio Indians to the veneration of San Pascual. Reportedly, as the saint had promised, the epidemic ended that same day. Nine days later, the Indian visionary died, fulfilling the entire prophecy.

Given the miracle and the efficacy of the San Antonio people's devotion to the new saint, his cult quickly spread to other Indian towns and ultimately throughout the Maya highlands. However, in the process, the Indians came to identify San Pascual with death itself and to represent him as a skeleton. The Spaniards were scandalized by this "corruption" (as Fuentes put it) and tried, without much success, to stamp it out by confiscating and burning all the skeletal images which had been carved and kept on the altars of nearly every Indian house. Even Holy Week observance in the capital had to be modified, because the Good Friday procession of Holy Burial of Christ, which began at the cathedral, was customarily preceded by a cart carrying as a prisoner a skeletal figure representing death, overcome by Christ's resurrection. So many Indians volunteered to pull the cart and lavished so much decoration on it as a means of publicly worshiping San Pascual as the patron of death that the authorities decreed that it should no longer be part of the procession.

Predictably, to the Spaniards the cult of the skeletal San Pascual was simply an aberration, resulting from ignorance, errors of transmission regarding the original content of the vision, and confusion over the identity of the saint. To the Cakchiquel and other highland Maya, however, it was a logical and emotionally useful response to an acute crisis. It was also not entirely unlike the response of the Spaniards' forebears two or three centuries earlier, who, along with the rest of Europe, had faced a similar crisis. The skeleton carried in the cart in the Holy Week procession was a Spanish introduction which dated to the late Middle Ages, the time of the Black Plague which wiped out at least a third of Europe's population. Given their preoccupation during this period with sickness and dying, it is not surprising that Europeans came to personify death itself, usually in skeletal or Grim Reaper guise. This mode of depiction endured into succeeding centuries, especially, as the above example illustrates, in religious contexts. The Cakchiquel were thus familiar with the personification of death in skeletal form and could easily have come to regard "him" as a powerful supernatural like those depicted in other images, the saints. Death on a mass scale could only be the result of some powerful supernatural, the "patron" of death. Indeed, based on the content of the Holy Week procession, "he" *was* a powerful being, since only Christ himself could defeat him. To those Maya living in towns other than San Antonio, where the cult began, it is easy to understand how San Pascual came to be associated with the skeleton; only death as a personified supernatural could control death as a phenomenon. Only now, the Indians knew the name of the patron of death—San Pascual—and how to deal with him. Of course, "he" was just like the other supernaturals; his aid could be enlisted, or he could at least be appeased, through offerings, veneration, and fiestas. In this way, even the catastrophic, mass death caused by imported diseases was not only made understandable (and thus perhaps slightly less frightening) but also amenable to at least some degree of human control.

BIBLIOGRAPHIC NOTE

Hunt (1977) presents a useful introduction to the Mesoamerican concepts of time and space. Berdan (1982) provides a succinct description of the workings of the Aztec calendars, and Edmonson (1988) delves masterfully into the history of Mesoamerican calendrical systems generally. Calendrical divination among the highland Maya is described in detail by Colby and Colby (1981) and by Tedlock (1982). López Austin (1988) reconstructs the forces which the ancient Mexicans believed to inhabit the body. Clues to their Cakchiquel counterparts were found in the Coto dictionary (Coto 1983, Hill 1990). Although Fuentes is our primary account of the origins of the San Pascual cult, additional detail and later developments are provided by Luján (1967) and Navarette (1982).

7 / Serving the Conquerors

Though the Kingdom of Guatemala, like the rest of Mesoamerica, had been conquered in the name of the Spanish crown, the conquerors themselves were motivated at least as much by the prospect of personal gain as they were by patriotism. The conquistadores were not regular Spanish troops (though many of them had been during the wars against the Moors and in Italy) but military entrepreneurs with license to conquer on the crown's behalf. In return for arming and equipping themselves, as well as for their exertions, they intended to realize large, immediate profits in gold or slaves. Nor were they pioneers seeking to build a new life for themselves on some distant frontier, but socially ambitious individuals intent on achieving the status of Spanish nobles and acquiring its attendant material emoluments. Indeed, as noted earlier, Alvarado's initial entrance into the Maya highlands was as much an organized looting expedition as a military operation. Dissatisfied with the pickings to be had in Guatemala, many of the conquerors (including Alvarado himself) looked about for new conquests in Peru or elsewhere as a way of making their fortunes. For those who remained in Guatemala (and despite his dissatisfaction, Alvarado moved his family there and retained lands and enterprises) it became clear that the only way to wealth, or even survival, depended on appropriating Indian labor and its products. Church and state came to understand this too as they established their respective institutions. Accordingly, much of the relationship between the Colonial Cakchiquel and the Spaniards was unabashedly exploitative, with the latter trying to extract as much as possible from the former. Many of the forms of exploitation were entirely legal (or, in the case of slavery, at least justifiable) under Spanish laws of the time. That was certainly of little comfort to the Cakchiquel. Yet there were illegal forms of exploitation as well, and even the legal ones could be and often were criminally perverted in practice. The result was an incredible series of demands from different Spanish individuals and institutions that the Cakchiquel somehow had to satisfy.

SLAVERY

Slavery was a phenomenon of the early Colonial period and was one of the worst of the conquistadores' excesses. As per contemporary Spanish law and military custom, those who resisted attempts at peaceful incorporation into the Spanish empire were fair game for military conquest (called "the just war"), and those who took up arms against Spanish forces could be enslaved legitimately. The same fate awaited those who (like the Cakchiquel of the Iximché polity) reneged on their initial submission to the crown. Unchecked by effective royal authority, the conquistadores used their slaves mercilessly in a variety of enterprises. Panning for gold in the region's placer deposits was highly labor-intensive, as was portage work across the Isthmus of Panama. Taken from their homes, their highland environment, and treated horribly, few survived for long. Those sent to perform agricultural labor on the conquerors' farms in the vicinity of the new capital of Santiago may have faired slightly better, but were still slaves nevertheless.

However justified slavery may have seemed to the conquistadores, the crown was convinced otherwise. After all, by virtue of their submission (whether peacefully or by force) the Indians were now Spanish subjects and becoming Christians, and therefore entitled to some protection. Accordingly, slavery was abolished by royal decree in the New Laws of 1542 and enforced in Guatemala by 1548. Yet this did not solve anyone's problems. The conquistadores and early colonists still both felt that they needed Indian labor and expected, as conquerors, to have it provided to them. The crown was concerned that, if it granted rights to Indian labor to the colonists in perpetuity, it would see the emergence of a New World noble class independent of royal power, just the kind of aristocracy which the Spanish monarchs Ferdinand and Isabella had finally reduced. Yet the crown also recognized that it owed both its initial acquisition and continued possession of its New World domains to the conquistadores' and colonists' loyalty. Therefore, some way had to be found to satisfy their demands for Indian labor while at the same time retaining royal authority and affording a measure of protection to the crown's Indian subjects. The way that the crown chose to do this was through *encomienda,* an institution based on a variety of practices developed in Castile during the reconquest of Spain from the Moors.

ENCOMIENDA

Originally, the term *encomienda* was applied to only one of the many forms of royal grant bestowed upon individuals and institutions participating in the reconquest. These grants were all basically feudal in that they involved the bestowal of rights (including jurisdiction to varying degrees) over land, its produce, and, frequently, people in return for loyal and continued military service to the crown.

As adapted for use in the New World, encomienda was, in theory, a royal grant of the specified labor, products, or cash tribute of so many Indians to a Spaniard in recognition of some service to the crown. Handily, there was no fixed number of Indians included in such grants, so they could be tailored to fit the rank and service of the grantee or *encomendero.* After two generations the grant reverted to the crown, which might thenceforth keep the tribute payment for its own use or reassign it to some other worthy recipient. In no instance did the crown grant feudal jurisdiction to the encomendero. In this way the crown hoped both to prevent the development of an independent New World nobility and to continue to hold out the potential reward of an encomienda for future services.

From the encomenderos' point of view, the system could be satisfactory only as long as the number of grantees remained sufficiently small that each had a large enough income from his grant or the Indian population remained large enough and productive enough to support them. We have already seen how the Cakchiquel population declined so precipitously in the sixteenth century and how slow it was to recover. Also, the crown found it very difficult to refuse requests for an encomienda grant. The net effect of these two trends was that over time more grants of ever fewer Indians were made, making the grants themselves less reliable as a source of livelihood for their holders. Moreover, by the early seventeenth century, many of the larger encomiendas were being assigned to Spaniards not even resident in Guatemala but in Europe, leaving the criollo colonists with ever-diminishing prospects of receiving a substantial grant. Those still in existence became subject to an ever larger number of charges against their incomes, intended to help fill the royal coffers. Of course, whatever they were worth to their holders, the Indians still had to produce the same amount of wealth to fulfill their tributary obligations.

By the 1600s the Spanish empire had fallen into an economic depression that would last most of the century. Conditions became so desperate for the criollos living in Guatemala that many of them abandoned the capital in order to take up farming and ranching as ways to support themselves. Yet, as conquerors, or by now the criollo descendants of conquerors, they were still unwilling to do much manual labor themselves. The crown's response to the colonists' renewed demands for access to the reduced Indian labor pool was the *repartimiento* system.

REPARTIMIENTO

Repartimiento was essentially a form of labor draft, under which Indian communities were required to supply a quarter of their able-bodied men each week for work on Spanish farms. The drafts were necessary since the Indians refused (not surprisingly) to work for free or for the low wages that Spaniards were willing to pay. Remember that the early 1600s in particular were a time of low population during which land was pretty much available for the clearing. Time spent by Indians working for Spaniards was time that could otherwise have been spent on their own enterprises. However, this reluctance was represented to the crown by the criollo colonists as simple indolence on the Indians' part, something which the crown would not tolerate among its subjects. Accordingly, the Indians would be required to work.

Still, the crown tried to design what it considered a just system of forced labor (despite the fact that this was a contradiction in terms). Royal officials with the title of *juez repartidor* were to oversee the entire process. They would determine the number of men to be called up from each Indian community. They were to ensure that all Indians subject to the draft served their turn, regardless of rank or wealth. The juez repartidor was also to enforce regulations regarding type of work and working conditions. The Indians were to be fed and housed decently by the Spaniard employing them, who was also to supply any tools needed for the task. They were to receive a standard wage of one real per day, including travel time. Finally, the travel time to and from the job were to be deducted from their total period at work. Ideally, a criollo landowner would simply inform the local juez repartidor of his needs and the workers would be forthcoming in the next week's draft. In reality, it never worked satisfactorily from anyone's viewpoint.

Criollo farm owners (or *labradores,* as they were called) complained of never having enough Indian laborers, of not getting them when needed, their cost, and the low quality of the work done. The idea that wages and the quality of work might be related seems not to have occurred seriously to anyone. More workers might be obtained by bribing the juez repartidor into assigning them more men or calling up more than a quarter of a town's eligible workers, but as more and more labradores adopted this tactic, the sizes of the bribes increased, only adding to the cost. Alternatively, labradores could hire Indian laborers to make up the shortfall in repartimiento workers by offering better wages, but this defeated the point of the exercise, which was to secure labor at minimum cost. However, we are concerned with repartimiento from the Indians' perspective, and clearly they were the most abused by the system, which invited abuse.

Our best information on the workings of the repartimiento among the Cakchiquel comes from two official inspections of practices in the vicinity of the capital, including the eastern Cakchiquel, in the later 1600s (*see* Borg 1986:112–126). According to these documents, each quarter of a town's eligible men were subject to work one week out of four, leaving with their labrador or his agent from their town early Monday morning, not to return until Sunday afternoon for mass. The Sacatepéquez-area people did not travel more than five leagues (about twenty-one kilometers) to work, which made it slightly easier for them and also for their labradores, who did not lose as much work to travel time. The Indians were to work from sunup to noon and, after an hour's rest, to just before sundown. They were to be paid one real per day, plus an extra real per week if they supplied their own tools. This contrasted with the one-and-a-half to two reales per day earned by hired laborers. In addition to workers' wages, the labrador was to pay one-half real per day per man of royal tax into the caja de comunidad of the men's hometown when he or his foreman collected them. The juez repartidor collected these funds periodically after first determining the number of eligible men from church marriage and death records. Any discrepancies, due to the fact that some eligible men had not gone to work or that the population had declined since the last tally, had to be made up by the Indian justices of each town.

The system was manipulated by everyone, with the poorest Indians suffering most. In addition to bribing the juez repartidor to assign more Indians to them, the commonest complaints against labradores concerned pay. Indians complained that payments were not made promptly according to regulations or in the specified amounts, with labradores playing various schemes to short them. A few even tried to pay the Indians in kind. Some workers were not paid for their travel time. Other grievances concerned too-long workdays and unreasonably heavy work loads.

Occasionally, a labrador would confiscate the tools the Indians had brought with them (presumably only iron tools, which were in chronically short supply and, hence, valuable; *see* Chapter 3). Fairly often, the Indians were employed in tasks other than those connected with wheat farming, the only legal use of repartimiento labor. Working in sugar mills and processing indigo dye were especially injurious to the Indians' health and were expressly forbidden, yet it occurred anyway. Finally, verbal and even physical abuse of repartimiento Indians was far from unknown.

The Cakchiquel themselves quickly learned how to manipulate the repartimiento system. It is hard to imagine, for example, Miguel Perez Pirir with all of his enterprises, wealth, and status or members of his corporate family with all of the work they did for themselves meekly shouldering hoes and heading off to work for a week on someone else's (and a Spaniard's at that) wheat farm. It is clear that individuals of even modest means could buy their way out of repartimiento obligations in any of several well-established ways. By the custom that the seventeenth-century Cakchiquel called *tacagual,* one Indian could hire another to take his place, paying two or three reales to someone in need of cash. If unable to recruit someone himself, an Indian wishing to avoid repartimiento paid four reales to his town justices, who would find a replacement. They called this practice *peyobal*. Under either peyobal or tacagual, the substitute worker received both the payment from whomever enlisted him plus his normal salary from the labrador. Alternatively, an Indian might pay his labrador to excuse him. This was probably the most expensive option, costing from four to ten reales for the week in cash or its equivalent in kind. A labrador might sometimes be willing to make such an arrangement, especially if he could then hire a replacement worker and still keep a couple of reales as profit. A small town like San Raimundo (obliged to send only forty-eight men per week) might consistently buy off the labradores and not send any workers or, at other times, only a few. Of course, at certain times of the year these two tactics might be difficult to use, especially at planting and harvesting when everyone was probably concerned with doing their own work. The tendency, then, was for wealthier Cakchiquel to buy their way out of repartimiento obligations and for the burden to fall much more frequently on the poor, who either needed the money to be made by replacing someone else or who could not afford to buy off the time.

All of these schemes for avoiding repartimiento service relied on the fact that Spanish officials and criollo labradores did not care which individuals showed up for work, only that the proper number of Indians were available. Sometimes, as we saw above, towns entirely paid off their labradores. Periodically, labradores did not need all of the laborers assigned to them. Both of these situations created additional problems, since, throughout most of the seventeenth century, the crown expected that the half-real tax it charged per worker would still be deposited in the town caja and collected on schedule by the juez repartidor. The Cakchiquel solved this problem by instituting the practice that on any occasion when fewer than the total quota of workers went out on repartimiento, those left behind themselves would pay into the town caja the half real normally paid by the labrador. The crown finally remedied this inequity in 1687 when it decreed that the half-real tax was to be collected only for those Indians actually sent on repartimiento.

before the image of the saint, whilst the Mass is celebrating. Some Indians will bring a bundle of a dozen candles, some worth a real apiece, others of three or four for a real. After the Mass the priest and the *mayordomos* [executives of the cofradía] take and sweep away from the saint whatsoever they find hath been offered to him; so that sometimes in a great town upon such a saint's day the priest may receive in money twelve or twenty reals, and fifty or a hundred candles, which may be worth to him twenty or thirty shillings [reales], besides some ends and pieces. Most of the friars about Guatemala are with these offerings as well stored with candles as is any wax-chandler's shop in the city. The Indians themselves when they want again any candles for the like feast, or for a christening, or for a woman's churching (at which times they also offer candles) they will buy them again of the priest, who sometimes receives the same candles and money for them again five or six times. (Gage 1958:236)

Cofradías also assisted with priestly support, as well as sacristy items and church furnishings. In Gage's time, maintenance alone amounted to two pesos per cofradía per month (Gage 1958:258). Responsible for the two Pokomám towns of Mixco and Pinula in the 1630s, Gage described his income in detail. His monthly support payments from the two towns' cajas and cofradías totaled some 69 pesos, or 828 pesos yearly. In addition, on a yearly basis he could count on 4 pesos from each of the eighteen guachibales in Mixco and the twenty in Pinula, plus about 3 pesos each in offerings. Thus, he could rely on 266 pesos per year from guachibales. Beyond even this he received sizable donations for official Church feasts— Christmas, Holy Thursday and Good Friday, Candlemas, All Souls Day—and for communion and confession during Lent. These added up to another 760 or so pesos annually, and a total yearly income from both towns of over 1850 pesos. Gage actually cited a figure of 2000 pesos, figuring in two reales each for christenings, marriages, and funerals (Gage 1958:259). Even though many cofradías produced the income to make their share of the payments through agriculture, land rental, livestock raising, and money management, they still represented a considerable drain of wealth away from Indian producers into non-Indian hands.

ILLEGAL EXPLOITATION

To this point, we have been discussing forms of exploitation that, while unjustifiable from our present-day viewpoint, were completely legal in principle under Spanish law. However, as we have already seen, these forms were all susceptible to illegal manipulation, usually on the part of some Spanish official in exchange for some gift, consideration, or bribe. Depending on rank, the illegal exploitation by these administrators could go far beyond simple juggling of numbers of repartimiento Indians and was just part of a larger pattern of official corruption which reached a peak in the seventeenth century (MacLeod 1973:313).

Spanish officials were probably no more inclined to corruption than their colleagues in other European nations of the time. Certainly, general economic circumstances, the system of appointments, and salaries had as much to do with the problem as did human greed. With the onset of the seventeenth-century depression in the Kingdom of Guatemala, export crops, industry, and commerce all but collapsed. In these conditions, royal offices became important sources of income, especially for men with aristocratic pretensions who would not engage directly in productive economic activities. Yet the crown was also pressed for cash, and the salaries of royal functionaries was one place where economies could be made. Accordingly, salaries were uniformly low. Another tactic used by the crown to raise money (and a measure of the desperation of the royal treasury) was to effectively sell offices to would-be holders. *Peninsulares* in particular, having often borrowed heavily to buy a high office, travel to the New World, and establish a suitably impressive, urban life-style, were under pressure to make as much money they could as quickly as possible. Each incoming official also typically brought with him a following of relatives and friends for whom some employment had to be found. Of course, officeholders also had to worry about making a profit on the venture sufficient to support them when their terms were up and they returned to Spain. Criollos were only rarely granted royal office of any importance (one cause of the antagonism they felt for peninsulares) but, given the lack of alternatives in seventeenth-century Guatemala, would still try to make it pay as much as possible.

A high-ranking officer such as the governor/president of the audiencia had many means open to him for making money while in office, including selling lesser offices to friends and associates, and direct exploitation of the Indians was not among the most profitable. It was thus the lower-level officials and, by all accounts, especially the *corregidores* who seem most commonly to have resorted to illegal schemes to exploit the Indians. The office of corregidor was created in the sixteenth century as a crown official to oversee the administration of a region's *(corregimiento)* towns not in encomienda. Later, his responsibilities were extended to encomienda towns as well. Appointed by the audiencia, he was the only normal point of contact between the Indians and the Spanish bureaucracy. Therefore, corregidores were in a unique position to exploit the Indians of their jurisdictions. Because such criminal activities were perpetrated by royal officials with ties to even higher officials, we do not have enough information tell how much of a burden such illegal exploitation was for the Cakchiquel to bear. About the best we can do here is to sketch some of the main forms of this exploitation.

One of the main duties of a corregidor was to perform a yearly *visita*, an inspection of the towns under his authority. As part of the visita, he audited the accounts of the caja de comunidad and performed any judicial duties that might be necessary (such as hearing or investigating disputes that could not be settled by the town justices; *see* Chapter 8). Then there was the matter of enforcing the myriad of royal ordinances designed to control even the most intimate aspects of Indian life. Gage wrote:

> The President of [the audiencia] of Guatemala, the judges of that Chancery, the govenors and high justices of other parts of the country advance and enrich their menial servants by making the poor Indians the subject of the bountifulness towards such. Some are employed to visit their towns as often as they please to see how much maize every Indian hath sowed for the maintenance of his wife and children; others visit them to see what fowls they keep for the good and store of the country; others have order to see whether their houses be decently kept and their beds orderly placed according to their families. (Gage 1958:241)

Citing documents from the northwestern Guatemala highlands, Collins provides additional specifics on the degree of detail such inspections involved:

> After the accounts had been taken, the corregidor sometimes made a tour of Indian dwellings. To pass inspection, houses had to be "well covered, clean, and furnished with images . . . crosses . . . rosaries . . . and [Papal] bulls . . . as well as with covers for sleeping, earthen pots and pans, grinding stones, and other kitchen utensils. The corregidor also checked to see that each house had beds above floor level, that each contained only one family, that children's beds were separate from those of their parents, and that male and female children had separate beds. On these occasions, the corregidor also checked to see that each family had sufficient clothing. . . . And, to help them better meet their tribute obligations, each household was required to have tools such as hoes, axes, machetes, and spades for working their fields and woodlands, and a regulation-sized chicken flock in a proper enclosure near the house. (Collins 1980:117–118)

This entire visita process was open to illegal manipulation, and some of the forms it took were so widespread that they even had names which everyone used to refer to them. Thus, while a corregidor was forbidden to draw a salary or expenses from the Indian cajas, he could require a *derrama* or *besamano,* an off-the-books gift of money (perhaps as much as several score tostones) upon his arrival. Corregidores were not to compel the Indians to support them while on inspection, but this did not apply to the official's entourage, which typically included a scribe, interpreter(s), an *alguacil mayor* (constable), servants, and, perhaps a couple official "witnesses" (cronies who attested to the correctness of the inspection), all of whom had to be entertained as sumptuously as the town could provide. The corregidor was well placed to withdraw funds from the caja and juggle its records to hide his tracks. He could also either exact "fines" for any infractions of the many royal ordinances or accept bribes to forget about them. Corregidores also typically charged a fee for confirming the results of the yearly elections of town justices.

To this point, we have considered only those forms of exploitation committed by corregidores in the performance of their duties. At least in some parts of the Kingdom of Guatemala, corregidores also used their positions of authority to become entrepreneurs, using the Indians as either a free labor force or as a captive market. Both of these practices went by the name of repartimiento. Under the abuse called the *repartimiento de algodón,* the corregidor purchased raw cotton in some commercial center such as the capital, then distributed it among the Indians of his district, requiring (under pain of fines or other threats) that the women spin and weave it into cloth, which he would then resell back in Santiago. If the quantities of cotton involved were large enough, the corregidor could realize great profits. The *repartimiento de bienes* involved the forced purchase at inflated prices by the Indians of goods supplied by the corregidor. Again, depending on the number of Indians and the price of the goods, the corregidor could enrich himself quickly.

Of course, as they were illegal activities, no records were kept and these practices come to our attention only through the records of proceedings initiated against the occasional unlucky, politically unconnected, or extravagantly greedy official. Therefore, we cannot determine either how widespread these practices were or the extent to which they affected the Cakchiquel. However, circumstantial evidence suggests that corregidores were generally worse in areas more remote from the capital than the majority of Cakchiquel towns.

THE COST OF SERVICE

What, then, was the expense to the "average" seventeenth-century Cakchiquel for the privilege of being a Christian subject of the Spanish crown? Given the unevenness of the documentary record, it is difficult if not impossible to arrive at such a figure. However, such information as is available does afford us an idea of the size of yearly, legally sanctioned obligations. In the Cakchiquel region, our best estimate can be made for the towns of Chimaltenango and Santiago Sacatepéquez.

In the later seventeenth century, Chimaltenango had 1600 full tributaries, which converts to a population of about 4000. The town thus owed 1600 tostones as their servicio del tostón, plus about 520 tostones in almud, for a total of 2120 tostones in royal tribute per year. However, Chimaltenango was also an encomienda town pertaining (until 1686) to the Condesa de Alba (Simpson 1966:244–250). As such, it owed the condesa a combination of agricultural products and money to the value of 168,384 tostones annually, nearly eight times what it owed in royal tribute! Such a ratio of encomienda to royal tribute was evidently not extreme for towns around the Spanish capital. On the other hand, the Cuchumatán mountains town of Jacaltenango owed 310 tostones of royal tribute in the 1660s versus about 962 tostones in encomienda tribute for a 1:3 ratio (Collins 1980:103). To the Chimaltenango sum we must add approximately 1600 tostones more, paid out of the caja de comunidad, to support the resident friar(s), giving us a minimum official town obligation of 172,104 tostones per annum. The term "minimum" is used since other community expenses (a land litigation against an encroaching Spaniard or another town, for example) would require additional funds, probably amassed via special collections made by the justices. Of course, the need for private priestly services, guachibal ownership, or cofradía membership all required additional expenditures though these might have amounted to only a few more tostones on a household basis. In any event, we arrive at a combined tribute figure of almost 108 tostones per full tributary (or nuclear household, which is what the unit represented in terms of productive potential) per year.

Yet Chimaltenango may represent only the middle range of such obligations. Fuentes reported that, in the later 1600s, the people of Santiago Sacatepéquez needed to realize 295,104 tostones annually in order to pay their encomienda and royal tribute as well as maintain their cofradías, guachibales, "and other things in their charge" (Fuentes y Guzmán 1969–1972, I:379). With only five hundred full tributaries during this period, each would have had a yearly obligation of about 590 tostones.

These are fantastic sums, especially if we keep in mind that a repartimiento laborer earned only one real per day (or a quarter-tostón) and hired workers only up to two reales. At the hired worker rate it would take a man 216 days to earn the 108 tostones due in Chimaltenango, while at the repartimiento rate it would take well over a year to earn one year's tribute! True, the Cakchiquel were reluctant to perform repartimiento labor, let alone rely on it as a source of income. Yet it still provides a baseline understanding of Colonial Cakchiquel obligations to the conquerors. Of course, a greater or lesser encomienda tribute would change dramatically the size of the burden on each full tributary. In mid-seventeenth century Jacaltenango, for example, it was only about six and a half tostones per year.

As we saw in Chapter 5, to meet these and other needs the Colonial Cakchiquel engaged wherever possible in a wide range of economic activities which, while we lack price data for the period, were certainly much more remunerative than weeding some Spaniard's wheat field. Corporate entities like towns and parcialidades attempted to defray as much of their tribute obligations as possible through community enterprises such as agriculture or stock raising carried out on parts of the group's common lands. Other communal resources, such as timber or minerals like lime, could also be exploited, with the town coffers receiving rents or percentages. While precise figures are lacking, it seems certain that this was almost never enough and that a substantial portion of a community's tribute had to come out of the pockets of its members.

Such donations could be earned by the entire household rather than just the husband or father. A wife and daughter who could weave cloth, make pottery, or even manufacture petate mats could make substantial contributions to the family coffers. Even today, women potters and weavers evidence a high level of self-esteem and demand a certain amount of deference from their spouses because of their moneymaking abilities. Unmarried, adolescent sons who could work almost as hard as their fathers but who were not yet counted as full tributaries were also assets, and the Indians kept their sons with them as long as possible at least partly for this reason. A corporate family like the Pirires was undoubtedly the best solution given the conditions. Certainly they all had to work hard, and as each son or grandson married he became a new full tributary with the attendant obligations. But they were doing more than just scraping by, as patriarch Miguel's rich gifts to the local church and his sponsorship of multiple guachibales clearly indicate.

This chapter may have given the impression that the Spaniards simply issued requirements to the Cakchiquel for their money, labor, and its products and that the latter simply complied. It is true that they had to make a substantial response to Spanish demands, especially in the realm of tribute and labor, but this is far from the whole story. The Colonial Cakchiquel also developed an astounding variety of ways to resist, circumvent, derail, and otherwise frustrate the conquerors, their programs, and their institutions.

BIBLIOGRAPHIC NOTE

The basic forms of Indian exploitation institutionalized by the Spaniards are all well known historically. See Sherman (1979) for the sixteenth century and Chamberlain (1939) and Simpson (1966) for extended discussions of encomienda. Collins (1980) and Borg (1986) contain important information on the local-level operation of the repartimiento system in two different parts of Guatemala. MacLeod (1973) provides a useful overview.

8 / Resisting the Conquerors

From their final military subjugation in the 1530s, the Colonial Cakchiquel never again rose up in a violent, coordinated way against their Spanish overlords, despite the injustices of the Colonial system. The absence of such uprisings is attributable to a variety of factors. First among these, especially early in the Colonial period, was the seeming totality of the Cakchiquels' final defeat after years of military resistance. Violent opposition to Spanish rule simply had not worked, and because of that, combined with the horrific population losses of the time, the Cakchiquel simply could no longer maintain armed forces in permanent conflict with the invader. Of course, as soon as the Spaniards achieved any degree of control they set about the task of dismembering the native polities, eliminating the rulers either in battle or later (as Alvardo did with Cahi Imox; *see* Chapter 2) and dispersing the members of the larger chinamitales among distant towns. In this way they effectively deprived the Cakchiquel of any form of overarching organization above the town level so indispensable for effective, coordinated resistance. Towns themselves ultimately came to compete against each other, as well as Spaniards, for land, and this created new antagonisms and distrust among the Cakchiquel (some of which endure even today). Population loss continued through much of the seventeenth century and could be locally devastating throughout the Colonial period. Finally, as a politically and economically subordinated population, the Colonial Cakchiquel simply had too much else to do on a practical, day-to-day level just to survive. Working to support themselves and contribute to their town's encomienda and royal tribute obligations, most Cakchiquel also had to labor for Spaniards under repartimiento as well.

Yet all this should not be taken to mean that the Cakchiquel simply surrendered to Spanish demands. As we saw in the preceding chapter, tribute and labor in some form were largely unavoidable. At the same time, however, resistance to Spanish rule was possible and even effective to a degree, especially if it was of a covert, nonviolent nature. Indeed, the Colonial Cakchiquel developed and made use of an impressive and generally efficient array of practices and institutions intended to keep the Spaniards at a distance or, at least, at bay. The efficacy of their efforts is attested to by the fact that the Cakchiquel survived the Colonial period and are still a thriving, culturally distinct population today.

FLIGHT

A potential option for members of any society faced with oppression is flight from the oppressor, and, indeed, this was a viable and much-used option among the linguistic cousins of the Cakchiquel living in the northern Yucatan peninsula. In a logical attempt to forestall flight, Spanish law forbade Indians from leaving their native towns permanently. Yet, in the Yucatan, there was always an open frontier to the south—the Petén forest—which, during the seventeenth century, was never under effective Spanish control (in fact, the last independent Maya polity, that of the Itzá of Lake Petén, was not subdued by the Spaniards until 1697). Yucatec Maya fed up with Spanish rule could relatively easily pack up and steal off to the forest where they could join fairly well-established populations of like-minded people. As the Spaniards pushed the frontier forward or attempted to round up these people for resettlement in communities controlled by them, these Maya simply pushed farther into the forest.

Such open frontiers did not exist for the Cakchiquel. True, the Petén forest did lie to the north to run to, but it was a long, difficult journey and involved descending into tierra caliente, which the highlanders typically detested and feared. Still, people did try to avoid the tribute, labor, and church-support obligations of town life. They did so by forming small, dispersed settlements in the mountains and ravines, which the Spaniards called *pajuides* (from the Cakchiquel *pajuyu,* "in the hill[s]"). Because access to the pajuides was difficult, they were unlikely to be visited by Spanish civil or religious authorities. To an extent, pajuides were also a natural result of the Cakchiquel preference to live close to their fields, which, given the nature of the highland terrain, could be located beyond easy walking distance of a town. Yet the Spaniards were self-righteously outspoken, even a little hysterical in their condemnation of pajuides. According to Fuentes, the residents grew sugar, used to brew vast amounts of chicha, which they sold without license to other Indians, engaged in all manner of wanton sexual behavior, and perpetuated their pagan cults. Of course, they also paid no tribute, performed no repartimiento labor, and gave no support to the church, leaving it to those who remained behind in the towns to take up their slack. Fuentes described a famous (or infamous) one along the Pixcaya river and its tributaries between San Juan Sacatepéquez and San Martín Jilotepéque, actually called Pajuyu:

> But no less noticeable are the great numbers of little sugar mills one sees among the Indians that, although each one does not produce much, the multitude of them make such an overage and superabundance of the stuff as to cause a drop in the price of sugar and other things fabricated from it. . . . But taking up the most important subject, which is the souls of these poor Indians . . . the sugars and shavings they fabricate from the cane are also used in chicha, and the distillation of liquor, which destroys them like flame to the straw . . . being born of this custom the continuous drunkeness in which they live: from which, apart from the many diseases and wounds which they receive from each other, results not only in the disordered union with their wives and concubines, but torpid beastiality with their daughters, mothers, sisters, sisters-in-law, and daughters-in-law, their lascivious drunkeness not even sparing girls of eight or nine years (I state [only] that which each day those of us who have been judges among them experience), and that which the holy devotion of the Dominican ministers cries to the Reverend Bishops upon seeing them live in the vegas of those rivers, in the place called Pajuyu, in these detestable sins, beyond the policing of towns, without being subject to the justices, and distant from Catholic teaching and doctrine. (Fuentes y Guzmán 1969–1972, I:316)

Despite the horror (real or feigned) that these settlements caused in the Spaniards, the continuity and even growth of town populations over time indicate that the majority of Cakchiquel were unwilling to move permanently from their ancestors' territories, a point to which we shall return. Therefore, they had to develop institutions and mechanisms short of flight to mitigate the effects of Spanish oppression.

"WEAPONS OF THE WEAK"

If organized, violent, "national" resistance or flight were not possibilities for the Cakchiquel, they did use an entire range of individual, anonymous forms of covert resistance. These "weapons of the weak," as they have been called by Scott (1985), are not only practical for securing some small advantage and for being personally satisfying to the individual utilizing them. Employed frequently enough by large enough numbers of people, they could be an effective means of frustrating both individual Spaniards and even the entire Colonial regime. Included in this arsenal were things like passive noncompliance, false compliance or overcompliance, feigned ignorance, foot dragging, and dissimulation. Such tactics are typically not well documented historically since, even in a more culturally homogeneous society where oppressors and oppressed share much of the same tradition, it is the oppressors who do most of the writing on which historians and ethnohistorians depend. As cultural aliens vis-à-vis the Cakchiquel, the Spaniards did not perceive that the Indians were employing specific tactics against them. Instead, Spaniards attributed stubbornness, sloth, deceitfulness, and the like to Indians as racial characteristics incapable of change. Accordingly, we have only limited glimpses of these "weapons of the weak" as employed by the Cakchiquel. Yet these are telling. For example, even as an official, Fuentes was especially irked by the seeming overzealous compliance of Indians drafted to run messages from one place to another:

> . . . and greatly annoying and troublesome are the Indian couriers because in giving the letter or letters they carry, they take up a position across from the door of the room most frequented by the president [of the audiencia, the highest-ranking royal official], corregidor [a regional official], priest, or private gentleman to whom they are sent, without leaving there either to eat or sleep, without speaking a word or asking to be discharged, obliging one to quickly send them off with the answer; for charity's sake to see him out of your house and to free yourself of the pain of seeing him there at all hours. (Fuentes y Guzmán 1969–1972, III:272)

Of course, the Indian couriers probably wanted most of all (short of being left alone entirely) to complete their missions so that they could return to their own work. Certainly, hanging conspicuously around until the return dispatch was written was an attempt to achieve this. But it is also easy to imagine the wry satisfaction in the mind of the courier who, while he could not avoid the obligation to serve, could at least upset the schedule of the Spaniard to whom he had been sent and, through his irritating presence, "require" that the latter draft an immediate response in order to get the bothersome Indian out of his sight.

But perhaps most frustrating was the Spaniards' inability to get any detailed information, or even a yes-or-no answer from the Indians:

> They guard secrets of importance to them better than any other race in the world, so much that they would die before revealing what they guard.
>
> They have the custom never to affirm what they see and know, because they always respond "perhaps it is so," "perhaps it will be," although they know that what they are asked is so and they have seen it: or although they have the thing asked of them. (Fuentes y Guzman 1969–1972, III:271)

Prelates fared little better. Gage wrote of his experience as a parish priest:

> If you ask them if they believe such a point of Christianity they will never answer affirmatively, but only thus: "Perhaps it may be so." They are taught the doctrine of Rome, that Christ's body is truely and really present in the Sacrament, and no bread in substance, but only the accidents. Yet if the wisest Indian be asked whether he believes this, he will answer, "Perhaps it may be so." (Gage 1958:237)

In his general discussion of these "everyday forms of resistance," Scott (1985:35) notes that these "individual acts of foot-dragging and evasion are often reinforced by a venerable popular culture of resistance." As we have already seen in part and shall see further, Colonial Cakchiquel culture was, to a great extent, literally a culture of resistance, and much more was involved here than simple, individual acts.

BROKERS AND BARRIERS

Although anyone and everyone could employ the weapons of the weak against the Spaniards or run away to a pajuyu, they did so basically as individuals (or perhaps families) and for individual ends. However, at least partly as a result of Spanish policy, certain Cakchiquel occasionally found themselves in the position of group representative and responsible for at least the outward compliance of their people with the foreigners' demands. Depending on how such representatives played their roles, they could either further oppress their own people or they could partially shield them from at least some of the effects of Spanish intrusion into local affairs. In the latter instance they became barriers or brokers vis-à-vis Spanish culture and the Colonial administration. In this case, according to MacLeod (1973:327), brokers and barriers are "institutions which seem intended, perhaps not consciously, to turn aside weak cultural and religious intrusion while giving in to economic exactions and trying to prepare for them."

The officers or justices of the cabildos (town councils), the alcaldes and regidores, though entirely Spanish creations, developed into preeminent barriers and brokers. During the sixteenth century the offices seem to have been monopolized to some extent by the surviving Cakchiquel aristocracy. This was also apparently a result of Spanish policy, which, though limiting terms to one year, also provided that the outgoing officers select their own replacements (though these had to be confirmed by crown officials). As long as these officials kept order and delivered their towns' tribute on time, they seem to have been left to run internal affairs pretty much as they wished. However, as traditional authority figures, these men were undoubtedly at least somewhat concerned with their subjects' well-being and probably initiated some of the practices that would make the Colonial cabildo a true barrier institution.

At the same time, the Spanish authorities appointed Indian "governors" (go-bernadores) of the towns. Again, early on, these governors were aristocrats, in some cases of the highest surviving rank. These were also one-year appointments, but they could seemingly be renewed at the discretion of the authorities. A gobernador was technically responsible for both the maintenance of order and tribute collection in his town, resulting in an overlap of duties between himself and the cabildo. Yet, at least early on, the gobernador owed his office to the Spaniards, not to the goodwill or esteem of his fellows. To avoid punishment or to hold on to the office and thus, perhaps, gain favors or receive preferential treatment from local crown authorities, he had to satisfy his Spanish masters. Thus, by the latter part of the sixteenth century we find that much of the highest native aristocracy had been co-opted by the Spaniards and reduced to the status of glorified tribute collectors. Undoubtedly, different individuals responded differently to this situation. While some aristocrat-governors probably carried on much as before the conquest, others saw an opportunity to aggrandize themselves at the commoners' expense and became petty despots. However, these cozy arrangements endured in different towns only as long as the indigenous aristocracy itself. As time wore on, the Cakchiquel aristocracy declined in numbers, wealth, and influence. As service as a town justice or gobernador became more onerous, more commoners came to serve in those capacities.

By the later seventeenth century at the latest, mechanisms existed by which towns could essentially purchase the office of gobernador for their own candidate. The practice was called prorogación and its use is documented specifically for the town of Sumpango in the late 1680s. As practiced then, the town principales (parcialidad heads) would make a collection from among all the households to defray the "costs" of having the man of their choice appointed as gobernador or continued in that office. In fact, the costs involved were minimal; the financially strapped audiencia was simply selling the office as a revenue-raising device. As a result, towns could select gobernadores of known character and loyalty, individuals unlikely to become drunk with power and certain to respect the wishes of the principales who had arranged for their appointments. In such instances, even the gobernador became a barrier/broker for his town and its true authorities, the parcialidad heads.

What could these officeholders do to protect their people from the Spaniards? In truth, not all that much, but something nevertheless. They could not avoid collect-ing tribute or sending men out on repartimiento, but they could, for example, engage in collusion to submit lower head counts than were actually the case. These both lessened the tribute burden somewhat and reduced the number of men a town had to supply for repartimiento. Lower head counts also functioned as a hedge against population loss in the intervening years until a new tally was ordered by the

Spanish authorities. These were not entirely selfless acts of courage on the parts of the men who engaged in this activity. While in office, the justices and gobernador were responsible for shortfalls in tribute or laborers. Once out of office, they were again subject to the same tribute and labor demands as their fellows. So, any advantage they could gain for their towns was worthwhile for them as well, both in and out of office.

Perhaps the most important (and least-documented) function of the justices was to represent their communities before visiting Spanish officials and keep them from prying too closely into town affairs. The juez repartidor made periodic visits to collect the fees paid for workers by labradores into the caja de comunidad. Corregidores collected tribute and made inspection tours. These Spaniards had to be handled so that they did not check head counts against church records too closely or audit the caja financial records too precisely. Bribes and acquiescence to a certain level of derramas (off-the-books gifts of money) were ways to achieve this, and it would have fallen to the justices to negotiate. Similarly, some unofficial arrangement would have to be worked out with each new priest or friar in terms of town support, prices for services, and sacerdotal intrusions into local affairs.

In no case did the justices deal from a position of any real strength. A politically well-connected official could get away with almost anything, and it was very dangerous to challenge directly the authority or integrity of a corregidor before the audiencia. Yet, for an official or friar to really "milk" a town was long, hard work. It was probably easier in most cases to strike a deal than try to wring every last drop from a town, especially as the latter course could, conceivably at least, come to the attention of higher authorities. This was probably even more likely in the case of the Cakchiquel towns close to the capital, where criollos, who particularly coveted such official positions (especially when held by a peninsular), would be more likely to denounce him. Indeed, bearing this out to some degree, the worst cases of extortion of Indian towns recorded come not from the Cakchiquel region but precisely from those areas farthest removed from the capital and with the fewest Spanish residents, such as Chiapas and the western Guatemala highlands (MacLeod 1973:314–317, 344–47; Lovell 1985:108–113).

The justices also represented their towns before the audiencia and its delegates in court cases concerning land and other community property. Any survey involving even a portion of a town's boundary had to be attended by the justices to ensure that the proper markers were used and to defend their town's interests if they were not. When such disputes could not be settled on the spot (as was usually the case), town justices would have to make the journey to the capital, retain Spanish counsel, and wait for the case to be heard and some initial disposition to be made. Afterward came the inevitable investigations, presentations of titulos, appeals, and counter-appeals.

All this could involve days of travel and weeks or even months of residence in the capital. It was time that the justices could otherwise have spent at their own homes, doing their own work. Also, money was needed for food and lodging, for the legal counsel, and for the costs of filing petitions and having duplicate documents of the proceedings drawn up as títulos for future reference (*see* below and Chapter 4). Funds might be taken from the caja de comunidad, but, as we have seen, its contents were already largely spoken for. Emergency contributions could be made from among a town's component parcialidades and wealthier residents, but the inevitable shortfall had to come from the justices' own pockets.

Finally, in terms of protecting their people from the Spaniards, the town justices attempted to resolve petty local disputes so that they did not come to the attention of the regional corregidor or the audiencia. This was a function granted the justices under Spanish law, but their effective performance meant that disputants were saved the time, expense, and potentially arbitrary, noncustomary (by Cakchiquel standards) decisions of Spanish administrators or courts. They also kept Spanish officials in the dark about internal community affairs (which, in turn, limits what we can reconstruct from Spanish records some three centuries later).

Cofradías served a similar barrier/broker function in dealings with ecclesiastical authority. As we have already seen, local churches and friars had to be supported, and the donations and payments for services from cofradías were an important part. Like cabildos, cofradías were required to keep financial records which would have to be verified by the parish priest, and perhaps even by a bishop. Yet, as long as the support was forthcoming, and maybe with an additional gift once in a while, the cofradía members could pretty much run their own affairs, organize and celebrate their respective patrons' fiestas, and perpetuate a great deal of traditional Cakchiquel belief and ritual in the process.

WRITING

The use of documents and writing has been alluded to or discussed in several places already. Far from being some peripheral activity controlled by the Spaniards, writing by Cakchiquel in Cakchiquel was a major medium of resistance to both Spanish rule and Spanish culture. This opposition took several forms, including nativism, innovation, and cultural resistance.

As participants in Mesoamerican civilization, the preconquest Cakchiquel were beneficiaries of a centuries-old, indigenous writing tradition. This does not mean that literacy was ever widespread among them. Indeed, it was probably limited to a small group of scribes, priests, and some members of the high aristocracy, who in turn were just the sort of people most likely to be eliminated by the Spanish conquest. Yet, early in the Colonial period, Spanish friars, who intended to instruct the sons of the surviving aristocracy, introduced alphabetic writing using European characters and materials. One friar, Francisco de la Parra, even developed new characters to represent sounds in Cakchiquel not present in the Spanish alphabet. A few other Cakchiquel may have been taught writing in order to act as town scribes—to keep the caja accounts, read dispatches and other official correspondence, and occasionally initiate administrative paperwork. "But, having in a sense let the genie of writing out of the bottle, the Spaniards were unable to control the range of uses to which the Cakchiquel . . . put writing" (Hill 1990).

Like other Mesoamerican peoples, the preconquest Cakchiquel seem to have had a fairly well-defined range of document types, though so far as we know no examples of any of these have survived into modern times. According to sixteenth-century Dominican friar/historian Bartolomé de las Casas, the preconquest Mexicans (and, by extension, other Mesoamericans) produced five kinds of "books." These included histories, books giving notice of the solemn and festal days of the year, books concerning dreams and auguries, books which told of the naming and "baptism" of children, and books describing rites and ceremonies (Las Casas 1958, II:341). The ancient Mesoamericans also produced other, shorter-length documents such as land boundary maps, and some of these may have accompanied the historical "books" to which Las Casas referred. Some Colonial Cakchiquel used the new, alphabetic writing to perpetuate at least two genres of preconquest documents for essentially nativistic purposes: calendrical divination manuals and dynastic or group histories.

Nativism is usually defined as a people's conscious attempt to perpetuate selected aspects of their culture as the result of some perceived threat. This is a common phenomenon of culture contact, since in such a situation a people may become cognizant of cultural differences vis-à-vis some other group, perhaps for the first time. Unfortunately, a common human reaction to such differences is to feel threatened by them, and nativistic movements of some sort are a result. Of course, in the case of the Colonial Cakchiquel, the threat to their culture was real enough. They were not simply a people in close contact with members of another, radically different culture. They were a people under siege culturally, and at least some Cakchiquel recognized the fact. Among them were some members of the indigenous aristocracy and higher-ranking ritual practitioners.

The divinatory manuals used by ritual specialists have a longer history in the Colonial period because, unlike aristocratic status, calendrical divination remained an important part of everyday life. While none of these texts has survived, they are described adequately in Colonial Spanish writings, right through to the end of the seventeenth century. Apparently, the Cakchiquel produced three kinds of manuals. The *vuh ahilabal q'ih,* or "book for counting birth dates," was the guide used to keep track of the 260-day divinatory calendar and was similar to the central Mexican *tonalamatl*. As discussed in Chapter 6, the day or "sun" under which an individual was born determined his or her natub, which conditioned each person's fate. The other days of the cycle also had special potentials, depending on the individual's birthday. With so many possible permutations, Cakchiquel calendar priests found it helpful to create reference guides in order to determine their clients' futures more readily. Divination through casting and counting seeds and crystals could also result in many possible outcomes. Accordingly, at least some diviners using this technique created a sort of handbook to which they could refer as they interpreted their lots. This book was called a *tzité q'am vuh*. The Cakchiquel also tracked the solar year, the agricultural cycle, and its attendant rituals in a type of book called *q'amutz*.

However much more was involved here than just the perpetuation of a quaint divinatory system. By preserving their way of tracking time, the Colonial Cakchiquel maintained the very structure and dynamics of their universe. The significance of this was lost on all of the Colonial Spanish writers, though Fuentes came closest to an appreciation of the Cakchiquel view of time when he wrote:

They believed with certainty in the immortality of the soul and afterwards, in a universal resurrection, they would return to have all their possessions such that they would not have to repair the defects and bad condition of their houses, saying that *thus they were left by their ancestors, and that thus they will return to possess the same lands that they possess at the time of their death.* And for this reason they keep hidden the silver mines and rich gold deposits. There is among them no promise or threat sufficient to reduce them to show them [to any Spaniard]. And, seeing themselves pressed, they respond that they know where [the mines] are but, *since the treasures are not theirs but rather of their ancestors who left them, they must exculpate themselves before the ancestors when they return to this world.* . . . (Fuentes y Guzmán 1969–1972, III:273)

. . . and this they did [bury grave goods with their dead in preconquest times] because they believed in the immortality of the soul. In this belief they have demonstrated their errors down to the present day [ca. 1690] as they say that there [after death] they needed to work and eat, needed servants to attend them, and that *they will return from there and once again possess their lands and treasures left buried and mines left covered up;* growing from this error, not being able to discover anything they know [about treasures and mines] because they say *what account would they give their ancestors when they return from that other world;* thinking and believing that they had gone to remote lands in which they were to labor as they did when they were here and that *they would return in the same appearance and beauty as when they had died.* (Fuentes y Guzmán 1969–1972, I:389–390), my emphasis)

No wonder the Cakchiquel were reluctant to leave their ancestors' lands; the latter were expected to return, and soon! As in the Fiesta del Volcán described in Chapter 1, the Cakchiquel concept of cyclical time meant that, eventually, the ancestors would return. Life would then be as it had been, before the Spaniards. A precondition for this happy state (and one which Fuentes in his effort to extract information from the Indians did not grasp) was the disappearance of the Spaniards. In this way, the Cakchiquel future was viewed as millenarian but also distinctly nativistic. They envisioned their future as a return to the "good old days" of their ever more distant, preconquest past.

These beliefs must have had a profound impact on the ability of the Cakchiquel to deal emotionally, psychologically, and spiritually with the facts of the conquest and their subsequent status as members of an economically exploited and politically subordinated population. Using a cyclical view of time, all of their problems could be understood as only part of a passing phase, not a permanent condition. It must, therefore, eventually elapse, and with the return of the ancestors to reclaim the domains guarded by loyal descendants, all Cakchiquel would be reunited in a world empty of Spaniards and free of their dominion. "Preserving their order of time through their calendars thus ultimately preserved both a vision of an orderly, comprehensible universe and hope for the future" (Hill 1990).

In contrast, Colonial-period historical writings in the indigenous tradition were a much more fleeting phenomenon, barely enduring until the beginning of our period, reflecting a less successful nativistic attempt.

In 1573, septuagenarian Francisco Hernández Arana Xahil began to set down in Cakchiquel a chronicle of his family, members of which had in the past been coleaders of the Iximché polity. This work has come to be known as the "Memorial de Sololá" (named after the town in which it was composed) or "The Annals of the Cakchiquels." In terms of content, it conforms to Las Casas' description of such "books." Las Casas stated that these dynastic histories contained notices of general events, fiestas, and the passage of the years; accounts of their wars, victories, and heroic deeds; the origin, succession and genealogies of their principal lords and the histories of their reigns; the weather, both good and bad; misfortunes, pestilences, other adversities, and under whose reign they had occurred; and the provinces and lands that had been conquered by the group up to the Spaniards' arrival (De Las Casas 1958, I:341).

Francisco himself was a direct descendant of Oxlahuh Tzii (Thirteen Dog, a calendrical name; he died in 1508), the most illustrious Xahil ruler. Because he was not born until the beginning of the sixteenth century, Francisco must have relied on some preconquest document or oral tradition for much of the chronicle, since family history and "national" history are merged and extended back into mythical times long before his own birth. This gave both the family and the polity the legitimizing aura of ancient lineage back to the times of the legendary Toltecs. The history continues in episodic fashion as per De Las Casas' description, recounting the major events during the association of the Xahil family's branch of the Cakchiquel with the Quiché of Utatlán, up until their separation following the revolt of the Quiché ruler's sons about 1470. Absolute history (with dates) begins here with the abandonment by these Cakchiquel of their old home near present-day Chichicastenango. The chronicle now records the genealogies of the Xahil and other ruling families of the new Iximché polity, their accessions, deaths, wars, and political maneuvers, climaxed by the Tukuché revolt in 1493. This event served as the starting point of the so-called Iximché calendar mentioned in Chapter 6, based on 400-day "years."

Francisco's own contributions include his boyhood memory of the arrival of Mexican ambassadors to Iximché in 1510 and a personal account of the Spanish conquest, with dates still tied to the Iximché calendar, suggesting that he or someone else had been keeping a register of events during that turbulent period. Yet, tellingly, Francisco did not end his chronicle with the conquest. Instead, he continued to make ever more mundane entries until his death about 1582. For twenty-three more years, another descendant of Oxlahuh Tzii, Pacal Francisco Diaz Xahil took up the task. Pacal was two generations younger than Francisco and also lived in Sololá. The trend of the entries to be more personal and commonplace accelerates. No longer is the succession of rulers discussed, but instead, the change of cabildo officers. Wars and palace intrigues have been replaced by accounts of assaults, drunkenness, and marital squabbles; the passing of lords replaced by the births and tragically frequent deaths of little children struck down by imported diseases. Pacal himself had no surviving children when he died in 1605, and evidently no other Xahil were concerned enough to continue the task.

Why had the chronicle been started in the first place and continued for two generations? The chroniclers' intentions were clearly nativistic. As members of what had been one of the highest-ranking families, they were acutely aware of their endangered status in a Colonial society in which the Spaniards had established themselves as the new aristocracy. How, in Cakchiquel terms, could that endangered status be perpetuated? The answer, at least in part, for Francisco and Pacal was to continue the chronicle, "effectively attaching an ongoing account of postconquest events to the end of a traditional, preconquest Mesoamerican family history, using the same basic format, chronological reference points, and system of time computation and including much of the same kind of information, despite the fact that the Xahil no longer enjoyed anything like their former preeminent social position" (Hill 1990). Theirs was an almost desperate attempt to perpetuate a social status rendered obsolete by the conquest.

Poignantly and inevitably, however, the effort was doomed to failure. Francisco and members of his generation had firsthand experience of traditional, preconquest Cakchiquel life, and for them at least some of the anxieties and emotional trauma of the conquest could be lessened simply by continuing the chronicle, thus retaining a direct physical link with their glorious past. Two generations later, a descendant like Pacal knew of such things and times only at second or third hand. He could only inscribe the everyday events of town life in an increasingly irrelevant effort to perpetuate a status with which he and others of his generation were unfamiliar. With Pacal's passing, the effort ended. Continuing the chronicle would have meant passing the job of family historian over two more generations, to individuals even more unfamiliar with their past and probably well on their way to the peasant status occupied by most of their fellows.

The Xahil were not alone in their attempt. In 1554, Alonso Perez Xpantzay, head of another prominent Iximché family, penned a shorter chronicle but one very similar in terms of subject matter to the Xahil history. In 1581, his son and successor, Felipe Vázquez Xpantzay, added a description of his chinamit's traditional boundaries, proceeding in the customary Mesoamerican manner of describing the circuit of its boundary markers. As an old man in 1602, Felipe wrote another document of a genealogical nature, in which he tried to bridge the immediate pre- and postconquest periods. His concern was to document that his own family members were the direct descendants of the last of the preconquest Xpantzay rulers, Hunlahuh Can, and that members of the Orozco family, who claimed a similar condition, were in fact nothing but the children of Hunlahuh Can's concubine slave, with no legitimate right to aristocratic status. Felipe seems to have taken the time late in life to create this genealogy in order to give his descendants some documentary evidence to present should their rank ever be contested by the Orozcos.

Yet the challenge never came. As with the Xahil family, the death of the second postconquest generation of Xpantzay saw an end to the family history, and presumably an end to concerns with documenting aristocratic status back to before the conquest as well. It was becoming clear to the Cakchiquel that elite social status in their communities during the Colonial period would depend more on wealth acquired through innovative combinations of Spanish and indigenous technologies, hard work, and luck than on simple descent from preconquest aristocrats. Miguel Perez Pirir claimed no such status for himself (though he was almost certainly entitled to it), nor did he feel any need to compose a family chronicle in order to validate his standing. His family, possessions, wealth, and gifts to the church were clearly enough.

In contrast to their western neighbors at Iximché, the preconquest rulers of the eastern Cakchiquel or Chajomá seem not to have had dynastic histories. Perhaps they were even more recent arrivals in their domains and had not yet consolidated their positions to the point that they could concern themselves with such matters. Perhaps paramount rulers, such as those of the Iximché polity, had not yet emerged. Perhaps such histories existed but have been lost or destroyed over the years. Whatever the case, the surviving Chajomá documents were all composed early in the Colonial period and are decidedly group or "national" histories. They lack the dynastic tack-ons of the western Cakchiquel aristocrats, and may thus represent an even more ancient form of Mesoamerican historical account (López Austin 1973).

The most comprehensive of the Chajomá histories is the so-called Título de los del pueblo de San Martín Jilotepéque, written in 1555 (Crespo 1956). This is the same document presented in 1689 by the San Martín people in their dispute with the group from Xenacoj (*see* Chapter 4). For these western Chajomá, group history begins with their departure from the Joyabaj area (probably in the late 1400s), an episode similar to the emigration of the western Cakchiquel from the Chichicastenango area. In proper Mesoamerican form, the history enumerates the succession of settlements occupied by the Chajomá prior to arriving at their final preconquest home and lists the sequence of rulers. It ends with a description of the group's territory, proceeding in the traditional manner from boundary marker to boundary marker, which corresponds very closely to the limits of present-day San Martín.

The eastern Chajomá of San Juan and San Pedro Sacatepéquez produced three much shorter documents with the participation and concordance of the San Martín people in 1550. These consist of a very brief history of settlement prior to the conquest, the sequence of leaders, and a boundary description accompanied by a map. These documents were all presented by the justices of San Juan in their 1707 dispute with the Pirir family (*see* Chapter 4). We cannot determine exactly why these Chajomá documents were produced when they were but there was apparently no effort to extend their chronological coverage further than the middle 1500s. Whatever their original purpose, it was evidently fulfilled by the one-time event of composition. Still, it is clear that the documents were revered by successive generations of these people and that they functioned effectively as group títulos throughout the Colonial period.

While the Colonial Cakchiquel waited for the flow of time to free them from foreign rule, they also had to deal pragmatically with the new order. Therefore, they went beyond using writing to perpetuate preconquest types of documents containing information of traditional interest. They also applied the new writing technology in innovative ways to a variety of problems and opportunities created by the Colonial situation. Most of these uses, both public and private, centered on the acquisition, retention, and inheritance of land. We have already seen in Chapter 4 that Spanish law was liberal in admitting almost any document as proof of prior ownership or use of land as the basis for its continued occupation in Colonial times. The Cakchiquel quickly recognized the value of written records, which they referred to by the generic term *títulos* in dealing with the audiencia, and developed their own range of documents to use as ammunition in court should the occasion ever arise.

Cédulas were rudimentary bills of sale for land, which accompanied many unofficial Indian transactions, usually executed at the request of the buyer. As will be remembered, the Colonial Cakchiquel could not legally buy or sell land unless they had previously purchased it from the crown via composición, and most of them never went to the expense or bother to do this. Still, given fluctuating population and uncertain individual or family survival, landowning Cakchiquel individuals in particular needed the flexibility to adjust the sizes of their holdings as the need or opportunity arose. One family could be all but wiped out by disease and unable to work all of its land; another could be in desperate need of cash to pay its tribute obligations or meet some other expense. A wealthy individual might be in a position to take advantage of such situations by purchasing the generally small plots of land put up for sale by people in such straights. However, the buyer would want some protection or assurance that his purchase was secure, that there would not be some future claim to the property by the sellers, their relatives, or descendants. Accordingly, these cédulas were drawn up, usually by the town scribe, as proof of the transfer of "ownership." At least in the late sixteenth century, such transfers, when conducted among aristocrats, were formal affairs witnessed by the town justices, who were later the guests of the buyer at a special feast. In this way, in addition to the cédula, the buyer could also call the justices to attest to the transaction should the need arise, even if they were by that time out of office. Through the use of cédulas, many petty, local land disputes were probably avoided or at least settled by town justices without the Spanish authorities ever hearing of them. Such official ignorance likely permitted the use of cédulas to become all the more ingrained in Cakchiquel practice.

The wills of two generations of the Pirir family suggest that the use of cédulas became more common as the seventeenth century wore on. In his will of 1642, patriarch Miguel Perez Pirir counted among his other holdings thirteen properties of various kinds, including houses, town lots, agricultural tracts, a forge, and a mountain hunting preserve. Undoubtedly, over the course of his long career, Miguel had bought and sold other properties as well. Yet he only mentioned having a cédula for the hunt lands, which may have been one of his last purchases. This suggests that, prior to midcentury, ambitious wheeler-dealers felt that there was no need for documenting their transactions. Probably the low population level and favorable man/land ratio meant that no one would need later to challenge transfers made during this period. In contrast, while Miguel's son and primary heir, Domingo, was no slouch when it came to buying real estate, he was much more careful to document his transactions. Of the dozen properties listed in his will of 1669 as having been purchased, he specifically noted his possession of cédulas for fully half of them. Domingo was also the one to petition for and receive a royal despacho de ámparo (restraining order forbidding expropriation) for the main Navorón holding. Conditions were changing. Spaniards were becoming more covetous of Indian land in the vicinity of the capital as the seventeenth-century depression lengthened. Cakchiquel populations may already have been showing signs of recovery. Much land had already been given over to livestock. Domingo was cautious.

Of course, acquiring land was of little benefit to individual Cakchiquel unless it could be passed on to descendants securely. For this purpose, the Cakchiquel developed *testamentos,* or wills (see Figure 8–1). Also written by town scribes, this type of document seems to have been most common in the seventeenth century, when social stratification among the Indians still existed. Although the wealthy would have more to pass on to their descendants, wills might be commissioned by anyone with something to protect and the fee for the scribe. An Indian will had little official binding force beyond the town of the testator. Yet both within and beyond the town, testamentos were useful documents. Within the town society, wills were at least as powerful as cédulas in terms of protecting property. Cakchiquel wills were deathbed statements, made before God and witnessed by the town justices, parcialidad leadership, and the beneficiaries. The testator's statements concerning property he or she owned were presumed to be true, all the more so if cédulas existed to back up the claims and in the absence of any contradiction from the town justices or other parcialidad members. The lack of argument from heirs at the time the will was dictated indicated their tacit acceptance of its conditions, leaving little grounds for squabbling over their inheritances later. Such arguments as did occur subsequently among the heirs could be more readily settled by the justices since they only had to review the provisions of the will and note that the disputants

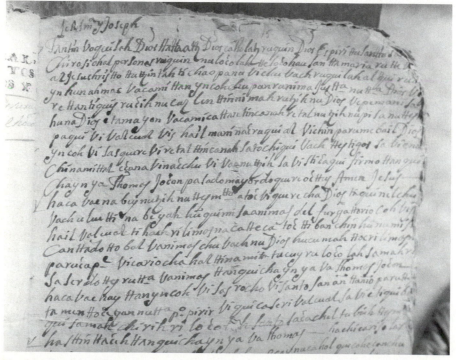

Figure 8 Detail of the first page of Thomás Jocón's 1708 testamento (photo by the author of the original document in the municipal archives of San Juan Sacatepéquez).

had agreed to them. Yet, as uncontested deathbed statements concerning land possession, testamentos could also function as títulos before the audiencia. Domingo Perez Pirir presented his father's testamento in support of his successful petition to be granted a royal ámparo in 1655. Juan de la Cruz Pirir submitted both Miguel's and Domingo's wills as evidence in the family's 1707 litigation with San Juan Sacatepéquez, where they were accepted as legitimate by both the town justices and presiding Spanish official and made some compromise by the town inevitable. Diego Perez Xpantzay introduced his mother's testamento as evidence in his 1689 dispute with members of the Poromá parcialidad of Tecpán, where it was central to his ultimate victory.

In contrast to the essentially private character of cédulas and testamentos, *convenios,* or covenants, were written agreements regarding the use, possession, or division of land or other property reached by larger corporate groups such as families, parcialidades, or towns. The contract between "foreign" and "native" Sacapultecos described in Chapter 3 is an example of a convenio. In it they settled a number of matters, including trespass on each other's lands, the division of town offices, the organization of town funds, and the maintenance of the town horse herd. Because convenios were records of agreements regarding land, the Indians carefully kept them like other títulos, in order to present them as evidence should any dispute ever arise. For example, the justices of San Juan Sacatepéquez presented in evidence a convenio from 1607 in their dispute with the Pirir family a century later in 1707. In addition, Diego Perez Xpantzay also submitted the convenio drawn up between his mother and uncle in 1635, witnessed (and thus approved) by the justices and local priest of the time, in his 1689 litigation.

In this discussion, writing by the Cakchiquel may have come to seem so commonplace, so normal an activity that we are in danger of missing its full importance. The very act of writing in the Cakchiquel language was an eloquent act of cultural resistance. It constituted a conscious rejection of the conqueror's language while, at the same time, appropriating his writing technology for their own ends. The uses of writing to perpetuate their view of time, the dynamics of their universe, and ties to the ancestors were also clearly attempts to resist Spanish pressures for change. Additionally, however, writing was (and is) power, and through writing the Cakchiquel were able to arm themselves with a "counter-corpus" of documents in their own language, incomprehensible to the vast majority of Spaniards, in response to the Spaniards' arsenal of documents whose content was impenetrable to all but a few Cakchiquel. Thus, the unique Cakchiquel identity, sense of apartness from the invaders, and a sense of control were reinforced "anytime one wrote, referred to, read from, listened to, or presented as evidence a document in that language" (Hill 1990).

TÍTULOS AND LITIGATION

From the preceding discussion, documents and legal action seem to have gone hand in hand for the Colonial Cakchiquel. While actual litigation does not seem to have been frequent, the Cakchiquel constantly prepared for it all the same. They carefully guarded as "títulos" the entire range of their own documents, plus the ámparos granted by the audiencia, and records of prior litigations against the day when they might be needed as evidence in court. For example, even the Xpantzay documents were not forgotten. On the contrary, they were carefully preserved as títulos and were presented as such in a litigation brought by the town of Tecpán against an encroaching Spanish landowner in 1659. The Tecpán people's ultimate victory in that case was due in no small part to the Xpantzay documents (especially the boundary description), which demonstrated Indian occupation of the disputed area long before their Spanish opponent's arrival.

But documentary evidence was only half the issue if litigation were contemplated. It was also necessary to enlist someone who was familiar with "the system," who knew how to file petitions with the audiencia, how to use the different títulos as evidence, who know Spanish law and legal custom and could thus structure and present an argument in the highly formalized setting of court. This was knowledge that no Indian possessed or was likely to acquire given the Spaniards' monopoly of the field. The Cakchiquel solution (one used by other highland Maya as well) was to retain Spanish counsel (or *procuradores*) to represent them before the audiencia. These men were professionals whose livelihoods depended on their reputations for giving their clients good service. A win in court was still a win, even if "only" on behalf of Indian clients. It still enhanced the reputation of an ambitious procurador. Besides, the Indians' money was as good as any Spaniard's. At the same time, a loss was a loss and a blow to the procurador's professional standing. Other potential clients might seek out someone else instead. Thus, for purely practical reasons, the Indians could be fairly sure of at least adequate representation in court.

Cronyism, venality, and collusion on the part of private Spaniards and officials were still distinct possibilities given the tenor of the times and the low salaries, but by the seventeenth century there were some safeguards, both intentional and accidental. First of all, royal officials were routinely instructed to give the Indians every consideration in legal matters, especially litigations. One high-ranking official, the fiscal, or crown attorney, was also required to function as *protector de Indios* (protector of the Indians) and to review all decisions made by the audiencia regarding Indian interests. Still, even these efforts to guarantee impartiality would have counted for little without two other factors. One of these was the institutionalized review of an official's tenure in office at the end of his term, called *juicios de residencia*. During such residencias, charges of misconduct were investigated, and, if proven, the guilty official was subject to fines and imprisonment. The other factor operating to ensure something of a fair hearing for the Indians during the 1600s was the unintentional fact of antagonism between criollos and peninsulares, and the fact that the crown overwhelmingly appointed the latter to administrative positions in the audiencia of Guatemala. While both were technically Spaniards, the criollos resented the fact that they were generally passed over for such appointments and were envious of peninsular officeholders. At the same time, peninsulares were usually disdainful of criollos, whom they felt were lazy and unsophisticated. The result of this mutual dislike was that peninsular officials did not necessarily have any bias in favor of criollo litigants in cases involving Indians. Indeed, impressionistically, the tenor of some statements of royal officials in a few of the land litigation records is one of paternalistic sympathy for the Indians and exasperation with the criollos. Of course, disputes among Indians were also exasperating for the Spanish officials involved, but barring the rare case of collusion between official and Indian litigant (*see* Hill and Monaghan 1987:104–110), magistrates generally had no personal interest in the outcome of the cases they heard.

The combination of *títulos* as documentary evidence and *procuradores* representing the Indians' interests before the *audiencia* proved to be a powerful combination. True, the Spaniards could not be made to disappear, nor could those Cakchiquel lands already in Spanish hands by the early 1600s be recovered. Yet, as illustrated by some of the cases referred to in this chapter, the Cakchiquel were able consistently to defend their remaining lands against further Spanish encroachment through the remainder of the seventeenth century, and indeed the rest of the Colonial period.

All of this should not be mistaken as an apology for Spanish colonialism. Especially by today's standards, it was a harsh system under which few would choose to live. However, it was a stable structure which ultimately endured almost three hundred years among the highland Maya. As we have seen in this chapter, the Cakchiquel early on developed ways to compromise and even resist it with no little success.

BIBLIOGRAPHIC NOTE

The broker/barrier concepts were first applied to Indian-run Colonial institutions by MacLeod (1973). Collins (1980) provides an in-depth treatment of this subject in a specific (non-Cakchiquel) town. Information on prorogación in Sumpango comes from AGCA document A3.12 Leg.2775 Exp.40097. The "Annals of the Cakchiquels" has been partly translated into English (Brinton 1885, Recinos 1957). The Xpantzay documents are accessible only in Spanish (Berlin 1950), as is the history of the Jilotepéque Chajomá (Crespo 1956). The eastern Chajomá documents are unpublished and contained in AGCA document A3.15 Leg.2787 Exp.40301, as are the Pirir wills (Hill 1989b).

9 / Patan: The Burdens of Life

The preconquest Mesoamericans were not very optimistic about life. A great measure of an individual's potential in life was determined at birth by the sun under which he or she had been born, and there was little that could be done about it. To a large extent, individuals simply had to accept their fates as determined by their natub/tonalli. Continued healthy existence depended in large part on fulfilling one's fate thus decided. Death awaited all, but for most, any afterlife was even drearier than existence in this world. This attitude is summed up succinctly and eloquently by one of the most famous of the Aztec speeches of greeting to a newborn:

> Thou hast come to reach the earth, the place of torment, the place of pain, where it is hot, where it is cold, where the wind bloweth. It is the place of one's affliction, of one's weariness, a place of thirst, a place of hunger, a place where one freezeth, a place of weeping. It is not true that it is a good place; it is a place of weeping, a place of sorrow, a place where one suffereth. (Sahagún 1950–1969, Book 6:176–177)

The preconquest Cakchiquel expressed much of their ambivalence about life through the term *patan*. Patan literally means "burden," the kind that Mesoamerican porters traditionally bore on their backs supported by a tumpline across the forehead. But the Cakchiquel extended the term metaphorically to denote a variety of the obligations of life. Paying tribute was patan, as was working in the fields or performing some service for others. Patan not only pertained to humans but was part of the cosmic order as well. "Gods and men, animals and implements, lords and commoners are . . . assigned their duties (which are by implication their functions and their positions in the cosmos)" (Edmonson 1971:17).

Even though much changed for the Cakchiquel with their conquest and Colonial administration by the Spaniards, they retained and even expanded their concept of patan. The Colonial Cakchiquel still paid tribute and performed labor service (though to new masters) and these remained patan. They now also supported the cult of the saints and increasingly served in public offices, which became ever more onerous, both financially and in terms of time spent away from family and work. Accordingly, we find the term patan extended to include both new activities. *Patanibal* ("burdensome thing") was a synonym for cofradía and *ah patan* ("he of the burden" or "burden carrier") was used to refer to anyone in public office. In a broader sense, life itself was patan, during the course of which individuals were obliged to shoulder a variety of burdens.

BIRTH AND CHILDHOOD

Childbirth is an inherently anxious time for parents and relatives. It was even more so for the Cakchiquel because the "sun" of the 260-day divinatory calendar on which the child was born determined the nature of his natub, which in turn decided much about his personality, talents, and fate in life (*see* Chapter 6). Indeed, the divinatory calendar itself seems to be related to the length of the human gestation period, measured from the beginning of the first twenty-day period in which a woman missed her menses and thus knew that she was pregnant. The developing fetus thus ran the entire round of possible fates as determined by the 260-day calendar, to be born on one specific day, a literal "wheel of fortune."

During labor and delivery, the mother was attended by one or more midwives who used massage to ease labor pains and assist with a difficult delivery. After the birth, mother and infant repaired to the nearest stream, where both bathed. Then they returned home, where they lay on a cane bed, under which a bed of coals was kept hot enough to make mother and child sweat. According to Cakchiquel thought, this practice helped avoid loss of the mother's natub and prevent "cold" illnesses. To these ends she also drank concoctions made largely from chiles. She rested for four days, then returned to her normal household duties. For the infant, the heat of the fire was a vital substitute for the heat of the sun. It would keep him alive but would not impart to him the natub, the latter being the single most important event in the individual's life.

To be born on an inauspicious day was a curse. Fortunately, Cakchiquel parents, like their counterparts in other areas of Mesoamerica, could do something about their child's natub. A special ceremony performed by an ah q'ih was necessary to fix the natub in the child, and this ritual could be performed on any of the days shortly following the birth (perhaps up to thirteen as in Aztec practice; *see* López Austin 1988:212). Thus, if the actual birthday was unpropitious, parents might obtain a better natub for their child by having the ah q'ih perform the name-giving ceremony on one of the succeeding days. According to Fuentes:

> . . . upon the day that a child was born they gave him [the ah q'ih] notice of it, he noted the day of the birth and, in due course went to the house of the child's parents; the mother came out with the child in her arms and presented it to him; he went with it behind the house and there, with many ceremonies, he invoked the devil who appeared, if the child had been born on the second of January, in the form of a snake. He requested [the snake] to protect and defend the infant from danger: he took the hand of the child and put it on the snake as a sign of friendship and recognition and with this returned to the house with the parents of this miserable and innocent child, responsible for taking it out every day at the same hour to the yard where the Nagual would again appear. . . . (Fuentes y Guzmán 1969–1972, I:280)

The "many ceremonies" most probably included the ritual bath, which constituted a symbolic rebirth of the child, after which he could be exposed to the sun and receive his natub. Otherwise, Fuentes confused the nagual (the animal form taken by the externalized uxla of a powerful person; *see* Chapter 6) with the *tona*.

According to this latter, widespread Mesoamerican belief, some wild animal was born at the same moment as each child, and thereafter both would share the same fate. Thus, if a person's tona were a deer and that animal were killed by another animal or a human hunter, the person would die at the same moment. In this way, each Cakchiquel was tied intimately to the natural world and sudden, unexplainable death with no other symptoms could be understood.

Most of the time, Cakchiquel infants were kept bound to cradle boards, much like those of some North American Indian tribes. As a result of this practice, Spanish friar and dictionary compiler Thomás Coto noted the tendency for Indians to have flattened occipital portions of their skulls. A wooden bow projected from the top of the board, which protected the infant's head should the cradle board accidently tip over. The board could be hung from two ropes attached to beams in the house, and the child gently rocked to sleep. Parents hung a cloth from the bow to protect the child from insects and dusty winds, as well as loss of his natub.

Like other Mesoamericans, the Cakchiquel believed that an infant's natub was fixed in him only tenuously and was thus most susceptible to loss. That was why children became ill and died so much more frequently than adults. And in a world with high infant mortality, children could be the objects of others' envy, which emanated as part of the uxla. Consciously or unconsciously, these noxious emanations could jar an infant's natub loose, and without it the child could last a much shorter time than adults. This belief is still widespread today and is called *mal de ojo* in Spanish, or "the evil eye." Effects of the evil eye could be avoided by concealing the child as much as possible, and when seclusion was impossible, by covering its face and head (the seat of the natub) with a cloth barrier to harmful emanations.

Some Colonial Cakchiquel may also have continued to follow the preconquest custom of using the umbilical cord in some context associated with the child's future. According to Fuentes, this involved cutting off a boy's umbilical cord with a new, unused obsidian blade, which was later thrown into a river as a sacred object. They burned the blood and held an ear of corn with variegated kernels in the resulting smoke. They kept the ear until planting time, when the kernels were carefully removed and sowed in the child's name. The resulting crop was planted again, with some of it used to feed him, and so on " . . . until he reached the age when he could plant for himself, saying that thus he not only ate by the sweat of his brow but of his own blood as well" (Fuentes y Guzmán 1969–1972, I:281).

Children reportedly were breastfed exclusively for their first three years and might be lulled to sleep while riding in a cloth tied to mother's back as she ground corn on her metate. The mother herself reportedly ate no other food but dishes made from corn, like tortillas and tamales. She would not touch meat, even if it was available. Similarly, once weaned, children ate nothing at first but foods prepared from corn, adding to this when older some sauce of chiles and tomatoes. Toddlers went naked (according to the climate) until four or five years, at which time boys received a pair of short trousers or a little loincloth. Girls presumably got short skirts and small huipiles.

At about this time, children were first introduced to the concept of patan in the first rite of passage of which they were conscious. As soon as a child could walk well enough, he or she was loaded with a small burden. This was probably a little load of wood for a boy and a tiny jar of water for a girl. Led by the hand by mother, they went to visit the grandparents, to whom they carried the load as a gift. Through his homey little ritual, children were introduced both to their adult roles, which involved carrying literal burdens, and to their lifelong obligations to others, which, figuratively, are also patan.

Childhood seems to have been short but was clearly distinguished from adulthood. For example, the Colonial-period dictionaries contain some terms for the toys parents fashioned for their children. These included dolls of baked clay or of carved wood and stuffed toys made from the skins of small animals or birds, filled with straw. The dictionaries also hint at the games children played. *Soq'* was the Cakchiquel version of "la gallina ciega," or blindman's bluff. Children could also bounce or play catch with a solid ball of native rubber (this in contrast to the ritual ballgame of Mesoamerica in which use of the hands was expressly forbidden). *Qakoh che* was a form of ninepins or bowling, using a wooden ball and pins. Still, as soon as physically capable, the appropriate parent according to sex began to train the child in all the tasks he or she would need to know as an adult.

Girls stayed at home and learned from their mothers how to grind corn, even having little metates and manos to work with. Weaving or pottery-making skills were also passed on in this way. According to Fuentes, girls from the better Indian families were carefully watched from the time they were about eight until they were married, lest they fall into bad company and fail to be properly industrious or, later, form sexual liaisons. Fathers were no less careful with their sons for the same reasons, but by the time boys were in their teens, men's work frequently carried them out of reach of parental control. Repartimiento obligations or wage labor could mean long periods away from home. Still, while bachelors, they were expected to bring all their earnings to their fathers, before whom they were to maintain a respectful silence until bidden to speak.

MARRIAGE

Full adult status came with marriage. However, this did not mean an end to obligations to parents and others of more senior generations. In a real sense, for both male and female, marriage meant assuming additional burdens.

The selection of spouses varied according to social stratum. For commoners, there appear to have been no specific rules. There may anciently have been some rule for chinamit endogamy, but this had broken down under the combined pressures of population loss and congregación in the sixteenth century. Thus, by the seventeenth century, one was not required to marry someone of the same parcialidad, but most people seem to have chosen a spouse from the same town. An ah q'ih was consulted to see if the spouses-to-be would be compatible, according to the "suns" of their birth, which had determined the characteristics of each one's natub. When potential spouses were from different parcialidades, the respective leaders of both groups presided over formal negotiations that might drag on for several months.

The main subject of these discussions was to establish the amount of bride price to be paid by the man's family or the nature of the bride service to be performed by the groom in compensation to the bride's family for the loss of a productive worker. Among commoners, bride service seems to have been the usual option since it involved no out-of-pocket expenses for the groom and his family. Bride service usually lasted a year and included such duties as working in the milpas of his future father-in-law, hauling wood and water to his house, and sweeping the grounds. These activities might be accompanied by such small presents as the groom could afford, perhaps an occasional gift of tasajo or cacao. The bride brought with her only her skills, though, especially if she were a skilled weaver or potter, she could be a valuable addition to the groom's family, balancing the inevitable loss of sisters and daughters to other families.

Once they had negotiated the precise terms of the marriage, they notified the town priest a year in advance of the actual wedding, and he noted the fact of the betrothal as well as its conditions in a formal document. Thus, according to Fuentes, the Indians were accustomed to respond to the question of whether or not they were married by saying: "I have my contract," by which they indicated that they were betrothed (Fuentes y Guzmán 1969–1972, III:271). If the contract were broken by, say, the groom not working to the satisfaction of his prospective father-in-law, or failure to pay the bride price when stipulated, the bride's father could cancel the agreement by reimbursing the man or his family for the goods and labor already provided.

In contrast, wealthy, aristocratic Cakchiquel were concerned generally to marry within their social stratum. For example, Miguel Perez Pirir's daughter, Petronila, married into the equally prominent Chamalé family, also of San Juan Sacatepéquez. This inherently meant a smaller pool of potential spouses and some corresponding differences in the contractual arrangements. In order to attract matches of the proper status for their children, parents employed both bride price and dowry. Thus, the groom's family would make some payment (perhaps very considerable) to that of the bride, while her family might bestow on her a piece of land or some livestock that her husband would work or manage for their children. In such cases, negotiations were probably very complex, with both sides trying to balance their desire for the "best deal" they could get with the need to acquire proper spouses for their children. On the other hand, a rich widow not too advanced in years might intentionally seek to marry a poor man to work her lands, hoping he would thus become dependent on her and likely to take good care of her. In his will, moderately well-to-do Thomás Jocón left his wife, Catharina, a tract of land, two cows and their calves, a mare and a mule, along with specific instructions to marry some pauper who would care for her (Hill 1989b:14, 88).

Regardless of rank, women generally went to live with their husbands in or near the house of the latter's father, a pattern called patrilocal residence. Yet exceptions could occur. A man might not have any sons, or perhaps more likely, due to the continuing ravages of imported diseases, have no surviving sons. In such instances, a wealthy father in particular might adopt his daughter's husband and entrust him with the family holdings. This seems to have been the case with Pedro Pirir (one of Miguel's grandsons) in the later seventeenth century, who apparently adopted Thomás Jocón as his son when he married Pedro's adopted daughter, Melchora.

BURDENS OF ADULTHOOD

As active adults, the burdens of family support fell to young and middle-aged husbands and wives. While in their child-producing years, they suffered the heartbreaking losses of their children to disease, both as infants and later as adolescents and even adults. Such insecurity in terms of children's survival must have resulted in an emotional hardening and caution against investing roo much feeling in a child, who probably would not live very long. This reluctance to nurture might, in turn, have caused strong parental feelings of guilt, resulting in a decidedly ambivalent attitude toward parenthood. It was unavoidable, even necessary, but still an emotional and physical burden.

Not only did adults support themselves and their children, they also cared for the husband's aging parents, as is common in preindustrial, agricultural societies. Much of the day-to-day burden in terms of actual care must have fallen to the daughter(s)-in-law. In a large corporate family like that of the Pirires, the individual load might have been lessened by sharing the responsibilities. On the other hand, there was considerable potential for resentment by full-grown and even aging sons at taking orders from an aged patriarch who would not surrender control of his lands and enterprises until on his deathbed. Sons and their spouses might also quarrel among themselves and jockey for their father's favor in anticipation of his dividing his estate. Perhaps this infighting could be controlled to some extent by having the sons and their families live away from each other on the lands they worked or managed. Miguel Perez Pirir evidently tried this, but with only limited success. The rancor among his sons grew steadily after his initial brush with death in 1642, when, with the dictation of his will, they first discovered their shares of his estate. The old man was finally forced to divide his goods prior to his death in order to stop the squabbling.

Married couples and their children formed the basic tributario entero unit, and tribute exactions and repartimiento obligations fell most squarely on them. Yet this was also the time of life when men were called upon to serve in the most important town organizations, the cabildo and the cofradías. Support of guachibales was also necessary for anyone with aspirations for higher social standing in his town. As we have seen, all of these activities required that people's time be spent on things other than their own work. Repartimiento and cabildo office also demanded that time be spent away from home. Cofradía and guachibal participation and cabildo service required cash outlays as well.

ILLNESS

As another, tormenting, life-threatening burden, some form of illness was practically inevitable. As noted in Chapter 6, the Cakchiquel interpreted most illnesses as the result of some imbalance among bodily forces or an assault on the natub, causing its departure. The condition could be corrected but successful treatment depended on an accurate diagnosis of the cause of the illness, rather than simply attending to the symptoms. This was why ill Cakchiquel quickly sought out an ah cun. As Friar Antonio Margil recorded for the Quiché of the Pacific piedmont at the beginning of the eighteenth century:

> On some man or woman falling ill, they immediately called on one of the assistants [ah cun] of their parcialidad. He would go, view the infirm one and tell him "Son (or daughter, if a woman), in order for me to cure you it is necessary that first you confess to me and tell me all of your sins." And if the Indian had fallen ill in a cacao grove, he [the ah cun] would say that the Cacao God had made him ill and, if it happened in the forest, he told him that the Lord of it had made him ill, and so on.
>
> Knowing the story, he told the infirm one: "Do not worry, because I go now to pray to the Lord of the Forest for you, and will take him his food [copal incense] in your name. Your obligation now is to tell me all of your sins."
>
> The sick woman or man, in order to recover, agrees. Later, he calls the wife of the sick man or the husband if it is a sick woman. The ah cun sits down and the husband sits by his side and then the doctor says: "Woman, have no fear, your husband will pardon you. This [confession] is necessary, because otherwise you will die. Sir! Grant her pardon, because we are all sinners and, perhaps, tomorrow you will lose the same thing as your wife." The husband then says: "Yes, sir, I do pardon her as it should be clearly stated." The sick woman begins to speak and says: "It is true, sir, that I have had thus-and-such men; it is true that the malice my husband had for so-and-so was not false, because so-many times I offended God with that man." And thus proceeded the confession, as true and faithful hopefully, as they confess to their true [Catholic] priests. This done, the ah cun says: "Daughter, your husband is now satisfied. I now pardon your sins. In the name of the Father, the Son, and the Holy Spirit, Amen. (Margil 1704 in Dupiech-Cavaleri and Ruz 1988:246–247)

Margil has condensed several different sources of affliction and different curative techniques. Offense to supernaturals could result in their causing illness by assaulting or capturing the offender's natub. Such beings might relent in return for an apology conducted on the proper day of the divinatory calendar, accompanied by a gift of the food (incense) that only humans could provide. Sexual transgressions were another matter. Anology to Mexican belief indicates that illicit sex in particular could cause emanations of the uxla, the bodily force which was the source of passions. Uncontrolled passions were inherently dangerous and such emanations could cause illness in the transgressor or his family, the death of domesticated animals, or the rotting of food and problems with other material goods (López Austin 1988:293). Confession is a traditional Mesoamerican means of both appeasing angry supernaturals and reestablishing bodily equilibrium. In the case of marital infidelity, confession in the spouse's presence was a way to dissipate the noxious uxla emanations and reattain the balance among bodily forces necessary for health.

Margil was also clearly outraged that unordained Indians should have assumed part of the priestly role by hearing confessions and granting absolution:

> And asked by us if those sins would also be confessed to the fathers [friars], they responded no, because God is greater than the priest and, therefore, it was not necessary to tell again that which God had already once forgiven. (Margil 1704 in Dupiech-Cavaleri and Ruz 1988:247–248)

Margil did not realize that confession was an indigenous practice. However, he did note that it could take several different forms:

These wretched ones [the ah cunes] had three modes of confession. The first and most common was to put a candle in the hand of the infirm one while he confessed and, with the confession concluded, for the ah cun to put [burn] the candle in the church so that God might pardon the infirm one, and the ah cun spoke thus to Our Lord: "Pardon a little bit, God; and perhaps I shall go to the forest to put your copal before that ancient one [deity or manifestation of the godhead]." This done, the ah cun left as a flash of lightning to the forest with the copal which the infirm one had given him, and he made a great plea to the Lord of the Forest, which they call Xaquicosal [Saki Coxol], who is the Devil, or Tzitzimite. He put the copal before one of the fat trees; or ceibas . . . in which they all had their faith and hope, and upon burning the copal, the tree and the area around it trembled.

   The other two methods of confessing used nine flowers or nine cacao beans in the hand of the infirm one, with the same ceremonies, and the nine cacao beans or flowers he [the ah cun] put upon the tombs of their ancestors. (Margil 1704 in Dupieche-Cavaleri and Ruz 1988:247)

In all cases, the pattern of confession was the same. Some object(s) absorbs the sins contained in the confession for transmission to some supernatural(s), a god, the ancestors, who, in turn, it was hoped, would forgive the transgression.

   Another possible cause of illness among the Colonial Cakchiquels was an imbalance between "hot" and "cold" substances to which the body was exposed. This hot-cold dichotomy is still widespread among Mesoamerican peoples, reflecting the traditional division of their universe into an upper, hot level (due to its domination by the sun) and a lower, cold one (due to its association with water and the subterranean). Things and even activities partook of these qualities, irrespective of their actual temperature. The Cakchiquel viewed man as an intersection of these two realms, partaking of both hot and cold but normally tending to be somewhat hot (due no doubt to the natub, which, as a force imparted by the sun, was naturally hot). While information on this subject is sparce, it seems that the Cakchiquel were most concerned with illness caused by cold imbalance.

   The standard treatment was to reestablish the balance between hot and cold by exposing the patient to some source of heat. This could include the rays of the sun itself, sweat baths, bathing in volcanic hot springs (as in San Antonio Aguascalientes during the mid-seventeenth-century epidemic; see Chapter 6), or eating "hot" foods. Alternatively, excessive heat, resulting from overexposure to the sun, for example, could be treated by bathing in cold water. "Cold" foods would be prescribed for illness resulting from overingesting "hot" foods, and so on. While most such hot-cold imbalances were the direct results of individual actions (such as eating) or environmental variables (such as intense sun), some "cold" diseases could also be sent by supernaturals associated with water. These included the guardian spirits of springs and rivers, such as those the Cakchiquel called the ah xulub.

   In any case, as we can see even from the limited data at our disposal, the multiple potential causes of illness meant that diagnosis was a complex process, yet absolutely necessary in order to effect a cure. Was the individual suffering from soul loss, from exposure to someone else's emanations, or a hot-cold imbalance? For each of these possibilities the cause had also to be determined. Was it a punishment from some supernatural being, the result of the individual's own, incautious actions, or, perhaps, sorcery? Curative techniques were specific, not general; it was useless to apologize to some supernatural when trying to cure an illness caused only by the patient's having eaten too much "cold" food. Accordingly, accurate diagnoses were both essential and difficult, and the failure of a particular practitioner to cure was understood as the result of a faulty diagnosis or insufficient power (in the case of treating illnesses due to sorcery), rather than as a fundamental flaw in the belief system itself. In such instances, as in our own society, one had to try another course of treatment or seek out another practitioner (as did Martín García Belesuy, though to no avail; see Chapter 6), perhaps one with more training, like an ah tzité or even an ah q'ih.

Illness was a burden only partly because of the suffering involved. There was also the expense. Practitioners like the ah cun, ah tzité, or ah q'ih did not perform their services for free. Unfortunately, we do not know how they charged for their services, but it probably involved both a scale for practitioners (with the ah cun charging the least and the ah q'ih the most) as well as clients (with richer Cakchiquel having to pay more for services). As illnesses lingered and cures failed, increasingly desperate people must have sought help from several, perhaps many, different practitioners. Many families must have been reduced to poverty in this way, a pattern well documented ethnographically among highland Maya in this century.

DYING AND BEQUEATHING

Death was understood as the result of some incurable illness. A final burden before leaving life was to dispose of one's property. The majority of Cakchiquel probably did not have many possessions to leave as an estate. As we have seen, most only held land by virtue of their membership in a parcialidad, so it could only be apportioned among heirs belonging to the same such group. Similarly, the bulk of the people probably would have had only limited movable property and few personal belongings. Most of these goods could probably be distributed verbally, with no need for elaborate documentation. On the other hand, for people with property or something else to pass on or protect, testamentos were both useful and necessary. The corpus of known Colonial Cakchiquel testamentos is small, limited to about a dozen, yet the regularities in both their format and patterns of property distribution indicate that these documents were not at all uncommon at the time and that testators generally conformed to their culture's norms in dividing their estates.

Wills were not dictated among the Cakchiquel until death seemed imminent. Both men and women could make testamentos, though our only example of a seventeenth-century woman's will was made by a member of the aristocracy, doña Francisca Yeol (Lolmay) (whose son, Diego Perez Xpantzay used it as evidence in the 1689 land dispute summarized in Chapter 4), suggesting that only women of this social stratum had the need or the social ability to create such documents. Testamentos had the emotional quality of being the testator's literal "last will." They also had the legal status of deathbed statements, meaning that the testator's claims concerning the possession of property and other goods were accepted as true, especially as they were typically witnessed by both the parcialidad leaders and the

town justices. This official sanction gave testamentos additional value as títulos, which would allow descendants to present them as evidence of their family's prior possession of land. Indeed, that is exactly how most of these documents were preserved. Like Diego Perez Xpantzay, Juan de la Cruz Pirir presented both his father's (Domingo) and grandfather's (Miguel) testamentos in his family's 1707 dispute with the town of San Juan Sacatepéquez (see Chapter 4). Several of the other known wills have similar histories (Hill 1989b).

The formats of the testamentos followed a fairly consistent format. First came a formulaic invocation of the Holy Trinity and an affirmation of faith, followed by an equally standard statement that the testator is making the will because he believes that he is on his deathbed. This could be followed by an enumeration of the testator's gifts to the church and the cult of the saints. In the case of Miguel Perez Pirir's will, the list ran on for a page and a half, including both past donations and endowments to be made upon his death, with all their cash values carefully noted and amounting to an impressive 6720 tostones. In contrast, a younger man of more modest means, such as Miguel Juan Queh of Santiago Sacatepéquez (who died while his children were still minors in 1662), could only endow four of the cofradías of his town with a fanega of corn each. A poor man, like Miguel Sanom of Patzicía, who died in 1627, left no endowment for the church and even had to beg that the town priest say a mass for his soul because he had no money to pay for the service (Hill 1990). This concern for the care of souls might constitute a separate section in the testamentos of better-off Cakchiquel; Miguel Perez Pirir set aside funds for three masses to be sung for his deceased wife. Domingo also left money for masses for his wife, Juana (who was still living at the time of his death), for himself, and for the other souls in purgatory. Otherwise, the testator typically proceeded to the actual distribution of his property. Sometimes he added a listing of loans owed to him or owed by him; Miguel Sanom died owing a total of seven tostones, while Miguel Juan Queh was owed well over three hundred tostones at the time of his premature death. Wills ended with a final invocation of the Trinity, an injunction that its terms not be challenged or disputed, and a statement that it has been witnessed by the parcialidad leaders and cabildo officers, terminating with the date of the document's composition. The town scribe entered the witnesses' names and office (if any) and signed the document, which was usually left in the family's possession.

As a general rule, men inherited land, though there were a number of circumstances through which women could also receive it. Again, the example of doña Francisca Yeol demonstrates that aristocratic women could inherit and control land; she even decided to swap plots with her brother. A younger widow might be left land by her husband either for her support or to attract a poor man as a husband who would work the land she owned and thus be dependent on her. Finally, unmarried daughters could receive land from their fathers that would serve as a dowry to attract desirable suitors. More rarely during our period, land might be given as an endowment for a cofradía or guachibal. In this way, individual saints' cults could become self-supporting to some degree, with the members acting more like custodians or managers of the assets.

In the case of a family corporation, one beneficiary, as head of the group, might be designated primary heir or successor. This was the case with Domingo Perez

Pirir, who, while not the eldest of Miguel's sons, seems to have been the only remaining brother with living sons of his own who could carry on the line. (Another brother, Ambrosio, also had children, but he seems to have quarreled with his father, Miguel, and left the family in the 1630s. He received a sizable inheritance nevertheless but was clearly left out of the family corporations's key holdings.) When sons were minors they were adopted by a paternal uncle who held their land in trust for them until they came of age. Alternatively, lands might be entrusted to *pairs* of adult brothers/sons. The practice could have resulted in the effective creation of new, smaller corporations and a fragmentation of family holdings, except for the high mortality rate of the period. As already noted, Domingo was the only one of Miguel's three remaining sons to have sons of his own in 1642. Of Domingo's six sons, only Juan de la Cruz was alive in 1707. Of Thomás Jocón's seven sons, only four were still alive seventeen years after his death. Thus, inheritance by pairs of brothers was apparently a strategy to ensure continued family ownership of important tracts of land, the idea being that at least one of the two brothers would have a surviving male heir.

Guachibales typically went to men as well. In 1642, Miguel Perez Pirir originally divided his four guachibales equally between Ambrosio and Domingo (who also received a feathered dance costume, the rental of which would at least partially offset the costs of the saints' day observances). However, in 1648 he angrily took Ambrosio's two guachibales away from him for failure to celebrate them properly and gave them to Domingo. In turn, Domingo entrusted three of them to pairs of his sons, just as he consigned to them the larger land holdings. He endowed the fourth with some land and a cow. All four were also to be supported with the profits from the remaining forge (Ambrosio got the other one), which all the brothers would presumably manage together.

Males likewise inherited most tools and household equipment, including even such feminine implements as metates and manos. Testators were usually quite specific in their division, especially with regard to the iron tools, which were so valuable in the seventeenth century. Otherwise, the kinds of goods passed on varied according to the wealth of the testator. Livestock was the most versatile form of bequest; cattle, horses, mules, and teams of oxen could go to males or females, adult or child, and even to cofradías or guachibales as endowments.

As part of their duties, cofradía members kept daily track of the sick and dying in order to inform the local priest of those in need of the last rites. They divided this work among themselves by parcialidades. Probably only residents of a town could expect to have the benefit of this service, and even then it could not always be performed in time. Thus, testators sometimes recorded instructions regarding rites to be performed after their deaths and left funds to ensure that they were carried out. Miguel Perez Pirir left one tostón to be paid to the church choir, which he evidently wanted to accompany his body on the way to his burial. He left six tostones so that the priest would pray over his body and left instructions that nine masses were to be sung for his soul. As a patron of his church, he had his wishes carried out and he received the honor of burial in its main chapel. Masses were sung for his departed soul over the following two months. Less ardent supporters of the church probably received correspondingly more modest rites, followed by burial in the church cemetery.

However, according to Cakchiquel belief, the dead were not entirely gone and not far away. At least one of the bodily forces (and perhaps both the natub and the uxla) remained in the area and retained an interest in descendants' actions and affairs. Indeed, as we saw in Chapter 8, the Cakchiquel expected the ancestors to return in the not-too-distant future to resume their traditional way of life. Even though over time their names might be forgotten, they were not gone. The ancestors' proximity, impending return, and the accounting that the living would be required to give at that time dictated that the living descendants be conservative, lest they provoke their anger and punishment in the form of illness. Fuentes wrote:

> They observe to the utmost the customs of their ancestors, and although the things that their ancestors did, erected, and fabricated are seen [by the living] to be erroneous, and badly done, but because their ancestors did it that way they learn it (Fuentes y Guzmán 1969–1972, III:271).

The ancestors' ways were thus to be maintained until their eventual return.

10 / Trends of the Later Colonial Period and Beyond

The Colonial regime did not end in 1700; far from it. In Europe, though in that year the Spanish branch of the Hapsburg dynasty (which had provided Spain with its king-emperors since Charles V in 1517) died out, it was replaced in 1713 by a branch of the French royal family, the Bourbons. Imbued with new blood and with new ideas from Enlightenment France, Spain embarked on an ambitious overhaul of its imperial administration known to historians as "the Bourbon reforms." These ultimately gave the empire sufficient strength to persist another century, until the Central American republics declared their independence in 1821. The reform effort even penetrated to remote Guatemala, where it figured in the shaping of the highland Maya culture that, in many respects, has endured down to the present.

THE FAILURE OF HISPANICIZATION

The sixteenth-century Spanish crown, its representatives, and the religious orders all seem to have envisioned that their combined program of religious indoctrination and civil organization would result in the rapid assimilation of New World peoples to Spanish culture. Yet, as early as the seventeenth century, it was clear to those with experience of highland Maya peoples that assimilation had already proceeded as far as it ever would under the prevailing conditions. Throughout the preceding chapters we have essentially documented various aspects of the failure of the hispanicization effort. Here we review briefly both some of the main areas targeted for change by the Spaniards and Cakchiquel responses.

Probably the most fundamental failure in the attempt to hispanicize the Cakchiquel occurred in the domain of language. There is nothing in the historical record to indicate that more than a few Cakchiquel ever acquired more than a smattering of Spanish. Perhaps the best evidence of this consists of the constant complaints of Spanish officials and prelates concerning the difficulties of communication with the monolingual Cakchiquel. These problems are mirrored by the necessity of using interpreters (as often as not criollos who had learned some Cakchiquel out of necessity) in conducting any official business with the Indians all through the Colonial period. While interpreters were required under Spanish law, given the way lower-level officials ignored other regulations pertaining to the Indians, they would not have bothered about this one unless interpreters were a necessity. Even much

written communication between Indian cabildos and the world of Spanish official-
dom was in Cakchiquel. This is an important point. The Cakchiquel did not need to
learn Spanish in order to become literate and enjoy many of the benefits of literacy.
As with so many elements of Spanish culture, they simply adopted the outer form
(in this case, writing technology), using it in their own ways and for their own ends.

The Colonial-period Cakchiquel borrowed only a few words from the Spanish
language. This is surprising given the number of elements borrowed from Spanish
culture: technologies, plants, animals, tools, beliefs, and institutions, which all had
to be named in order to be spoken about. While a detailed discussion of linguistics is
beyond the scope of this volume, the Colonial dictionaries reveal two clear patterns
of naming things of Spanish origin. The more common pattern was for the Cakchiquel to identify the foreign thing with something familiar and somehow similar in
their language, to which they added prefix or suffix "*castilan,*" meaning Castilian
or Spanish. A few examples:

> Olive = castilan q'inom ("Castilian plum") (Coto 1983:59)
> Mint = castilan izk'ih ("Castilian goosefoot") (Coto:290)
> Sugarcane = castilan ahih ("Castilian cane") (Coto:88)
> Arquebus (a seventeenth-century firearm) = castilan pub ("Castilian blowgun")
>   (Coto:43)
> Peacock = q'uq' castilan ("Castilian quetzal") (Coto:401)

The other pattern involved naming the thing entirely in Cakchiquel:

> Mule or ass = umul queh ("rabbit-deer" (Guzmán 1984:95)
> Horse = mama queh ("elder deer") (Guzmán:105)
> Goat = chicop tentzun ("Mexican-animal animal") (Coto:80)

The Cakchiquel saw a similarity between long ears of mules or asses and those
of rabbits, while the deer was the largest indigenous quadruped. Ultimately, queh
alone came to be used almost exclusively for mule, a measure of its importance to
the Colonial Cakchiquel. The Mexican word *mazat* was borrowed to refer to deer.
The use of mama as "elder" was intended to give the idea of size and wisdom that
are the products of age. The Cakchiquel were mistaken technically in attributing the
origin of the goat to Mexico, though that may have been the route through which
they were introduced into the Maya highlands, perhaps with the first conquistadores. In any event, it was not necessary for the Cakchiquel to learn very
much, or even any, of the Spanish language in order to borrow and utilize elements
of Spanish culture.

Religion was another domain in which the Spaniards had an overt, concerted
program for change. Yet, we have already seen that the Cakchiquel adopted
Christianity as an addition to their existing beliefs and practices and that they
themselves saw no conflict between the two. The cult of the saints was one of the
main tools the missionary friars used to introduce the Indians into the Catholic faith,
and we saw how the Cakchiquel merged the saints both conceptually and ritually
with traditional supernatural beings (especially the patronal gods and the ancestors).
By nearly all accounts, the Cakchiquel engaged in many of the other Catholic rituals

(such as confession, communion, etc.) only infrequently, if at all. The Cakchiquel co-opted Catholic concepts of the afterlife and resurrection as part of their millenarian, nativistic view of the future, in which all of the ancestors would return to life in a traditional, Spaniard-free world.

The Spaniards really did not have a formal program for a technological transformation of the Indians, yet this was a domain in which some of the greatest changes occurred. For the most part, the Cakchiquel seem to have been left to examine the Spanish technological inventory and select those items which they judged to be most potentially useful. These included the iron-working complex, cattle raising, horse/mule/oxen breeding and use for transport, crops (especially commercial crops such as wheat, sugarcane, etc.), and writing. While they also adopted money and exploited its utility, this was forced initially on the Cakchiquel by the demands of the Spanish tribute system. While the Cakchiquel made technological additions which, in a real sense, transformed their Colonial-period economy, they managed many of these changes themselves. Therefore, it would be inaccurate to say that the Cakchiquel had been hispanicized technologically. Rather, they developed their own technological inventory in which they combined indigenous and imported elements to create a distinctive Colonial Indian economy.

The Spaniards did have a program for Indian civil organization, and this is one domain in which they achieved considerable success. They managed to congregate the Cakchiquel into towns ordered on a Spanish model. They instituted cabildos and cajas and introduced municipal offices, all of which endured and became central institutions of Cakchiquel public life. However, the Cakchiquel did not implement these things in exactly the ways that the Spaniards had planned. They built towns but preserved parcialidades as residential areas and social units. They supplied men to be town justices, but the offices had to be apportioned among a town's parcialidades and filled by the traditional leaders of these groups. With officeholders owing primary loyalty to their parcialidad or town, not to the Spanish crown which created the offices, justices became effective barriers and brokers for their people vis-à-vis the Colonial regime. Tribute had to be paid and labor performed, but the Spaniards did not see these as constituting a program of change. Rather, they justified them partly as being simply a continuation of the sorts of preconquest obligations that Mesoamerican Indians in general had to fulfill for their indigenous rulers.

In sum, the Colonial Cakchiquel differed in many ways from their preconquest ancestors. But most of these differences were fairly superficial in nature. They had borrowed (or been forced to borrow) many elements of Spanish culture but had incorporated them as they saw fit, often relying on traditional principles and practices to do so. The net result had been not hispanicization, but rather the creation of a new culture with many strong and basic ties to the past. Although hispanicization had failed and the Cakchiquel developed their own Colonial-period culture, the latter was not changeless. Developments in the later Colonial period and beyond created pressures to which the Cakchiquel had to respond. In the process, they developed some of the features so characteristic of Mesoamerican Indians as known from ethnographic studies in this century.

PEASANTIZATION AND DEVELOPMENT OF THE CIVIL-RELIGIOUS HIERARCHY

During the seventeenth century, aristocratic and corporate families had been able to generate sufficient wealth to maintain their enhanced social status and distinct life-style. Populations had been small enough that, for most of the period, access to land was not a difficult problem. Sufficiently large families could thus fairly readily engage in profitable, diversified economic activities such as stock raising and commercial agriculture. By the end of our period and extending through the eighteenth century, population growth made this kind of enterprise much more difficult. We have already seen evidence of population pressure near the end of our period in cases involving both an Xpantzay aristocrat and the Pirir family against other residents of their respective towns. Ultimately, such people simply could no longer gain or maintain control over sufficient lands to generate the income necessary to support their status. The net effect was socioeconomic leveling, with nearly all Cakchiquel becoming subsistence-oriented peasant farmers.

But some important functions traditionally discharged by aristocrats and the wealthy remained, especially cabildo officeholding, sponsorship of guachibales, and service in the cofradías. As the Cakchiquel became poorer, these sorts of obligations, which used to be prerogatives of the elite, became burdens, financial liabilities to the peasant farmers who now had to perform them. We have already seen the outlay time and money that cabildo office could entail. The celebrations associated with guachibales (even those endowed with money, land, or other goods) seem to have declined during the eighteenth century to the point that they consisted only of a mass in church and a modest meal at the house of the holder, attended by the friends and relatives, who had made donations needed to help meet even these nominal expenses (Hill 1986:68, 72).

Cofradías had also declined. For example, there is no mention of cofradía-run livestock estancias for the eighteenth-century Cakchiquel (though these did continue in other parts of the Maya highlands). Some cofradías of this period seem still to have had capital in the form of money that could be lent forcibly to community members. However, by this time we see new variations and forms of fund-raising. For example, sometimes the forced loans were made only to the cofradía members as a main condition of their participation. They bore this burden on behalf of their fellows. They were apparently supposed to invest the funds in merchandise that they would buy in one place and sell at a profit somewhere else. If they failed to raise sufficient funds for the saint's day celebration through the use or reinvestment of the loans, they were required to make up the difference out of their own pockets. In return, they might be partially compensated for their expenditures of time and money by work done on their lands by grateful neighbors (called *q'uchubal* in Cakchiquel) or through gifts of various kinds of goods (called *k'exelobal*), as opposed to cash contributions. Other cofradías lacked any kind of endowment and ran entirely on voluntary contributions (Hill 1986:70–72).

The demands on Cakchiquel peasants of both cabildo office and cofradía service in terms of time and money meant that they could not serve continuously in these positions. Rather, they could participate only occasionally and with long periods between terms in order (they hoped) to save up a financial cushion, which would be expended while in office. The eventual result was the development of civil-religious hierarchies in Cakchiquel towns.

Such hierarchies are characteristic of all highland Maya communities studied ethnographically. Their operation involved the rotation and alternation of officeholders over the years. Ideally, a man began his public career in a lower-ranking civil or religious post in early adulthood. After a period of several years without holding any office, he would serve again, this time in a position in the opposite side of the hierarchy. If he had begun as an *alguacil* (errand-runner and constable) in the cabildo, he would serve next as a member of one of his town's less important cofradías. Over the course of his career, a man would thus serve in a variety of positions, both civil and religious. Though they all involved outlays of time or money, a man was rewarded with the prestige which accrued to him for the successful performance of his duties. After a lifetime of service, a man emerged as one of the town's *principales,* the revered body of elders who were the true managers of town affairs.

Unfortunately, we lack the kind of detailed, personal information about individuals' officeholding careers in the eighteenth century that would allow us to be more precise about the timing and process of civil-religious hierarchy emergence among the Cakchiquel. However, information on the religious institutions of the town of Patzún during this period suggest some of the features involved.

In 1744, the town's gobernador, justices, principales (at this time probably still referring to the parcialidad heads), and cofradía members prepared a detailed report on cult-related expenses as part of an inquiry on the part of the fiscal (royal attorney) of the audiencia. At that time, the town boasted six cofradías. Yet the interesting information is that the six did not make anywhere near equal yearly expenditures. Indeed, the Patzún cofradías can be grouped in pairs according to the sizes of their budgets. Those devoted to San Nicolás and Santa Cruz had modest yearly expenditures of 46 and 47 tostones respectively. Those of San Francisco and Santa María each spent rather more, 63 and 66 tostones. On the other hand, the cofradía devoted to the town patron, San Bernardino, and that of El Santísimo had impressive yearly expenses amounting to 152 and 144 tostones. From the amount of money each pair of cofradías spent, it would seem that they were hierarchically ordered, similar to the ways in which such organizations are arranged in contemporary communities with civil-religious hierarchies. Thus, in eighteenth-century Patzún we might expect that younger men with more limited funds served in the San Nicolás and Santa Cruz cofradías, those with more experience (and perhaps larger families to assist with the expenses of service) in the intermediate San Francisco and Santa María cofradías, and only mature men with distinguished records of past officeholding being permitted to serve in El Santísimo and the patronal San Bernardino. While we lack explicit statements about any direct integration of civil and religious offices, evidence from elsewhere in the Maya highlands indicates that cabildo scribes kept the cofradía accounts. This suggests that a formal connection already existed between Indian towns' civil and religious institutions (Hill 1986:70, 76–77).

THE DEVELOPMENT OF COMMUNITIES

As recorded ethnographically, community has been a key organizational principle for all highland Mesoamerican peoples, most typically in the form of "closed, corporate communities." As originally defined, these are "closed" entities in a social sense; membership in the community is based on birth in it, people tend overwhelmingly to marry within the community of their birth, and outsiders (if tolerated at all) can never really gain full acceptance or participation in community affairs. Such communities are "corporate" in that they hold land and other economic resources (such as woodlands, grazing areas, sources of clay for pottery making, lime deposits, etc.) as a group. Individuals traditionally cannot sell or otherwise alienate community property; they only have rights to use or exploit these resources based on their community membership (Wolf 1955, 1957).

At least among the highland Maya, each Indian town has its own "community culture," consisting of the institutionalized forms of belief, behavior, and organization that make each community unique and better than all others in the eyes of its members (Tax 1937, Reina 1966, Reina and Hill 1978). These include such things as language (even among towns whose residents speak the "same" language, such as Cakchiquel, there are still some differences that are perceived by speakers as significant), the unique costumes worn by each community's members, the particular constellation of saints worshiped, and the economic specializations (such as pottery making, weaving, woodworking, or stonework, etc.) practiced in each.

Yet, as we saw in Chapter 3, sixteenth- and seventeenth-century Cakchiquel towns were artificial creations, the by-products of the Spanish congregación program, under which numbers of previously autonomous parcialidades were resettled together forcibly. Far from merging their differences, these parcialidades retained their identity, and to some extent their autonomy, dividing among their leading families the offices of the Spanish-introduced cabildo and retaining control of their traditional lands, with their members pursuing as diversified an array of economic activities as possible. When and how did the transformation occur from towns as collections of semiautonomous parcialidades, each with internal social stratification, to communities composed of undifferentiated peasants? What were the factors that brought this change about? Given the unfortunate state of our knowledge of Cakchiquel ethnography, it is not at all certain that the transformation sketched above ever really happened to completion in all of their towns. Certainly, parcialidad organization remains vibrant in some Quiché towns to the northwest of the Cakchiquel area (Hill and Monaghan 1987). Still, by adopting a longer-term view of the community formation process, we can identify some of the factors involved.

Of course, Cakchiquel parcialidades were themselves corporate entities, especially with regard to landholding, so the principles of group ownership and responsibility were an integral part of their pre- and postconquest culture. With continuing population loss through the sixteenth century and persisting uncertainties regarding individual survival throughout the seventeenth century, group possession of land remained both viable and logical. This undoubtedly predisposed the Colonial Cakchiquel to think about landholding in terms of some group (parcialidad, corporate family, etc.) rather than individually.

However, as we have seen, the Cakchiquel population was not static but began to rebound in the later seventeenth century, reaching a Colonial-period high in the late eighteenth century. Though their numbers remained far below those of pre-conquest times, the Cakchiquels' losses of land to Spaniards and the adoption of livestock as part of their economy made it increasingly difficult for the rising population to support itself. We saw an early manifestation of this trend in the late seventeenth and early eighteenth centuries in which commoners, out of desperation, began to challenge the large landholdings of Cakchiquel aristocrats and wealthy corporate families. However, even if these estates were dismantled, they would not have provided more than a short respite from the pressure of an increasingly unfavorable man/land ratio. By the later eighteenth century, we see competition for land taking place not within towns but between them, each town trying to protect its land base, in part by taking advantage of the Bourbon reforms as they affected landholding. Their actions, combined with Spanish law, inevitably made the town, as such, the most important landholding entity.

Since the time of their formation in the sixteenth century, Spanish law tended to treat Indian towns as corporate entities. Tribute, encomienda, and repartimiento obligations were all assessed on a *town's* population, and the town as a unit was held responsible for meeting these responsibilities. Despite a few cases where the crown granted title via composición or an ámparo to a parcialidad or corporate family, towns were also clearly intended to be the main Indian landholding units. The town, for example, was the entity granted the square league of ejido (*see* Chapter 4). However, it was not until the implementation of the Bourbon reforms with regard to landholding in the eighteenth century that the audiencia of Guatemala got around to granting formal titles to towns for their ejidos. As part of their surveys needed to lay out a town's ejido, Spanish officials typically inspected the boundaries of the lands claimed by town residents, calling for representatives from neighboring communities to attend and confirm the common boundary. If land disputes among towns had not already come to the audiencia's attention, the arguments over boundaries occasioned by such surveys made it clear that there was a crisis brewing in the Indian countryside. Some of the conflicts between towns lasted decades; for example, one between Comalapa and San Martín Jilotepéque concerning their common boundary ran off-and-on for fifty years, from 1722 to 1773.

Only towns, by making collections among all their residents, could afford the costs of litigation (for lawyers, petitions, copies of all documents, etc.) over such extended periods. When these boundary questions were finally settled, eighteenth-century Cakchiquel towns sought to protect their hard-won holdings by purchasing their lands from the crown via composición, receiving a legitimate, royal título. Again, however, it was the town which was granted title to the land, because (owing to the poverty into which the Cakchiquel had fallen by this time) only entire town populations could amass the necessary sums. Thus, in 1752, the town of San Juan Sacatepéquez paid the crown 1200 pesos for just over 480 caballerías of land. In 1761, the town of San Pedro Sacatepéquez paid just over 1391 pesos for its 442 caballerías of land. The town of San Martín Jilotepéque paid 244 pesos for 122 caballerías of land in 1764 (an additional 26 caballerías were granted free as ejidos to the town) and 106 pesos for another 70 caballerías in 1792. Both of these latter purchases were made only after years, even decades, of petitions to the audiencia and litigations over boundaries with neighboring towns.

Accordingly, towns became increasingly important entities as residents necessarily pooled their resources in this way and as towns received titles encompassing all of their inhabitants' lands. People's livelihoods and economic security became dependent on the success of the town as a landholding and land-protecting entity. Residents also became much more dependent on each other as co-contributors to the funds (caja) and institutions (cabildo, cofradías) which defined the town as a social and legal entity.

The development of communities can also be seen in the documents which came to be presented as títulos by the eighteenth century. Basically, as the town became the main land-protecting entity, it appropriated for use as town títulos documents which had formerly served as títulos for its component groups (corporate families and parcialidades). This trend was already underway by the later seventeenth century. Thus, the justices of Tecpán presented the Xpantzay family documents described in Chapter 8 as town títulos in 1659 as evidence of prior possession of land in their successful litigation against an encroaching criollo landowner. The justices of San Martín Jilotepéque presented the Chajomá history written in 1555 in their 1689 litigation against people from Xenacoj. The justices of San Juan Sacatepéquez submitted the sixteenth-century Chajomá documents in their possession in the 1707 dispute with the Pirir family.

The relative scarcity of land and the resulting disputes among towns also caused residents to become concerned with being able to differentiate easily between members and nonmembers of the community. At a time when populations were reaching their postconquest peak, people no longer necessarily knew each other just by sight. Who was that man clearing land on that hillside? Was he one of "us," or a trespasser/squatter from some other town who should be run off? The Cakchiquel met this need to identify community members in part through the development of community-specific costumes, which also served to reinforce visually a sense of social solidarity among members of a now homogeneous community of peasants, united against outsiders, both Spanish and Indian. Significantly, however, the prototypes for these costumes were not the traditional clothing of the commoners, nor that of the Spaniards. Rather, the clothing of the indigenous Cakchiquel aristocracy served as the models.

The more radical departures from commoner-style dress occurred in the men's costumes. As noted in Chapter 5, commoners traditionally wore only a loincloth and a cloak, usually made of coarse, unadorned bast or henequen cloth, in accordance with preconquest sumptuary laws. In creating the community-specific costumes, the aristocrats' knee-length cotton trousers, secured by an embroidered cotton sash, replaced the loincloth. The short-sleeved cotton shirt became a common item of costume that displaced the cloak. This latter may have been transformed into the elaborately embroidered cloth called a *tzute*, worn either around the shoulders or as a head covering. For women, the embroidered cotton huipil replaced its plain plebeian counterpart. In many communities today, even more elaborate costumes are reserved for ritual events such as patronal fiestas.

It may seem contradictory that, at the same time in which all Cakchiquel were being reduced to peasant status, they chose modified versions of elite-style dress for their community-specific costumes. Yet, given their situation, this is entirely logical. When permitted, peasants the world over tend to imitate the fashions of more elite social strata. What could have been more predictable, then, than for the commoner majority of Cakchiquel to adopt styles and materials so long denied to them? The fact that the Cakchiquel were also determined to maintain their identity in large part through ties to their past also made it logical to identify with the costume of the indigenous elite as symbols of a glorious past that would, someday, return.

It is difficult to be precise about the timing of these developments in costume design and function. None of the seventeenth-century sources even hint at community-specific costumes. Even Fuentes, writing near the end of that century, was struck by the differences in dress between Indian commoners and aristocrats rather than variations among towns, and he had traveled widely and lived all of his life in the Maya highlands. In fact, the earliest reference to community costumes dates to 1759. In that year, as part of an investigation into a supposed uprising by the people of Tecpán (see the next section), testimony was taken from the Indian gobernador of Patzicía, who claimed to have received a letter requesting his town's support. Though the document bore no signatures, he was sure that it came from Tecpán because of its bearers' distinctive clothing (Hill 1989a:184). Unfortunately, he was not asked by the presiding Spanish official to describe the characteristics of the costume for the record. Yet it is clear that this method of identifying people by their town of origin according to their costume was already well established and acceptable even in a criminal investigation.

Even the saints became community members as they were adorned by their worshipers in the local costume. Describing some of the "abuses" committed by the Cakchiquel of Comalapa around 1770, Archbishop Cortés y Larraz wrote that they dressed the saints with many garments and put *paños* (tzutes) on their heads, the same way that the men dressed. When the local priest reproached them for this practice, he was told that it was the custom of the ancestors and that, accordingly, they would continue to observe it (Cortés y Larraz 1958, II:89).

THE DEMISE OF PARCIALIDADES IN EIGHTEENTH-CENTURY TECPÁN

Sometimes, unpredictably, Spanish officials unwittingly promoted the process of community formation. In one well-documented case involving the town of Tecpán, the alcalde mayor (the eighteenth-century equivalent of corregidor) of the district effectively outlawed parcialidades in the town. Up to that time, the eight parcialidades of Tecpán had retained many of their traditional functions. They were still probably the main landholding units as Tecpán did not formally gain title of all its lands until 1773. Most of the parcialidades had two heads, who still made collections (cotzunes) from among their people for group and town-related expenses. Parcialidad heads (by this time called *calpules*) also retained significant judicial functions within their groups. They heard and adjudicated disputes between parcialidad members, without reference to the town justices, who officially should have performed this function. In disputes concerning wrongdoing that merited punishment, parcialidad heads also inflicted whippings in their homes on guilty members, who were hung by the wrists using ropes hung from the rafters. Calpules kept both the cords and whip on their household altars, indicating the sanctity of the punishments. Again, technically, only a town's justices or its gobernador could impose corporal punishment legally.

All of this might have endured indefinitely had not the calpules challenged the authority of the alcalde mayor. This official had appointed one of his cronies as town scribe for Tecpán, a post usually filled by an Indian resident. While details are lacking, it seems that the new scribe managed to anger just about everyone in town. The town justices, realistically but, on the whole, timidly, refused to make any complaint. But the calpules, as the real (though unofficial) authority figures of the town, were outraged and wrote a petition to the alcalde mayor in which they asked for the scribe's removal. The alcalde mayor was not about to have his authority or his appointments questioned by Indians. He sent an order to the town justices to arrest the upstart calpules on the grounds of their technically illegal (but entirely traditional) practices (outlined previously) and for having unlawfully circumvented the legal authorities of the town in filing their petition. The town justices were in a difficult position. They were legally responsible for carrying out the alcalde mayor's orders but at the same time had probably been chosen by the calpules to fill the cabildo positions. As an out, they reported lamely that they had been unable to apprehend the calpules and suggested what they probably saw as an unrealistic alternative—that the alcalde mayor send troops to capture them.

Everyone in Tecpán was probably shocked when the thirty-man "squadron" of mounted Spanish militia arrived in town late in the evening of Saturday, April 28. Seeing their bluff called, some of the calpules turned themselves in and were locked up in the town jail. But the militia's timing had been bad. The following Sunday was the Octave of Easter, and most of the town's population spent the night celebrating in the plaza. As news of the militia's mission spread, the people became angry. From the anonymity of the crowd people hurled insults at the cause of all the trouble, the scribe. He and some of the militia cowered in the cabildo with drawn swords, thinking that the crowd had formed in response to their arrival and that they would soon attack. Nothing happened, though the next day a crowd formed at the jail and released the prisoners, before the town friar herded them all off to mass. The militia quickly mounted and left town, one man who injured himself slipping from his saddle in the hurry to leave being the only casualty in the group.

The alcalde mayor blew events out of all proportion in his report to the audiencia, giving the impression that the long-dreaded Indian uprising against Spanish rule had begun! The fact that an uprising *had* occurred in Chiapas almost fifty years earlier predisposed all Spaniards in the region to believe his story. Accordingly, he was given sweeping powers to deal with the situation, including the use of eighty militia from the Patzicía-Itzapa area (probably all of its adult male Europeans). Such was the hysteria caused by the story of a revolt that little attention was paid to the flaws in the alcalde mayor's investigation. For example, he had never established how many prisoners had been in jail, their identities, or even that the lock had been broken! Nevertheless, he returned from Tecpán on May 6 with over ninety prisoners, among them the calpules and half a dozen women. All were imprisoned until the end of May, when the fiscal of the audiencia ordered the alcalde mayor to interrogate them. More irregularities occurred. The town friar was never asked to make a statement on the events as he witnessed them. The prisoners were not represented by legal counsel, nor were they allowed to tell their side of the story. All were simply asked a few exact questions that left no room for elaboration.

The fiscal of the audiencia noted all of these deficiencies but was convinced that some kind of crisis had only narrowly been averted. Severe punishment was needed, if only to set an example for other Indians of the area. Accordingly, he recommended that all the prisoners be whipped, even though they may only have been part of the festive crowd celebrating the night before an important Church day. The audiencia agreed, specifying that each of the calpules should receive one hundred lashes, each of the women fifty, and the other prisoners between twelve and twenty-five lashes, according to their sex, health, and age.

The fiscal also approved the alcalde mayor's recommendations concerning ways to curtail the power of calpules and the integrity of parcialidades. The alcalde mayor had advised that the calpules should be expressly forbidden to hear and settle members' disputes, to administer punishments, to make collections from among their groups, or to make petitions on behalf of their people to the Spanish authorities. He now urged that these prohibitions be extended to *all* towns in his district (which included most of the Colonial Cakchiquel towns). The audiencia agreed and further decreed that the town justices of Tecpán notify the alcalde mayor of the calpules' identity each year in order to keep a close watch on these troublemakers, lest they attempt to regain some of their former position in town affairs. (Having made his point, the alcalde mayor evidently showed some forbearance. Only the calpules and the six women were to be whipped. Their sentences were reduced, and it does not seem that they were ever carried out.)

From the Spanish authorities' standpoint, the measures worked better than they could have hoped. Although the documentary record is too incomplete to permit us to track events through the rest of the century, by the early 1800s it is clear that calpules and the parcialidades they used to lead were gone. Even today, the town of Tecpán has only four neighborhoods, or *barrios,* but these do not extend beyond the town proper into the countryside in the way that parcialidades did, and no one can remember the old system (Hill 1989a:179–187). While eliminating parcialidades was not explicitly part of Spanish policy, such units could become inconvenient enough to be done away with. Once gone, only the town remained as an overarching social entity.

LAND AND LABOR IN THE LATER NINETEENTH CENTURY

The Cakchiquel had made adaptations to a relatively stable Colonial regime by which they could have maintained themselves indefinitely. However, the Colonial period ended and power passed from royal officials with at least an ideal obligation to protect Indian interests to criollos accustomed to using the Indians as a ready source of cheap labor. Criollos divided into two camps, the liberals and the conservatives. Just after independence the liberals gained control of the government and legislated many measures to dismantle leftover Colonial institutions. In brief, their program met with considerable opposition from both the urban elite as well as rural ladinos, and to a lesser extent, Indians. The liberal regime was toppled, replaced by conservative factions which annulled their predecessors' reforms. As a result, Guatemalan Indians passed through much of the century in conditions little different from those of the Colonial period, except perhaps that they were generally left much more to themselves.

All of this changed drastically when a new liberal regime installed itself in 1870. Imbued with a belief in economic development as the path to social and political progress, the liberals promoted the growth of commercial agricultural exports to world markets, especially coffee. As part of their program, the liberal regime sought to bring as much land under this sort of moneymaking cultivation as possible, removing it from unprofitable subsistence agriculture. Accordingly, laws were passed which empowered the government to declare portions of Indian communities' ejidos as being in excess of their needs and thus subject to sale. The result around the turn of the century, particularly among the more easterly Cakchiquel towns, was a land grab by outsiders on a scale not seen since the late 1500s. This had the effect of removing even more land from the hands of an ever-growing Indian population, forcing many into dependence on work as agricultural laborers on others' lands. In part, this is just what the liberals had in mind. The Indians, they thought, could never become "civilized" as long as they were economically self-sufficient subsistence farmers. They had to be forced to work as laborers in order to be freed from their traditions and ignorance and dragged if necessary into the modern world.

Of course, these ideas went hand in hand with the labor needs of commercial agriculture. Coffee entrepreneurs had to be assured that cheap, plentiful labor would be available when necessary, especially at harvest time. Since the Indians would not willingly leave their homes for extended periods for such work in the unhealthy lowlands at low wages, the liberals initially revived a version of the Colonial repartimiento. Called *mandamiento* (order), the system provided that plantation owners could apply to the *jefes políticos* (regional political bosses appointed by the central government) for as many Indians as necessary for employment as laborers. The jefes políticos were, in turn, empowered to draft as many as sixty Indians at a time for periods of two to four weeks from each of the towns in their districts to fulfill planters' needs.

Several forms of debt peonage also became legally sanctioned. Basically, these were practices in which an Indian was advanced money by a planter or his *habilitador* (labor agent). The Indian *jornalero habilitado* (cash-advance laborer) signed an agreement stipulating that he would work off the debt on the planter's *finca* (plantation) when harvest time came. *Colonos* (colonists) agreed to a long-term contract under which they would live and work for set wages on the planter's finca for up to four years. These people were intended to provide the necessary year-round labor for the finca. Many schemes existed whereby the debt was never fully paid off. These included additional loans, advancing the workers credit to buy foodstuffs and other goods from the finca (an updated version of the repartimiento de bienes), and fraudulent bookkeeping with regard to the amount of the debt and the extent to which it had been worked off. Severe sentences in jail awaited anyone who failed to appear for work or who ran off before his debt was paid. Vagrancy laws were also used as a legal means of forcing Indians with little or no land of their own and no other occupation to spend part of the year as finca laborers (Jones 1942, McCreery 1983). The highland Maya communities studied by ethnographers in this century all had their institutions and integrity assaulted and even partially dis-mantled as a result of such policies. The communities and their cultures were not entirely destroyed, but, by the beginning of the twentieth century, they bore about as much resemblance to their Colonial-period counterparts as Colonial Cakchiquel culture bore to that of the preconquest era.

FOR THE FUTURE

On the other hand, modernization in the last forty years has provided the Cakchiquels with many new, previously unimagined opportunities in tourism, commerce, agriculture, transportation, and industry. In a very real sense, we are on the verge of a reemergence of significant socioeconomic differentiation in Cakchi-quel society. Along with the new opportunities have come new ideologies, most commonly in the form of evangelical Protestant creeds which proclaim that Cakchi-quel and other Indians can change their traditionally low socioeconomic status and that the accumulation of wealth is, in itself, a good thing. However, according to the evangelists, the attainment of these goals requires a sacrifice; many of the old ways, much of their traditional culture, the Cakchiquel are told, must be aban-doned. To date, while Protestantism has made considerable progress among the Cakchiquel, few converts have made as complete a break with their culture as the missionaries demand. One probable reason for this is the absence of a defined social status into which such progressively minded and upwardly mobile Cakchiquel could move. While many Cakchiquel have historically abandoned their Indian identity to become ladinos, such a change has usually meant leaving their home communities for life in the cities or some other non-Indian part of the country. Many of those who choose to remain Cakchiquel have a well-developed dislike for their non-Indian countrymen, grounded in the memory of the conquest and centuries of oppression, regularly reinforced by the discrimination they face whenever they enter the ladino world. Many Cakchiquel still fully expect that the ladinos and other "foreigners" will someday disappear. As recently as the 1940s the Cakchiquel of Patzicía rose up and slaughtered all the ladinos living in the town at the hint that the time of their ultimate deliverance had come (for the personalistic account of a witness *see* Pettersen 1976:184–187).

Must the Cakchiquel abandon their identity as Cakchiquel in order to modernize successfully in a country with as sizable an Indian population as Guatemala? Not necessarily. Despite the real problems they currently face, the Cakchiquel, if left to make their own choices, will develop their culture as they always have and adapt to new and ever-changing conditions while remaining Cakchiquel.

BIBLIOGRAPHIC NOTE

Civil-religious hierarchy is a time-honored topic in Mesoamerican ethnology. Among the major statements are Carrasco (1961), Cancian (1965), Reina (1966), and Rus and Wasserstrom (1980). Community characteristics are an equally massive subject. Important statements have been made by Tax (1937), Wolf (1955, 1957), Reina (1963), and Reina and Hill (1978). Information on the composición of ejidos for San Pedro Sacatepéquez comes from AGCA document A1.45.1 Leg.5325 Exp.44882, for San Martín Jilotepéque from A1 Leg.2141 Exp.15255 and A1 Leg.2145 Exp.15299.

Martínez Peláez (1970) has suggested that community-specific costumes were Spanish creations which grew from the needs of administrators and encomenderos to be able to identify the town of origin for any given Indian in order to prevent flight to some other town as a means of evading tribute and labor obligations. The flaw in Martínez' argument (and one which he acknowledges) is the absence of any official directives on this subject in the massive archives of both Guatemala and Spain.

Information on the "uprising" in Tecpán comes from a copy of the investigation proceedings in the Archivo General de Indias (AGI) document Guatemala 539. Another copy is listed in the holdings of the AGCA as A1.21.3 Leg.2141 Exp.15247 (see Hill 1989a).

Glossary

ah cun A ritual practitioner concerned with the diagnosis and treatment of illness

ah itz A sorcerer

ah q'ih A calendar specialist

ah tzité A ritual practitioner capable of divination using tzité seeds and rock crystals representing days of the 260-day calendar

ahilabal q'ih A manual for calendrical divination

alcalde The higher-ranking of the two main offices of a Colonial-period cabildo

alcalde mayor An eighteenth-century office, essentially a replacement of the office of corregidor

alguacil Typically the lowest-ranking office in the civil-religious hierarchies which began to emerge in Cakchiquel communities during the eighteenth century

almud de los soldados de Granada A tax imposed on the Indians in the seventeenth century to support a Spanish garrison in Nicaragua

ax waab' The executive council of a parcialidad in some Quiché-speaking communities

caballería A unit of land measurement equal to about 111 acres

cabildo As used in Colonial times, both a town's municipal office and its council

cacaste A wooden packframe used by human porters to carry merchandise

cacique An Arawak-language term used by the Spaniards to refer to any Indian in a position of authority

caja de comunidad A community chest or coffer in which town monies and records were kept

calpul As used in Colonial Guatemala, a parcialidad or such a group's leader; in the latter sense it was somewhat interchangeable with principal and cacique

cédula In this case, an informal bill of sale executed between Indian buyers and sellers of land

chinamit The basic unit of preconquest highland Maya society, roughly equivalent to the central Mexican calpul

cholol q'ih The Cakchiquel version of the 260-day Mesoamerican divinatory calendar

cofrade Member of a cofradía

cofradía A group of laymen dedicated to the veneration of a particular saint

colono A laborer in modern times who agrees to a multiyear contract with his employer

composición The legal procedure through which individuals and groups purchased land from the Spanish crown

congregación The sixteenth-century Spanish program which brought together the scattered, remnant Indian population into nucleated town settlements

convenio An Indian contract or covenant concerning the division or use of land

corregidor A royal official charged with the administration of a district or corregimiento

cotzún A Cakchiquel term for a type of collection made from residents of a town or members of a parcialidad

criollo A Spaniard born in the New World

despacho de ámparo A royal writ which functioned much like a restraining order, protecting its holder from summary action by a third party; Colonial-period Indians frequently sought this kind of protection for their lands rather than purchase them from the crown via composición.

ejido In Colonial times, lands granted by the crown to towns as corporations

encomendero The grantee or recipient of an encomienda

encomienda A royal grant of the tribute otherwise owed by a group of Indians to an individual Spaniard, usually in recognition of some meritorious service to the crown

estancia A ranch for breeding livestock

fanega A unit of dry measure equal to about 150 pounds

fiscal A royal official similar in function to a state's attorney; in Colonial Guatemala he had the additional duty of protecting Indian interests in matters brought before the audiencia

gobernador An Indian appointed by Spanish authorities to be responsible for tribute collection and the maintenance of order in his town

guachibal An individually or privately endowed cult, devoted to the veneration of a specific saint

habilitador In the recent past and today, a recruiter of Indian laborers

indios de confesión Indians who were eligible to receive communion

jefe político In the nineteenth and early twentieth centuries, a political appointee of the national government charged with the administration of one of the departments into which the country is subdivided

jornalero habilitado In recent times, a laborer who agrees to work in exchange for an immediate cash advance

juez repartidor A Spanish Colonial official responsible for administering the repartimiento of Indian laborers in a district

juicio de residencia An official review of a Spanish officeholder's conduct at the end of his term

k'exelobal A gift made to a Indian cofradía member to assist him in meeting his financial obligations

labrador Spanish wheat farmer in Colonial Guatemala

mandamiento A late nineteenth century reincarnation of Colonial-type labor drafts

maxtlatle (or maztlatle) Nahuatl-language term for the Mesoamerican-style loincloth

mecapal Tumpline strap passed around the forehead when bearing burdens

medios tributarios Half-tributaries such as widows and widowers

metate and mano Grindstone and handstone used in processing corn

nagual An individual with the ability to project his/her uxla into another form

natub A divine force believed to dwell in the head of each individual, the nature and potential of which is determined by the day of the individual's birth

nut A collection made from among residents of a town or members of a parcialidad

pajuyu A dispersed Indian settlement in an area away from direct Spanish control

parcialidad The Spanish term for a chinamit or its equivalent in Colonial times

patanibal A Cakchiquel term for cofradía, literally "burdensome thing"

patronazgo The right to endow the church with land; as practiced in Colonial Guatemala, Indian donors retained effective control over such endowments, affording them some protection from Spanish usurpation

peninsulares Spaniard residents of the New World born in Spain

peso The basic unit of Spanish coinage, equal to two tostones or eight reales

petate A woven rush mat

posesión jurídica Formal, legal possession of a tract of land

principal Originally used by the Spaniards to denote the head of a parcialidad, the term was later applied to those distinguished individuals who had passed through their community's civil-religious hierarchy

procurador A Spanish legal counselor

q'uchubal Communal work performed by neighbors on the lands of a cofradía member

real A unit of Spanish coin equal to one-eighth peso or one-quarter tostón

regidor A councilman, the lower-ranking of the two main offices of a Colonial Indian cabildo

repartimiento The Colonial labor draft which required Indian towns to send a quarter of their able-bodied men each week to work on Spanish-owned farms and other enterprises

reservado An Indian exempted from tribute because of advanced age or service in the cabildo or church

servicio del tostón The basic head tax imposed by the Spanish crown on its Indian subjects

testamento A will or testament

tierra caliente Land below about 1000 meters

tierra fría Land above 2000 meters

tierra templada Land between 1000 and 2000 meters

tierras realengas Patrimonial lands belonging to the Spanish monarch

título Literally a land title, the term was used by the highland Maya to refer to any document which justified the possession of land

tona An animal companion spirit which shares the same fate as its human counterpart

tostón A unit of Spanish coin equal to one-half peso or four reales

tributario entero A full tributary, the basic unit of Colonial taxation

tzité q'am vuh A manual for interpreting the results of divinations using tzité seeds and rock crystals

uxla A divine force believed to dwell in the liver of each individual, responsible for desires and other strong passions

visita An inspection made by Spanish civil or ecclesiastical officials

vista de ojos A visual inspection or survey of land conducted by a Spanish official

xulú A variety of lesser supernatural beings believed to inhabit springs, rivers, ponds, and certain large trees

Bibliography

Berdan, Frances E.
   1982 *The Aztecs of Central Mexico*. New York: Holt, Rinehart and Winston.

Berlin, Heinrich
   1950 "La Historia de los Xpantzay." *Antropología e Historia de Guatemala,* vol. 2, no. 2, pp. 40–53, Guatemala.

Borg, Barbara E.
   1986 "Ethnohistory of the Sacatepéquez Cakchiquel Maya, Ca. 1450–1690 A.D." Ph.D. dissertation. Columbia, Missouri: University of Missouri.

Brinton, Daniel G.
   1885 *The Annals of the Cakchiquels*. Philadelphia: Brinton's Library of Aboriginal American Literature.

Bunzel, Ruth
   1952 *Chichicastenango*. American Ethnological Society Publications, vol. 22.

Cancian, Frank
   1965 *Economics and Prestige in a Maya Community*. Stanford, Calif.: Stanford University Press.

Carmack, Robert M.
   1973 *Quichean Civilization*. Berkeley, Calif.: University of California Press.

Carrasco, Pedro
   1961 "The Civil-Religious Hierarchy in Meso-American Communities: Pre-Spanish Background and Colonial Development." *American Anthropologist,* vol. 63, no. 4: 483–497.

De Las Casas, Bartolomé
   1958 *Apologética Historia de las Indias,* 2 vols. Biblioteca de Autores Españoles, nos. 105, 106. Madrid: Ediciones Atlas.

Chamberlain, Robert S.
   1939 "Castilian Backgrounds of the Repartimiento-Encomienda." Washington, D.C.: Carnegie Institution of Washington, Contributions to American Anthropology and History, no. 25.

Coe, Michael D.
   1984 *The Maya* (3d ed.). London: Thames and Hudson.

Colby, Benjamin N. and Lore M. Colby
   1981 *The Daykeeper, the Life and Discourse of an Ixil Diviner*. Cambridge, Mass.: Harvard University Press.

Collins, Anne C.
   1980 "Colonial Jacaltenango, Guatemala: The Formation of a Corporate Community." Ph.D. dissertation. Ann Arbor, Mich.: University Microfilms.

Cortés y Larraz, Pedro
1958 Descripción Geográfico-Moral de la Diocesis de Goathemala (2 vols.). Guatemala: Sociedad de Geografía e Historia, Biblioteca "Goathemala," vol. 22.

Coto, Thomás
1983 *Thesaurus Verborum: Vocabulario de la lengua Cakchiquel u Guatemalteca, nuevamente hecho y recopilado con sumo estudio, travajo y erudición.* (René Acuña, ed.) Mexico: Universidad Nacional Autónoma de Mexico.

Crespo, Mario
1956 "Títulos indígenas de tierras." Guatemala: *Antropología e Historia de Guatemala,* vol. 8, no. 2: 10–15.

Dubois, John W.
1981 "The Sacapultec Language." Ph.D. dissertation. Berkeley: University of California.

Dupiech-Cavaleri, Daniele and Mario Humberto Ruz
1988 "La diedad fingida, Antonio Margil y la religiosidad Quiché del 1704." Mexico: *Estudios de Cultura Maya,* vol. 17: 213–267.

Edmonson, Munro S.
1971 *The Book of Counsel: The Popol Vuh of the Quiché Maya of Guatemala.* New Orleans: Middle American Research Institute, Tulane University, Publication 35.
1988 *The Book of the Year: Middle American Calendar Systems.* Salt Lake City: University of Utah Press.

Feldman, Lawrence H.
1985 *A Tumpline Economy.* Culver City, Calif.: Labyrinthos.

Fuentes y Guzmán, Francisco Antonio de
1969–1972 *Obras Históricas de don Francisco Antonio de Fuentes y Guzmán.* (Carmelo Sáenz de Santa María, ed.) (3 vols.). Madrid: Ediciones Atlas.

Gage, Thomas
1958 *Travels in the New World (1648).* (J.E.S. Thompson, ed.). Norman: University of Oklahoma Press.

Gillespie, Susan D.
1989 *The Aztec Kings: The Construction of Rulership in Mexico History.* Tucson: University of Arizona

Goldman, Irving
1970 *Ancient Polynesian Society.* Chicago: University of Chicago Press.

Gruzinski, Serge
1989 *Man-Gods in the Mexican Highlands.* Stanford, Calif.: Stanford University Press.

Guillemin, George F.
1967 "The Ancient Cakchiquel Capital of Iximché." Philadelphia: *Expedition,* vol. 9, no. 2: 22–35.
1977 "Urbanism and Hierarchy at Iximché." In N. Hammond, ed., *Social Processes in Maya Prehistory.* London: Academic Press: 227–262.

Guiteras-Holmes, Calixta
1954 "Background of a Changing Kinship System among the Tzotzil Indians of Chiapas." Unpublished manuscript, Escuela Nacional de Antropología e Historia, Mexico.

Guzmán, Pantaleón de
1984 *Compendio de nombres en lengua Cakchiquel*. (René Acuña, ed.). Mexico: Universidad Nacional Autónoma de Mexico.

Hill, Robert M.
1984 *Chinamit and Molab: Late Postclassic Highland Maya Precursors of Closed Corporate Community*. Mexico: Estudios de Cultura Maya, vol. 15: 301–327.
1986 "Manteniendo el culto a los Santos: Aspectos financieros de las instituciones religiosas Mayas en el altiplano Colonial." Antigua, Guatemala: *Mesoamerica*, vol. 11: 61–77.
1988 "Instances of Maya Witchcraft in the Eighteenth-Century Totonicapán Area." Mexico: *Estudios de Cultura Maya*, vol. 17: 269–293.
1989a "Social Organization by Decree in Colonial Highland Guatemala." Durham, N.C.: *Ethnohistory*, vol. 36, No. 2: 170–198.
1989b *The Pirir Papers and Other Colonial Period Cakchiquel-Maya Testamentos*. Nashville: Vanderbilt University Publications in Anthropology No. 37.
1990 "The Social Uses of Writing among the Colonial Cakchiquel Maya: Nativism, Resistance, and Innovation." Paper read at the annual meeting of the Society for American Archaeology, Las Vegas.

———— and John Monaghan
1987 *Continuities in Highland Maya Social Organization: Ethnohistory in Sacapulas, Guatemala*. Philadelphia: University of Pennsylvania Press.

Hunt, Eva
1977 *The Transformation of the Hummingbird*. Ithaca, N.Y.: Cornell University Press.

Jones, Chester L.
1942 "Indian Labor in Guatemala." In A. Curtis Wilgus, ed., *Hispanic American Essays: A Memorial to James Alexander Robertson*. Chapel Hill: University of North Carolina Press, 299–323.

Juarros, Domingo
1823 "A Statistical and Commercial History of the Kingdom of Guatemala." In *Spanish America* (J. Baily, trans.). London: J. Hearne.

LeRoy Ladurie, Emmanuel
1974 *The Peasants of Languedoc* (John Day, trans.). Urbana: University of Illinois Press.

López Austin, Alfredo
1973 *Hombre-Diós, religión y política en el mundo náhuatl*. Mexico: Universidad Nacional Autónoma de Mexico.
1988 *The Human Body and Ideology: Concepts of the Ancient Nahuas* (T. and B. Ortiz de Montellano, trans.). Salt Lake City: University of Utah Press.

Lovell, W. George
1982 "Collapse and Recovery: A Demographic Profile of the Cuchumatán Highlands of Guatemala (1520–1821)." In Robert M. Carmack, John Early, and Christopher Lutz, eds., *The Historical Demography of Highland Guatemala*. Albany: Institute for Mesoamerican Studies, State University of New York at Albany, Publication No. 6: 103–120.
1985 *Conquest and Survival in Colonial Guatemala*. Montreal: McGill-Queen's University Press.

Luján Muñoz, Luís
1967 "La devoción popular del rey San Pascual." Guatemala: *Folklore de Guatemala*, no. 3: 15–38.

Lutz, Christopher H.
1983 *Historia sociodemográfica de Santiago de Guatemala, 1541–1773*. Antigua, Guatemala: Centro de Investigaciones Regionales de Mesoamerica.

MacBryde, Felix W.
1934 *Sololá: A Guatemalan Town and Cakchiquel Market Center*. New Orleans: Middle American Research Institute, Tulane University, Publication 5: 45–152.
1947 *Cultural and Historical Geography of Southwest Guatemala*. Washington, D.C.: Institute of Social Anthropology, Smithsonian Institution, Publication 4.

MacLeod, Murdo J.
1973 *Spanish Central America, A Socioeconomic History 1520–1720*. Berkeley: University of California Press.

McCreery, David
1983 "Debt Servitude in Rural Guatemala, 1876–1936. *Hispanic American Historical Review,* vol. 63, no. 4: 735–759.

Martínez Peláez, Severo
1970 *La patria del Criollo: ensayo de interpretación de la realidad colonial Guatemalteca*. Guatemala: Editorial Universitaria.

Murdock, George P.
1949 *Social Structure*. New York: Free Press.

Navarrete, Carlos
1982 *San Pascualito Rey y el culto de la muerte en Chiapas*. Mexico: Universidad Nacional Autónoma de Mexico.

Pettersen, Carmen L.
1976 *Maya of Guatemala: Their Life and Dress*. Seattle: University of Washington Press.

Polo Sifontes, Francís
1977 *Los Cakchiqueles en la Conquista de Guatemala*. Guatemala: Editorial "José de Pineda Ibarra."

Recinos, Adrián
1957 *Crónicas Indígenas de Guatemala*. Guatemala: Editorial Universitaria.

———— and Delia Goetz (trans.)
1953 *Annals of the Cakchiquels and Title of the Lords of Totonicapán*. Norman: University of Oklahoma Press.

Reina, Ruben E.
1963 "The Potter and the Farmer: The Fate of Two Innovators in a Maya Village." *Expedition,* vol. 5, no. 4: 18–31.
1966 *The Law of the Saints*. Indianapolis: Bobbs-Merrill Co.

———— and Robert M. Hill II
1978 *The Traditional Pottery of Guatemala*. Austin: University of Texas Press.

Rus, Jan and Robert Wasserstrom
1980 "Civil-Religious Hierarchies in Central Chiapas: A Critical Perspective." *American Ethnologist,* vol. 7: 466–478.

Ruz, Mario H.
1985 *Copanaguastla en un Espejo*. San Cristóbal de las Casas, Mexico: Universidad Autónoma de Chiapas, Centro de Estudios Indígenas, Serie Monografías, 2.

Scott, James C.
1985 *Weapons of the Weak: Everyday Forms of Resistance*. New Haven: Yale University Press.

Sherman, William L.
1979 *Forced Native Labor in Sixteenth-Century Central America*. Lincoln: University of Nebraska Press.

Simpson, Lesley B.
1966 *The Encomienda in New Spain: The Beginnings of Spanish Mexico*. Berkeley: University of California Press.

Smith, A. Ledyard
1955 *Archaeological Reconnaissance in Central Guatemala*. Washington, D.C.: Carnegie Institution of Washington, Publication 608.
1965 "Architecture of the Guatemala Highlands." In *Archaeology of Southern Mesoamerica*. G. R. Willey, ed., *Handbook of Middle American Indians*, vol. 2. Austin: University of Texas Press.

Tax, Sol
1937 "The Municipios of the Midwestern Highlands of Guatemala." *American Anthropologist,* vol. 39, no. 3: 423–444.

Tedlock, Barbara
1982 *Time and the Highland Maya*. Albuquerque: University of New Mexico Press.
1986 "On a Mountain Road in the Dark: Encounters with the Quiché Maya Culture Hero." In *Symbol and Meaning Beyond the Closed Community,* Gary H. Gossen, ed. Albany: Institute for Mesoamerican Studies, State University of New York at Albany, pp. 125–138.

Vassberg, David E.
1984 *Land and Society in Golden Age Castile*. Cambridge: Cambridge University Press.

Vázquez, Francisco
1937–1944 *Crónica de la provincia del Santísimo Nombre de Jesús de Guatemala* (4 vols.). Guatemala: Sociedad de Geografía e Historia, Biblioteca "Goathemala."

Veblen, Thomas T.
1982 "Native Population in Totonicapán, Guatemala." In Robert M. Carmack, John Early, and Christopher Lutz, eds., *The Historical Demography of Highland Guatemala*. Albany: Institute for Mesoamerican Studies, State University of New York at Albany, Publication 6: 81–102.

Wolf, Eric R.
1955 "Types of Latin American Peasantry: A Preliminary Discussion." *American Anthropologist,* vol. 57: 452–471.
1957 "Closed Corporate Peasant Communities in Mesoamerica and Java." *Southwestern Journal of Anthropology,* vol. 13. no. 1: 1–18.

Ximénez, Francisco
1929–1931 *Historia de la provincia de San Vicente de Chiapa y Guatemala* (3 vols.). Guatemala: Sociedad de Geografía e Historia, Biblioteca "Goathemala."

Index